Supervision of Teachers:

A Guide to Improving Instruction

Isobel L. Pfeiffer
School of Education
West Georgia College

Jane B. Dunlap
College of Communications
The University of Tennessee

ORYX PRESS
1982

The rare Arabian Oryx is believed to have inspired the myth of the unicorn. This desert antelope became virtually extinct in the early 1960s. At that time several groups of international conservationists arranged to have 9 animals sent to the Phoenix Zoo to be the nucleus of a captive breeding herd. Today the Oryx population is nearing 300 and herds have been returned to reserves in Israel, Jordan, and Oman.

Copyright © 1982 by The Oryx Press
2214 North Central at Encanto
Phoenix, AZ 85004

Published simultaneously in Canada

Printed and Bound in the United States of America

Library of Congress Cataloging in Publication Data

Pfeiffer, Isobel L.
  Supervision of teachers.

  Includes index.
  1. School supervision.   I. Dunlap, Jane B.
II. Title.
LB2801.A1P43   1982   371.2'01   82-8150
ISBN 0-89774-045-9   AACR2

Table of Contents

Preface

This book was written to present basic concepts of supervision in a straightforward manner. Since improving instruction must be the ultimate goal, the focus remains on those aspects of education which affect teaching-learning activities. Materials in this text were organized and used for a graduate course in educational supervision; suggestions from the students in these classes have been incorporated.

After a general introduction to the different ways supervisory services may be provided, the first section, Using Supervisory Tools, introduces specific procedures in supervision: Microteaching, Staff Development, Clinical Supervision, The Supervisory Conference, Analysis of Teaching, Curriculum Skills, and Alternate Strategies. In each chapter, the processes are described with examples and pertinent research.

From special supervisory techniques, the reader proceeds to a broader look at improving instruction in the second section, Using Management Skills. The Organizational Process, Leadership, Coping with Conflict and Stress, and Evaluation are presented in relation to the educational milieu and instructional improvement.

The final section, Using Human Resources, deals with Communication, Change, and Public Relations. Educators who are aware of these general areas can use them to enhance their supervisory effectiveness.

A variety of resources and research is given to provide a sound base for the concepts presented. The novice in supervision will find materials to describe roles, problems, and goals in educational supervision. Experienced supervisors and administrators will find instruments for evaluation, guidelines for planning programs, and ideas for helping teachers improve instruction.

Topics discussed which are not usually found in books on supervision include microteaching as an inservice technique, handling stress and conflict, and public relations. It is a useful reference for principals, classroom teachers, teacher educators, and guidance personnel, as well as supervisors.

Chapter 1
Supervision:
An Introduction

Supervision in education is a process with one major goal: improvement of instruction. It is a multifaceted interpersonal process—dealing with teaching behavior, curriculum, learning environments, grouping of students, teacher utilization, and professional development. Also, there are miscellaneous responsibilities which may include writing proposals for grants, providing public relations services, or fulfilling assignments which superordinates decide to delegate. The continuum of supervisory activities extends from an inservice meeting for all the teachers in a system to clinical supervision on a continuing one-to-one basis. The supervisor may need to help a teacher in planning units, preparing materials for individualization, setting up student evaluation programs, arranging parent conferences, or accomplishing other teacher tasks. In addition, coping with stress and handling conflict are areas in which the supervisor can give assistance to teachers.

Working with people to bring about the achievement of specific goals is the purpose of supervision in many areas—education, business, industry, and nursing. Though spheres of activity and end-products may differ, all supervisors require many human relations skills, as well as knowledge about motivation, values, and changing behavior. There is one overriding similarity in the supervisory responsibility: constant effort to help workers to improve. Ideally, this is in consonance with personal development of all supervisees, aiding in their growth to full individual strength. Industrial supervision often relates to products which can be counted. The product in schools—student learning—is more difficult to assess because it deals with intangible human development and is concerned with goals, both long and short range. Some cognitive and affective learning cannot be really evaluated in the school environment. Whether or not Dick and Jane will apply problem-solving processes when they are adults can only be conjectured. Both tangible and intangible results are important and must be recognized.

Overall, school productivity is not well-defined; therefore, supervisory efforts which are expended to achieve it may be similarly hard to describe. This situation also holds true in nursing where patient care involves human response. In short, where people are reacting to a human action or a sequence of actions, outcomes may be difficult to measure. Nevertheless, a common base for supervisory activity seems to exist. Contrasts and comparisons of the supervisory process in education, nursing, business, and industry are valuable because each arena of activity provides a rich source of information. Research in industry has been a particularly fertile ground for educators.

In industry, supervisory functions are often delegated to middle management with such job designations as group leader or project director. Education has developed job titles, too, with different names for oftentimes remarkably similar tasks. Some of these designations are director of elementary education, cooperating teacher, and building principal. Before examining the titles, the jobs, or the actions now involved in educational supervision, one should briefly consider a historical change in the profession through the past century.

Initially, the term ''school supervisors'' referred to individuals who checked on teachers to see whether or not they were following prescribed courses of study and maintaining required codes of conduct for both themselves and their students. Such restrictive, ''I spy'' activities have been almost eliminated from the professional actions of supervisors in today's educational milieu. Currently, there is much less formidable observation. Supervisors do watch, do listen, do observe— but with the goal of helping teachers develop their own unique styles according to individual choices rather than imposed values. The profession now has a wide spectrum of titles. Some of these appear to have been selected not just for identification purposes, but also for reasons of neutralizing the original negative image. Consider such affirmative-sounding names as the following—all of which are common in today's American schools: department head, resource teacher, coordinator, team leader, helping teacher, curriculum specialist, assistant superintendent. In addition to these people who devote much of their time to supervision, many administrators now allocate portions of each day to teachers for ''stopping by,'' ''looking in,'' ''dropping in to help,'' ''discussing ideas for solving a problem.'' What are all of these activities? Supervision.

An experienced teacher who shares ideas with a beginner is supervising informally. In some schools, a new teacher is assigned a ''buddy'' who has worked in the system and can help orient the newcomer to the system, i.e., who acts as a supervisor. The effective supervisory program evolves as teachers, supervisors, and administrators cooperate. Effective supervision requires a concerted effort.

At no time can educators settle for supervision that is based on a cold, theoretical, measurable relationship because, at the core of these relations, there is a real and human bond between supervisor and supervisees. The exciting truth is that a warm "human connection" is built between one individual who is helping and another who is being helped. There is interest, concern, joy, irritation, encouragement, hope, resentment, and gratification involved. But, all of these responses are good—in fact, in some cases they are necessary.

IS EDUCATIONAL SUPERVISION NEEDED?

The need for educational supervision today is increased by current economic, political, and social factors. With a decrease in student enrollment and an apparent abundance of certified teachers, teacher mobility has almost disappeared. Teachers are keeping their jobs until there is a specific opportunity for advancement or until they retire. A school system can no longer rely on "automatic turnover" which used to happen because teachers were moving outward and upward. Different approaches and fresh ideas, formerly brought in by new personnel every year, now must be devised by local talent. Faculty renewal, therefore, assumes increased importance. Faculty development programs become essential if the teachers, supervisors, and administrators are to be stimulated and challenged to work in new and better ways.

Of course, many self-motivated teachers will continue to pursue their own educational improvement. But, after certification requirements are met and maximum salary levels are reached, further incentives for professional growth may be required to motivate teachers toward a continuing upgrading of skills and knowledge. Some teachers need external encouragement to gain the experiences which enable them to improve student learning in their own classrooms. Although motivation is often considered a problem by teachers as they work with students, there may be problems in motivating teachers to learn about new material in their content areas and current discoveries in the world of teaching and learning.

Katz (1972) has suggested that teachers at different stages in their careers have different needs. In the first, or survival, stage, a teacher requires understanding, reassurance, and encouragement. Instruction in skills and insight into the causes of behavior would be beneficial in these years. Then, after the teacher has acquired a few years of experience, a consolidation period occurs. The teacher is ready to focus on individual students and their learning. Having on-site assistance with access to specialists and finding opportunities for collegial activities are advisable in this second stage of professional development. It is hoped that most teachers move toward a comfortable and satisfactory teaching style—expressing their own personalities in unique ways. After three or four years of experience, teachers may reach a third phase, the renewal stage, a time when getting into a pattern of redoing the same thing (getting in a rut) is imminent. The teacher needs the stimulation of professional meetings, classroom visits, professional journals, teacher centers, and exposure to new procedures, such as videotaping for self-analysis. Eventually, perhaps after five years of teaching, most teachers have reached the final career stage of maturity. Higher education or postgraduate courses, degree programs, professional literature, seminars, conferences, and institutes are some of the resources which could promote their development as professionals. Mature teachers have developed teaching competence and self-assurance by this period; however, they never outgrow the pressing need to improve and expand both as persons and as teachers.

The importance of individualizing instruction for students has long been recognized in the classroom. But, individualizing the professional development programs for teachers has not received much emphasis, although it has commensurate importance. Usually, all teachers in a building are expected to attend the same meeting. The speaker may present material which is helpful to some faculty members, but s/he rarely takes care of the needs of all the teachers. When supervisors recognize the developmental stages of teachers, as well as their unique strengths, styles, and interests, then the planning of individual programs for professional growth can and must be fostered. Not only will time and effort be saved, but improved teacher attitude toward inservice activities will be gained.

Indeed, educational supervision is needed. Since public confidence in schools is at an all-time low, as indicated in polls, news reports, periodicals, and rejected levies, supervisors are essential—to help teachers improve instruction, to motivate professional growth of teachers, and to implement curricular developments. Such services contribute to better student learning and to public confidence.

HOW IS SUPERVISION DEFINED?

No single definition or description of supervision is universally accepted. Wiles and Lovell (1975, p. 6) provide the following:

Instructional supervisory behavior is assumed to be an additional behavior system formally provided by the organization for the purpose of interacting with the teaching behavior system in such a way as to maintain, change, and improve the provision and actualization of learning opportunities for students.

Ben Harris (1975, pp. 10-11) states:

> Supervision of instruction is what school personnel do with *adults* and *things* to maintain or change the school operation in ways that *directly* influence the teaching processes employed to promote pupil learning. Supervision is highly instruction-related but not highly pupil-related. Supervision is a major function of the school operation, not a task or a specific job or a set of techniques. Supervision of instruction is directed toward both maintaining and improving the teaching-learning processes of the school.

In their book, *Supervision: The Reluctant Profession,* Mosher and Purpel (1972, pp. 2-3) include this description:

> We consider the tasks of supervision to be teaching teachers how to teach (in which working with teachers as people is a significant subfunction), and professional leadership in reformulating public education—more specifically, its curriculum, its teaching and its forms.

Human resources supervision is the emphasis proposed by Sergiovanni and Starratt (1979, p. 13) as they indicate "more emphasis is given to integrating individual needs with school objectives and tasks." Their definition of supervision is "a process used by those in the schools who have responsibility for one or another aspect of the school's goals and who depend directly upon others to help them achieve these goals" (p. 15).

Supervision, as used in this book, refers to the process of interaction in which an individual or individuals work with teachers to improve instruction. The ultimate goal is better student learning. The achievement of this goal may involve changing teacher behavior, modifying curriculum, and/or restructuring the learning environment. Not just one, but many relationships go together to form the complex bond which is recognized as "the supervisory connection." As one person works with another person or persons, there is a series of interpersonal contacts in which something indefinable happens. The result is human change. Perceptions may be sharpened, motivations clarified, and behavioral actions accelerated or transformed. These results, at any level, constitute supervision, whether superordinate-to-subordinate or peer-to-peer.

WHAT ARE SUPERVISORY ACTIVITIES?

The main thrust of supervision must result in improvement of student learning by procedures such as:

1. Changing teacher behavior.
2. Modifying curriculum.
3. Restructuring the learning environment.

Changing teacher behavior often is assumed to be the main job of the supervisor. An expected activity is working in a one-to-one relationship in a five-step clinical supervision model which includes a preobservation conference, observation of teaching, analysis of collected data, post-observation conference between the teacher and supervisor, and subsequent follow-up. However, this model is time-consuming, and only a few supervisees can be served, since it requires continuing one-to-one attention.

Another one-to-one relationship is a professional counseling approach, called "ego counseling," by Mosher and Purpel. The major thrust of this approach is not specific teaching behavior but teacher attitudes. The discrepancy between reality and teacher expectation must be recognized, and the teacher should develop ways of coping with such discrepancy. Some supervisors develop counseling skills and they can deal directly with these professional problems; other supervisors choose to refer the teachers to professional counselors. Both clinical supervising and "ego counseling" focus on professional behavior—the former on teaching activities, and the latter on teacher attitudes.

An alternate approach for supervisors is to work with large or small groups of teachers. Such instructional supervision may involve one teacher, four or five in a group, or as many as 100 when a process or a new educational development is explained. For example, a group may learn about individualizing instruction using computer assisted instruction (CAI) through an inservice program. Microteaching may be used to expand the repertory of a few teachers or of a large group. At other times, changing teacher behavior is achieved by a brief process of sharing an article from a professional journal. In short, many teachers must be aware of other methods of teaching before they are stimulated to upgrade their own performance. For example, a teacher who has never experienced learning stations will probably never develop learning stations for his/her own classroom use.

In addition to modifying teaching, supervisors also exert effort toward changing the curriculum itself so that student learning is altered or increased. In fast-changing times, obsolescent material must constantly be updated, and new ways of pointing out relevance of lessons in the "real world" must be continually developed.

Especially in the past 10-15 years, innovative efforts have been emerging toward interdisciplinary teaching approaches. In such projects, a topic is studied from many disciplines, rather than from just one. For example, expressed conflict between labor and management may involve history, economics, literature, journalism, and speech, rather than simply the history of the struggle. In these curricular changes, a supervisor or administrator may work directly with one teacher or a group of teachers—perhaps even with a department or a committee. At other times, supervisory activity may be indirect. A teacher may be given new material, and the eventual reading and assimilating of this material may then result in expanding the limits of learning for the students.

Some curricular changes may involve a single teacher, while others extend to overall planning, K through 12. The articulation of a course of study from grade-to-grade within one school is often a challenge. Coordinating a program from school-to-school is more complicated, but it is not an impossible supervisory achievement. Whether language arts, mathematics, science, social studies, art, health, or physical education is the principal emphasis, all students should be provided with an opportunity to retain basic concepts of learned material and advance to more complex and interesting levels as they progress through school. Expert supervisory assistance is essential in planning and implementing such programs across different schools (i.e., elementary, middle, and high school), because teachers have diverse teaching styles which, in turn, produce different effects on students who have widely varying learning patterns.

Restructuring the learning environment is a way of improving instruction that involves changes both in curricula and teacher behavior. A teaching team can provide large group, small group, and individual instruction, thereby adding varieties of instruction and creating a provocative climate which can increase student attention. Cross-age teaching (the use of older students as tutors) adds understanding between groups and brings to the surface an understanding of content which only the young teaching the young can provide.

Continuous progress in reading or math can be a drastic shift from a self-contained classroom if students of different ages, but similar achievement, work together. Emphasis on providing special opportunities for gifted children may involve special classes or special activities within a regular classroom. Supervisors may be involved in planning and implementing such changes, and they provide support and help to teachers in these circumstances.

Teaching personnel may need to be reorganized in order to activate improved instruction. Teaching teams, aides, departments, dyads, and houses all involve the development of a cooperative approach to teaching students. Facilitating the work of such groups may require supervisory assistance.

Expanding opportunities for students to learn may mean the use of different learning environments. Outdoor education is an example of moving into the community for educational experiences. Field trips, cooperative programs, and alternative schools all require community resources. Recognizing resources and encouraging their propitious use in the educational program is a valuable supervisory service.

WHO SUPERVISES IN EDUCATION?

Supervision, then, is a process which involves not only administrators as they work with others to improve the instruction in their schools, but which also involves personnel who develop curricula (coordinators, directors, department heads, team leaders). Helping teachers, resource teachers, and cooperating teachers are supervisors who observe teachers and work with them individually to improve student learning. Principals supervise as they help teachers improve their lessons. Teachers are supervising when they help other teachers develop stations for a teaching unit or when they share a game to provide math drill in a new guise. Counselors supervise as they, with teachers, develop programs for particular students who seem to need more challenge and less structure or for students who need remedial work. Many different individuals perform supervisory activities. (See Figure 1.) Some individuals perform supervisory tasks as a part of their jobs; others perform supervisory tasks unofficially.

Supervisory activities occur at the building level, the school system level, sometimes the district level, and the state level. Building and system supervision is probably most important to the individual teacher, although the district level—which might be a county, township, district, or area—may influence certain programs and teachers. Currently, in many states, the special education supervisors for a district have considerable impact on procedures and curricula. Vocational supervision is frequently provided on a state and district basis. State supervisors usually serve as consultants. Occasionally, supervisors at the state level are instrumental in implementing legislated action or state department decisions.

WHAT SKILLS AND RESOURCES ARE NEEDED?

Successful supervision seems to require specific skills and characteristics. Since the supervisor is a helper, the Florida Studies suggest the importance of a positive self-concept. Developing good interpersonal relations requires a basic recognition of self-worth before respect for others can be generated and communicated (Combs, Avila, and Purkey, 1971). Awareness and empathy are needed. Since supervision involves group activities, as well as one-to-one communication, group dynamics must be

Figure 1. Personnel Involved in Supervision.

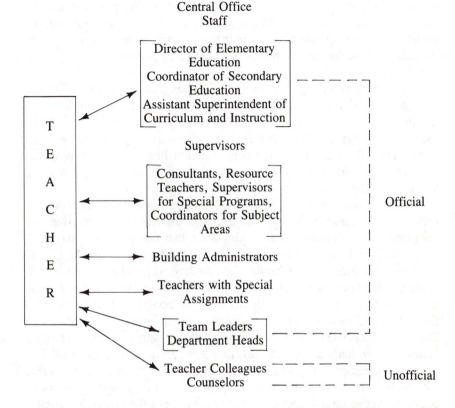

understood. Communication skills must include oral and written, verbal and nonverbal, sending and listening. Knowledge about teaching and learning is essential. Analysis of teaching requires observational skills and familiarity with various instruments for collecting classroom data. In addition to human relations, the effective supervisor must be able to manage time, handle conflict, and cope with stress—three areas of increasing concern in today's culture.

Supervision is a complex and diversified area of study. No one theory of supervision is generally accepted. Several different approaches to supervisory leadership seem to be observable in the ''real world'' today. In the article ''People, Program, or Power—The Supervisory Puzzle,'' Pfeiffer (1978) described three orientations:

1. Humanistic—valuing people and process.
2. Technological—valuing program and product.
3. Managerial—valuing power and position.

From the humanistic stance, goals and decisions emphasize personal needs, individual development, and involvement of personnel in supervisory activities. A technological approach attends to the program and the student product, e.g., scope and sequence of curriculum and measurable student learning. A supervisory/managerial approach fosters a power structure with decisions and policy determined by persons in the organizational hierarchy.

Although many supervisors function using combinations of these, recognition of the tripartite division may facilitate understanding some of the differences in supervisory activity. Diversity in value systems complicates supervision and the supervisory relationship. Not only is the leadership style affected, but interpersonal relationships with supervisees become changed. Supervisory techniques, motivation, and rewards are just a few of the basic factors involved.

In this hodge-podge of supervision, some basic skills and resource materials are generally acceptable. The Association for Supervision and Curriculum Development is an organization that functions on a national, state, and area level. Its publications include yearbooks, pamphlets, and the periodical *Educational Leadership*. Another organization that is concerned with supervisory activities is the Association of Teacher Educators, which also publishes bulletins and yearbooks. *Action in Teacher Education* is its new periodical. Many educational journals include articles useful to supervisors, since new curricula, teaching strategies, learning factors, and other educational developments are pertinent to them. Research information is especially important, since one supervisory service for teachers may be translating the research into more useable form. Supervision can help decrease the time lag between the research "discovery" and application of the finding in the classroom. Supervising staff should be familiar with the publications of the American Educational Research Association.

SUMMARY

Supervision in education is multifaceted. Individuals who supervise have different titles and perform many different services. The overall goal of improving instruction is sought through a variety of activities. Professional development has assumed a greater importance in today's schools, and individualizing programs for faculty growth is essential.

Some procedures for improving student learning include changing teacher behavior, modifying curriculum, and restructuring learning environments. In the one-to-one and group processes of supervision, specific skills and characteristics are needed. A positive self-concept, communication skills, knowledge about teaching and learning, and understanding of group dynamics are some of the requirements. Professional organizations, especially the Association for Supervision and Curriculum Development and the Association of Teacher Educators, provide publications and support for supervisors.

REFERENCES

Combs, A.W.; Avila, L.; and Purkey, W. *Helping Relationships: Basic Concepts for the Helping Professionals*. Boston: Allyn and Bacon, Inc., 1971.

Harris, B.M. *Supervisory Behavior in Education*. 2d ed. Englewood Cliffs, NJ: Prentice-Hall, Inc., 1975.

Katz, L. "Developmental Stages of Preschool Teachers." *Elementary School Journal* 73 (October 1972): 50–54.

Mosher, R.L., and Purpel, D.E. *Supervision: The Reluctant Profession*. Boston: Houghton Mifflin Co., 1972.

Pfeiffer, R.T. "People, Program, or Power—The Supervisory Puzzle." *OASCD* 2 (Fall 1978): 10–12.

Sergiovanni, T.J., and Starratt, R.J. *Supervision: Human Perspectives*. 2d ed. New York: McGraw-Hill Book Co., 1979.

Wiles, K., and Lovell, J.T. *Supervision for Better Schools*. 4th ed. Englewood Cliffs, NJ: Prentice-Hall, Inc., 1975.

Using Supervisory Tools

Chapter 2
Microteaching as a
Supervisory Tool

Microteaching began as a preservice experience in teacher education and has since become a recognized phase of many preservice and inservice teacher education programs. Originated in 1963 at Stanford, it provided a realistic and functional experience for teacher education students prior to their actual classroom responsibilities. This scaled-down teaching encounter involved a short time period (4-20 minutes), a small group of students (3-10 students), and a focus on a particular teaching skill. Videotape was used to provide immediate feedback. After viewing and analyzing the lesson with a supervisor, the teacher reorganized and taught the lesson to another group of students. The video replay was again followed by a brief conference with a supervisor to evaluate the changes. A repertoire of practiced skills was acquired by the neophyte to take into the classroom during this teach-critique-reteach-critique sequence. The teacher's flexibility and versatility were increased by building up this repertoire (Association of Teacher Educators, 1971).

In 1968, according to Johnson's survey of teacher education programs, 44 percent of the colleges and universities preparing teachers used some form of microteaching (Allen, Cooper, and Poliakoff, 1972). However, there were adaptations of the original format.

Initially, in the Stanford program, teaching skills were selected by extensive analyses of actual teacher tasks in a classroom situation. Skills were identified and defined so they could be isolated for observation and study. Then, appropriate teacher behaviors were specified, and training protocols were developed. These protocols included filmed and videotaped examples or written descriptions and scripts. A few examples of the more than 20 skills in the Stanford program are positive reinforcement to stimulate student participation, set induction to get students ready for the learning experience, and the provision of examples and applications to relate concepts to student experiences (Allen, Cooper, and Poliakoff, 1972).

In contrast to the teacher behavior in the preceding skills, a micro-teaching program can have specific objectives stated in terms of student behavior. Basic teaching tasks of this type have been used at the University of Texas at Austin. If clarity of objectives is the teaching task, then the appropriate student behavior would be that the student can state the goal for the lesson. Behavioral objectives are an integral part of such an emphasis.

When the skills were selected in the Stanford program, ways of teaching each skill were developed. Sometimes written descriptions, faculty discussions, demonstrations, role playing presentations, typescripts, audiotapes, videotapes, or films were used. These served as examples or models for each skill. One or more used in combination have often been effective. Some programs use specific media, e.g., the minicourses of the Far West Regional Educational Laboratory are inservice courses in which models are supplied by films. The teacher must comprehend what each skill involves and what kinds of teacher behavior are appropriate. This information must be presented with enough flexibility to the teachers to encourage individuality. There is the possible danger of restricting teaching behavior and putting all teachers into the same mold; however, a study by Orme, McDonald, and Allen found that individual creativity could be maintained when models were used (Olivero, 1972).

ADVANTAGES OF MICROTEACHING

Teaching is a complex, multidimensional process. While fulfilling some of these dimensions during a school day, most teachers play roles, such as discussion leader, media expert, librarian, diagnostician, guidance counselor, planner of lessons, and disciplinarian. Becoming expert in all of these is a continuing responsibility. A teacher must be concerned about planning the lesson, individualizing, motivating, involving students, using a variety of teaching strategies, maintaining classroom control, evaluating students, achieving objectives, following school policies, and promoting favorable attitudes toward learning. Without experience in coping with them in a controlled environment, all of these concerns can be overwhelming. Appropriate experiences can be provided through microteaching. If a teacher wants to work on one specific aspect of teaching, there is little possibility of isolating that part in a regular classroom situation. However, the factors in a microteaching environment can be limited so the teacher can direct attention to a particular skill or task.

In addition to practiced skills or tasks, the teacher gains experience in planning and timing. A lesson which has a brief time limit must be carefully planned or the goals cannot be achieved. The setting up of behavioral objectives, selecting appropriate and effective teaching strategies, and evaluating whether or not the objectives have been achieved requires identification of desired student behavior and possible teaching activities, as well as development of feedback procedures. The teacher recognizes the need for effective planning in the scaled-down situation. With supervisory assistance, s/he should improve the three areas of planning: objectives, strategies, and evaluation. These ingredients are the same for a microlesson, a daily lesson, a unit, or a course of study. Through microteaching, the teacher experiences and reviews the basic processes in planning which can then be applied to other educational situations.

It appears that secondary teachers have sometimes limited their teaching strategies to instruction for the class as a group. Although individualization, continuous progress, and nongraded programs have been implemented on the secondary level, there are schools where traditional class activities continue relatively unchanged. Successful experience in the teaching of small groups of students—as in microteaching—can often extend into more gratifying instructional encounters in "real life" classrooms.

Self-analysis is a professional skill that teachers need. Professional growth is based on the assumption that teachers perceive themselves as continuously learning new skills and developing into more mature and creative teachers. Those who are videotaped in the microteaching process probably have more opportunity to analyze their teaching than they will have at any other time in their educational careers, since the supervisor, students, and videotape provide data. Students complete rating forms dealing with the task or skill which the teacher is practicing. Self-analysis is encouraged as the supervisor and teacher discuss student learning and relate evidence of such learning to the objectives of the lesson.

Videotape feedback supplied in a supportive and stimulating environment can increase understanding of self and encourage better use of one's assets. Thus, positive self-concept, a requisite for effective teaching, is strengthened.

The first part of the microteaching process is the *teach*. This, in brief, is a short lesson taught to a small class with the teacher following a set of his/her own established objectives. The activity takes place in a setting which contains functional equipment, uncluttered background, a blackboard for instructional use, and an arrangement of desks and chairs which puts both the teacher and the students into the range of either one or two cameras. The teacher and supervisor watch this taped sequence together and share their reactions, specifying strengths of the lesson and considering possible alternatives. If an objective was not reached, they consider ways of achieving this. Students evaluate the teaching using appropriate rating forms which may also be scrutinized. These suggestions are summarized into one or two definable statements.

The process of viewing the film, exchanging opinions, and mutually trying to arrive at specific improvements in the lesson is called the *conference*. Following the conference, the teacher reorganizes the lesson, incorporating the suggestions, and returns to the classroom to teach the lesson again to different students. This second attempt is called the *reteach,* which may be followed by either a formal or informal *final conference.*

Frequently, time limits will prevent complete viewing of the taped reteach and a formal conference; however, the teacher must be given an indication of how successfully the suggested changes were implemented. The supervisor, of course, is vitally interested in whether or not the conference suggestions are incorporated in the reteach, because this implementation is the criterion for determining the success of the supervisor's conference.

In summary, there are four principal parts to the microteaching process: the teach, the conference, the reteach, and the final conference. The first three parts are recorded experiences which provide an objective, taped portion for individual or shared analysis. Just as the replay of a major league baseball game explains to a viewer why a team wins or loses, so the videotaped classroom action provides answers about teaching experiences. Videotape feedback is the key part of microteaching, since it provides the material for analysis by self, peers, superordinates, and subordinates. A teacher can clarify his/her own strengths and weaknesses with the supervisor's guidance during the conference. The worth of the experience is especially evident when one notes the sharp improvement in quality of performance in the reteach, as contrasted with the teaching demonstrated in the initial teach. This development of the one being analyzed is an indication of the growth of a teacher and the growth of a person as well. The development of the teacher as a person is a facet of professional growth (Wilhelms, 1973).

MICROTEACHING FOR INSERVICE STAFF DEVELOPMENT

Although microteaching was first used in preservice education, it has been successfully used for inservice programs presented to groups of experienced teachers at many levels. Schools in Jefferson County, Colorado, and El Dorado County, California, used microteaching for inservice with favorable results, i.e., new teacher behaviors were used in actual classroom experiences (Allen, Cooper, and Poliakoff, 1972). Many colleges and universities have contributed to the increasing use of microteaching for inservice education, and the technique has been used to improve college teaching (Allen, Cooper, and Poliakoff, 1972). It is heartening to note that the effects of microteaching seem to be lasting.

Three years after the use of a minicourse from the Far West Regional Laboratory, Borg found that changes in teacher behavior persisted (Fuller and Manning, 1973).

In addition to improving teaching skills, another value of microteaching for experienced teachers is the development of instructional skills models. These videotaped models become resources, and they are available for inservice use, particularly with beginning teachers. Furthermore, microteaching can be used to test new instructional materials and techniques. Not only does the teacher become more familiar with the new material, but s/he can draw clear comparisons between techniques and materials.

A teacher may want to investigate whether students learn more about Puerto Rican native arts by group projects or by individual study. One class may be organized into groups to study such crafts as pottery making, rug weaving, and furniture construction. Each group would present its findings in some way—skit, demonstration, display, or report. Another class might study Puerto Rican crafts with individual assignments. Again, the results of the investigations would be presented as reports, demonstrations, discussions, or displays. These presentations would be videotaped. Analysis of the tapes, along with cognitive tests and attitude surveys, would give the teacher a comparison between techniques. Reactions of other teachers to the videotapes would be helpful. These tapes should then be added to the learning resource center so that individual students, as well as groups of students, could use the tapes for makeup, enrichment, or review.

Such short, taped sequences which show the incorporation of materials and techniques can be enlightening to teachers who are always seeking the many ways to make an instructional period memorable, instead of forgettable. Microteaching can be used by experienced teachers who are helping less experienced teachers. In this way, a peer is serving as an on-site supervisor. Additionally, curriculum specialists can use this medium as a stafff development tool.

The value of microteaching for staff development can be summarized under four major headings:

1. Microteaching is a way of looking at and describing aspects of teaching so that an individual teacher working with a supervisor or peer can deal with specific weaknesses and problems and also discover some strengths which can be increased and developed.
2. Microteaching provides a professional growth process for groups of teachers. They can review and improve their skills by interacting with one another and using the replayed videotape as a basis of professional analysis and discussion.

3. Microteaching creates an opportunity for teachers who want to work alone at self-improvement. It is quite possible to have a camera functioning in the classroom, turned on, focused on the microteaching and eventually turned off by the teacher or a student. The tape can be replayed privately for the teacher to view and assess.
4. Microteaching offers a procedure for testing teaching materials and techniques. A short lesson for a small class using specific materials requires a ''low risk'' investment. Sometimes, a single replay of a class which is piloting a new system can show whether or not the materials and/or techniques are effective.

MICROTEACHING AS A PART OF SUPERVISOR EDUCATION

When supervisors work with an individual teacher to improve instruction, evidence of a supervisor's effectiveness is hard to find. The supervisor's next visit usually means an observation of different content, perhaps different students, or a different phase of a unit. Consequently, the suggested changes for improvement may not be appropriate. For instance, if the supervisor and teacher decided there should be more opportunity for students to investigate a variety of ideas related to the topic as the unit was begun, the supervisor may observe, at the next visit, some of the final activities related to the unit. But, recommended changes in teacher behavior cannot be checked in the new lesson, so the supervisor cannot assess his/her success.

In contrast, the effectiveness of supervision can be determined in microteaching. Too often, such readily observable data are not available in the everyday activities of a teacher. The teach segment of a microteaching experience makes the object of analysis a consistent, unified target of observation. Subsequently, the reteach gives the supervisor an opportunity to determine whether or not the instructional behavior has changed in accordance with conference suggestions.

Videotaping of the conference also gives a supervisor objective feedback material. Analysis of these videotapes allows the supervisor to decide what verbal and nonverbal communication techniques should be maintained, changed, or eliminated. Such procedures allow the supervisor to work toward a unique conference style.

The microteaching format encourages the supervisor to examine the teacher's objectives for the lesson. No observation can be fair, unless the observer knows what the teacher is trying to do. Then, teaching is observed and appraised on two bases:

1. Were the objectives of the lesson achieved?
2. Were items on the rating scale for the teaching task fulfilled?

Since the supervisor cannot observe everything in a teaching situation, some limitations must be set. In microteaching, the objectives of the lesson and the rating scale limit the appraisal.

A portion of a Microteaching Manual for teacher education students is provided in Appendix A. This material can provide a basis for understanding the potential of microteaching for teachers and supervisors, although the tasks are simplified for use with neophytes. Experienced teachers would require more sophisticated task levels.

MICROTEACHING PRACTICUM

Supervisory relationships involve interpersonal contacts. Reading and talking about situations and problems of teachers may broaden the understanding of supervisors and potential supervisors. Exploring possible causes and alternative solutions can be helpful and interesting. However, the supervisory role is best comprehended when the role is actually assumed. Role playing is helpful but, the more real the situation is, the more highly motivated and challenged the supervisor will become. Consequently, a microteaching practicum is recommended as an opportunity for supervisors. In this experience, a preservice supervisor "gets the feel" of the often highly charged interactions which are part of supervisor-teacher communications. Enacting the part of supervisor in a microteaching practicum can aid in the development of skills of analysis; also, it gives rich experience in observing and communicating during the conference process.

When a microteaching practicum is possible, students from a supervision class should work in pairs. One of them should serve as supervisor for the first teacher while the other acts as operator of the camera in the classroom or station. (See Appendix B.) The roles should be reversed for the second teacher. Figure 2 is a checklist which assumes that two teachers will be teaching lessons in a microteaching station, a location which should be equipped with a blackboard, teacher's desk, student chairs, and videotaping equipment. The practicum provides actual practice in supervisory conferences, the "analysis sessions." A supervisor's success is indicated by whether or not the teacher incorporates suggestions from the conference in the reteach.

(The forms in Figures 2-5 were developed for use as part of the supervisory practicum in the Microteaching Laboratory at The University of Akron.)

Figure 2. Checklist for a Microteaching Practicum.

1. Test mike and equipment. *Operator*
2. Prepare name tags. *Supervisor*
3. Introduce self to all. *Operator/Supervisor*
4. Discuss rating forms with students. *Supervisor 1st group only*
5. Write proper information on board for each teach, conference, and reteach. *O*
   (Names of teacher and supervisor along with designation of teach, reteach, or conference)
6. Look at lesson plan objectives. *S*
7. Record teach and conference; mark log accurately. *O*
8. Follow teacher's action with camera and get students' responses. If split screen is available, focus one camera on students. *O*
9. Give teacher 2 minutes' warning after 10 minutes. *S*
10. Have students complete rating forms and collect them before conference. *S*
11. View tape with teacher. *S*
12. Mark your own rating form of teach with check marks. *S*
13. Tape conference. List names on blackboard. Use *one* camera. *O*
14. Use indirect approach in conference: encourage self-evaluation, be supportive and honest, do not flatter, be specific in suggestions for change and praise, SUMMARIZE. Steps in conference: make teacher feel relaxed, establish rapport, agree on changes for improvements, reinforce strengths. Be specific in suggested alternatives and be specific about what was good. *S*
15. List suggestions for reteach at bottom of your rating form (write yes or no if change is made in reteach and mark same form with ''X'' for reteach). *S*
16. Exchange students before reteach. *O*
17. Teach 2—Operator and Supervisor change roles, repeat 5-16.
18. Reteach 1—Repeat 5-10. Mark rating form with ''X'' for reteach and indicate whether changes were made.
19. Replay segments of tape. Have short conference, not videotaped. Focus on changes made and encourage teacher in reference to next micro lesson. *S*
20. Fill out form inside front of folder; put plan and ratings in folder.
21. Reteach 2—See 18-20.
22. Complete log with both names and footage. Include names of both individuals for the conference.
23. If there is additional class time, view and discuss conferences.
24. Rewind tape and put it in the container. Slide folded log in the box. Mark tape with *supervisor names* and place in correct file drawer.
25. If observer is also present in the station, observer should assist whenever possible (1-5, 8, 16). S/he should operate the camera during the conference. The observer should complete evaluation forms for the supervisor and confer informally about strengths and improvements for the conference.

To provide feedback to the supervisor, the teacher is asked to evaluate the supervisor. Figure 3 is an example of a form that has been used for this purpose.

Figure 3. Evaluation Form.

Task. Supervisor's Name _____
Evaluation of supervisor (circle one):

A   A-   B+   B   B-   C+   C   C-

Please check appropriate phrase:

____ extremely helpful   ____ very interested
____ somewhat helpful   ____ relaxed
____ little or no help   ____ a bit nervous
____ uninterested   ____ tense and "uptight"
____ somewhat interested

The supervisory checklist in Figure 4 can be used by the operator to evaluate the conference or by anyone viewing the videotape of the conference.

Figure 4. Supervisory Checklist.

Supervisor _____
Evaluator _____

YES   NO

____   ____   1. Was supervisor indirect?
____   ____   2. Was supervisor supportive?
____   ____   3. Did supervisor give teacher an opportunity to express his/her views?
____   ____   4. Were suggested changes limited to one or two?
____   ____   5. Did both supervisor and teacher verbalize the changes?
____   ____   6. Was conference summary given?
                      7. What were strengths of conference?

_____

                      8. What improvements do you recommend for the conference?

_____

Self-evaluation may be facilitated by encouraging the supervisor to look for specific data. Figure 5 is an example of a self-analysis form.

Figure 5. Conference Self-Analysis Form.

Name _____

Date of conference _____

Task _____

1. How would you describe your conference generally?
   ____ direct   ____ indirect   ____ nondirective
2. How many questions did you ask? ____
3. How many open questions did you use? ____
4. How did you establish rapport?
   _____

5. How were you supportive?
   _____

6. What specific changes were agreed upon?
   _____

7. Who summarized the conference?
   _____

8. What ways would you improve the conference?
   _____

SUMMARY

Microteaching is a useful tool which provides preservice and inservice experiences for professional development. It focuses on student behavior, the timing of lessons, and cohesive plans which base activities and evaluation on the behavioral objectives for the lesson. Opportunities for practicing self-analysis skills and developing positive self-concept can be provided, while developing a more sophisticated level of task refinement. Using microteaching for experimentation with curriculum and methodology can also build a resource of tapes for individualizing instruction and for use as models for inservice activities.

Microteaching can help build supervisory skills, especially conference techniques. A microteaching practicum can be a valuable activity in a supervision class.

REFERENCES

Allen, D.; Cooper, J.M.; and Poliakoff, L. *Microteaching*. No. 17 in the Series of PREP Reports. Washington, DC: US Department of Health, Education and Welfare, 1972.

Association of Teacher Educators. *Microteaching: Selected Papers*. ATE Research Bulletin 9. Washington, DC: Association of Teacher Educators, 1971.

Fuller, F., and Manning, B.A. "Self Confrontation Reviewed: A Conceptualization for Video Playback in Teacher Education." *Review of Educational Research* 43 (Fall 1973): 469–528.

Olivero, J.L. *Microteaching: Medium for Improving Instruction*. Columbus, OH: Charles E. Merrill Publishing Company, 1970.

Wilhelms, F.T. *Supervision in a New Key*. Washington, DC: Association for Supervision and Curriculum Development, 1973.

Chapter 3
Staff Development

One important supervisory responsibility is staff development, often termed inservice education, staff renewal, professional growth, continuing education, on-the-job training, and/or professional development. Harris (1980, p. 21) defines inservice education as "any planned program of learning opportunities afforded staff members of schools . . . for purposes of improving the performance of the individual in already assigned positions." Such a definition has many interpretations and results in great diversity of plans.

VARIED EMPHASIS

Staff development in the school setting implies a program for promoting the professional and personal growth of staff members so they can improve the teaching-learning opportunities for students. A wide variety of developmental programs are provided by different schools. Some schools will have a total staff meeting at the beginning of the school year, often with an "inspirational speaker" to get the teachers "psyched up" for the year's work. At this time, the superintendent may present his/her charge for the year, hoping to encourage the faculty to better efforts and cooperative endeavors. Then, the principals of the buildings may present more specialized sessions for their faculties. After these preliminary meetings, some school systems delegate responsibility for further inservice to principals who believe that a faculty meeting, biweekly or monthly, satisfies their requirements. Other schools have extensive preliminary orientation and planning sessions with continuing group and individual opportunities. Teachers may join study groups, take classes, visit other schools, attend conferences, and pursue specific interests in a variety of ways. School systems may have their own study groups and classes or cooperate with nearby colleges and universities to bring credit courses to the community. Because of specific school programs, administrators may encourage individual teachers to visit schools with similar programs or to attend conferences dealing with related topics. Supervisors often play an active role in developing inservice meetings.

The master contract of a school is a crucial part of its staff development program. Many of these contracts specifically limit the frequency and length of required meetings; these agreements may also list options for evaluation and observations. Working in compliance with such contracts puts a new emphasis on the flexibility of persons in supervisory roles. Also, the importance of developing positive teacher attitudes toward professional growth is emphasized, for only when teachers value such opportunities for their own development can significant provisions be negotiated. Building good interpersonal relations and "selling" a sound inservice program to teachers become survival tactics for the supervisory staff.

Teachers are less mobile as a result of declining school enrollment, so the school system cannot depend on new personnel for fresh ideas; therefore, the teachers in a system must be the basis for educational improvements. New information in content areas and research about human behavior, especially learning, should have an impact on the activities in a school, and newly developed theories about organization and management should be adapted to the educational setting. Motivating the professional and personal growth of staff members becomes a necessity for good schools.

PLANNING INSERVICE PROGRAMS

Mention the next inservice meeting to a group of teachers, and the typical responses are moans, protests, and dour looks. Professional development, in theory an opportunity for growth and personal enrichment, has in practice produced boredom and negative responses. Why is there such a divergence between theory and practice? How can aversive reactions be changed? What promotes favorable attitudes toward inservice? These questions are crucial in planning inservice activities and must be considered by supervisors involved in planning and facilitating these activities.

A commission study of staff development efforts in some 1,300 school systems was sponsored by Phi Delta Kappa (PDK), and an extensive data bank concerning current staff development practices was compiled (King, 1978). Analysis of the data indicated that there is no best way to structure staff development that is "regarded as helpful, constructive, relevant and worthwhile" (p. 18). When either teachers or administrators unilaterally determined the content and processes of inservice programs, these were rated negatively. King concluded that "there appeared to be a real advantage in assigning the responsibility and the authority for staff development to a fairly well-balanced committee of teachers and adminis-trators'' (p. 18).

This study found that 10 factors seemed to be vital for effective planning (King, 1978):

1. There should be consideration of objectives. Since staff develop-ment is an instructional program, the planners must know what they are seeking to accomplish.
2. The target population, the recipients of the inservice program, should be determined. When the intended participants are known, then the planners can use information about these people to select materials and procedures appropriate to the sophistica-tion of the group.
3. The time for the staff development should be designated. Such a decision should relate to how much time is needed, as well as what time of year, what day of the week, and what time of day are most practical.
4. Selection of type or types of offerings should be made based on the objectives, capabilities of the school system, and appeal to the target population. Some possibilities, in addition to institutes, courses, and workshops, are ''demonstrations, personnel ex-changes, seminars, visitations, consultations, retreats, teacher centers, symposia'' (p. 20). The fact that teacher experiences, interests, and abilities vary may require more than one type of offering to cover a topic effectively, e.g., a program for teachers who are working with their first student teachers and another for teachers who have already supervised several student teachers.
5. Planners should select appropriate sponsorship. Although build-ing or school system sponsorship is frequently used, King men-tioned other alternatives, such as self-sponsorship by a motivated individual or interest group, state department of education, edu-cational foundations, professional associations, and universities. In fact, he recommends whatever arrangement will provide the needed resources without diverting from the objectives and the local needs.
6. Activities for the staff development program should be specified from the wide variety of learning experiences available. Criticiz-ing the frequent use of listening, King (p. 21) proposed:

    > In addition to such proven methods as demonstrations, skill practice, observation, lecture, group discussions and buzz sessions, consideration should be given to analysis and synthesis exercises, role playing, gaming, problem solving, in-baskets, decision-making, travel, brainstorming, fish

bowling, round robins, packaged audio-visuals, simulations, computer assisted instruction and micro-teaching. A common thread running through our responses (to the PDK survey) was "Good staff development consists of doing as well as listening."

7. Planners should choose media appropriate to the objectives and participants, if these media meet the quality of instruction desired. Printed materials, films, tapes—audio and video, slides, telelectures, and computer programs are some of the choices available.
8. Location and facilities should receive careful attention. Availability at the scheduled time is not the only consideration. The room should provide an attractive setting and be large enough for the group and for the activities. The necessary facilities should be present and working, e.g., if the overhead projector is needed, it should be properly functioning. The location should be accessible with adequate parking.
9. The factor in the study which correlated most positively with superior staff development was the regularity of evaluation of the staff development effort of the system. Such evaluations provide data on accomplishment of objectives and give information to the planners for improvement of future programs.
10. Finally, the incentives to be employed should be described. Although, in general, schools have not been highly creative in providing rewards for inservice activities, stipends, release time, professional growth credit, certificates or awards, publicity, administrative and supervisory approval, college credit, and opportunities for promotion are sometimes used. Individuals often are motivated by personal satisfaction, peer approval, certification requirements, or self-actualization.

Planning for effective staff development is a complex task. However, as a result of the PDK study, the following was concluded: "Any school system can have quality staff development if they will approach the task with purpose, determination, imagination and commitment" (King, 1978, p. 18).

NEEDS ASSESSMENT

A frequent reaction to inservice meetings is "It isn't relevant to what I'm doing," or "Why should I have to spend time hearing the same old stuff I've heard for years?" Teachers often feel that someone in the administration who is unfamiliar with classroom survival needs has read an article, heard a speech, or talked with another administrator and found an idea which is intriguing. This idea becomes the basis for the next professional meeting in the school system, without any regard for teachers' needs and concerns.

One of the essential tasks in planning a staff development program is determining what is needed and desired in the school, for good staff development programs are built on perception of needs. The process of obtaining this information, which becomes the basis for planning, is a needs assessment. Undoubtedly, the teachers' concerns (needs, wants, desires) should be a priority; administrators, students, parents, and community members may also have suggestions for areas of professional growth.

A needs assessment should establish both general and specific goals for faculty. General needs encompass the school system or a cluster of schools in a system, while specific ones apply to a teacher, a department, a grade level, a team, or a school. The assessment has both formal and informal aspects, but someone must be delegated to prepare or find an assessment instrument, collect data, and interpret it. Supervisory personnel are often the ones responsible for the needs assessment.

The person in charge of conducting a needs assessment may adapt an instrument previously used in that school system or one used in another system. Figure 6 is an example of a form used by one city school district; sometimes originating a questionnaire to fit a particular system seems more appropriate. In either case, knowledge about the current issues, as revealed in educational periodicals and local publications, provides ideas for items to include in the instrument. These sources, along with informal contacts with administrators, teacher organization leaders, supervisors, paraprofessionals, board members, students, and interested community members, are the significant base for the preparation of an instrument. Friends in other schools, the state department of education, members of accreditation teams who have worked in a system, and university personnel familiar with the school may also provide valuable suggestions. There should be an opportunity for teachers to add their concerns to the basic list and to assign priority to these needs. Administrators and supervisors should have similar input.

Preferred strategies and structures for meetings can also be determined by a needs assessment. Knowing when individuals prefer to meet is an advantage, for experience has shown that an afterschool meeting prevents the attendance of coaches who schedule practice then. Also, some teachers are least productive immediately after completing their teaching for the day. Early mornings, evenings, Saturday, and other possibilities should all be considered.

Figure 6. Assessment of Educator Inservice Needs.*

Name _____

School and Grade Level/Department _____

YOUR HELP IS NEEDED! It is essential that we know your high priority inservice topics and possible speakers for the coming school year. Only then can we provide inservice programs that meet your needs. Please complete and return to your building principal.

5–Strongly needed and very important for many educators; I would choose to participate when possible.
4–Strongly needed and very important for many educators; I probably would participate.
3–Well worth considering for program development.
2–Not of high priority at this time.
1–Should receive little, if any, consideration.

Rank 1-5   Suggested Speaker
_____ 1a. Individualization of instruction   1a. _____
_____ 1b. Teaching composition skills   1b. _____
_____ 1c. Providing for individual learning styles   1c. _____
_____ 1d. Teaching the basic skills in any subject   1d. _____
_____ 1e. Teaching children with learning problems   1e. _____
_____ 1f. Teaching of reading   1f. _____
_____ 1g. Teaching of mathematics   1g. _____

Classroom Management:
_____ 1h. Grouping for instruction   1h. _____
_____ 1i. Improving student self-concept—human   1i. _____
          development
_____ 1j. Organization and recordkeeping   1j. _____
_____ 1k. Discipline techniques   1k. _____
_____ 1l. Behavior modification   1l. _____
_____ 1m. Effectively using test information   1m. _____
_____ 1n. Student evaluation   1n. _____
_____ 1o. Communication techniques—teacher,   1o. _____
          administration, community
_____ 1p. Improving student motivation   1p. _____

Teacher Methods:
_____ 1q. Learning centers   1q. _____
_____ 1r. Questioning techniques   1r. _____
_____ 1s. Role playing—simulation   1s. _____
_____ 1t. Using multimedia   1t. _____
_____ 1u. Student tutoring and conferencing   1u. _____

* Source: David Enderle, Assistant Superintendent, Wooster, OH.

Figure 6. Assessment of Educator Inservice Needs (cont'd).

_____ 1v.	Mastery learning	1v. _____
_____ 1w.	Independent learning and study methods	1w. _____
_____ 1x.	Teaching study skills	1x. _____
_____ 1y.	Career education	1y. _____
_____ 1z.	Energy education	1z. _____
_____ 2a.	Teaching gifted students	2a. _____
_____ 2b.	Mainstreaming special education children in the regular classroom	2b. _____
_____ 2c.	Utilizing educational television	2c. _____
_____ 2d.	Metric education	2d. _____
_____ 2e.	Instructional program—articulation and coordination	2e. _____
_____ 2f.	Elementary—Organization, program, etc.	2f. _____
_____ 2g.	Middle School—Organization, program, etc.	2g. _____
_____ 2h.	High School—Organization, program, etc.	2h. _____
_____ 2i.	Recognizing needs of multi-ethnic groups	2i. _____
_____ 2j.	Outdoor/environmental education	2j. _____
_____ 2k.	Utilizing the fine arts in the classroom	2k. _____
_____ 2l.	Parent-teacher conferencing	2l. _____
_____ 2m.	Using newspapers in the classroom	2m. _____
_____ 2n.	Developing effective bulletin boards and displays	2n. _____
_____ 2o.	Integrating economics education into the curriculum	2o. _____
_____ 2p.	Planning effective teaching units	2p. _____
_____ 2q.	Getting the most out of field trips	2q. _____

Check Topic(s):

NAME OF SPEAKER
(Include address or place of employment, if possible)

_____ Language Arts   _____

_____ Math   _____

_____ Science   _____

_____ Social Studies   _____

_____ Fine Arts   _____

_____ Practical Arts and Vocational   _____

Figure 6. Assessment of Educator Inservice Needs (cont'd).

_____ Foreign Language	_____
_____ Health—Physical Education	_____
_____ Counseling—Guidance	_____
_____ Reading	_____
_____ Music	_____
_____ Educational Media— Library	_____
_____ Driver Education	_____
_____ Special Education	_____
_____ Administration	_____
_____ Outdoor Education	_____
_____ Business Education	_____
_____ Speech and Hearing	_____
_____ General	_____
_____ Other	_____

There is always risk in asking about inservice strategies. Teachers, as human beings, may hesitate to become involved, preferring to be entertained. However, the popularity of "Make and Take" sessions seems to indicate that relevant activities are appreciated. Consequently, participant suggestions about strategies and format may be helpful to planners.

When the data are collected and analyzed, needs of administrators and supervisors, as well as teachers, should be categorized. A good professional growth program should include all the staff and not be limited to teachers. Such a broad program provides balance and gives the total staff of a school system equal responsibility for continuing professional development.

In summary, a needs assessment can furnish the background for setting up an overall program. It shows priorities for general meetings, building sessions, and inservice days.

INDIVIDUALIZATION

In addition to group needs, general and specific, individual needs should also be met in a good professional development program. Job targets have been one way to approach individualization. This approach, originated by George Redfern (1972), has been adopted in various forms by many schools. The basic concept involves the formulation of specific objectives for a teacher's progress, usually for a school year. These goals are determined sometimes by the individual teacher, sometimes by concerns in an evaluator's recommendation, and other times by the results of an evaluation procedure. The assessment may be based on a form originated by the school system or one adapted from another source. Redfern's model, for example, is often modified for local use. When the Battelle Self Appraisal Instrument (McFadden, 1970) is used, the teacher is profiled in the four areas of teaching: instructional leader, social leader, promoter of healthful emotional development, and communicator. Since this analysis of teaching is based on a careful examination of the literature and categorization of teachers' experiences, this instrument can help a teacher recognize both strengths and areas of weakness. The teacher and principal, or supervisor, should discuss this data and consider potential activities to build up selected areas. (See the Teacher Self-Appraisal section of Chapter 12 for more information about the Battelle Self Appraisal Instrument.)

The job target plan is usually a phase of both the evaluation and staff development programs of a school system. Evaluation, which is a sensitive area usually involving promotion, tenure, and termination, arouses teacher antipathy. Yet, any professional growth program requires the collection of data to determine needs. This process may be called assessment, appraisal, or evaluation, but it is a necessary step.

Job targets may be determined in numerous ways, such as self-analysis, analysis of observer data, superordinate suggestion, consideration of available activities, and specific school goals. The number and complexity of job targets should be limited—enough to challenge a teacher, but restricted to avoid frustration. Job targets which are too easy foster complacency; those too difficult cause frustration. Working with teachers to formulate these targets, then, requires an understanding of the individual, his/her professional strengths and weaknesses, motivations, responsibilities, and interests. With such knowledge, more realistic objectives can be established.

The next step is the planning of how to accomplish these targets. Such planning includes the procedures, timing, and check points. If the teacher is going to improve questioning techniques in class discussion and testing, then planning should include the use of books on questioning, e.g., those by Sanders (1966) and Hunkins (1976), college courses which focus on improving questioning, inservice and/or conferences which deal with questioning, and perhaps clinical supervision. With these activities specified, a time line is established so that teacher progress can be determined. Instruments for collecting data (e.g., electronic recording and/or recording by observers) and methods for evaluating the data must be determined. Selection of instrument depends on the specific objectives. Is raising the level of student thinking the criterion? Is increasing student participation important? If the level of questioning is an issue, then categorizing of questions requires use of some classification system, such as Bloom's *Taxonomy* (1956) or Taba's categories (1966). If the involvement of students in discussion is indicated, Flanders' Interaction Analysis (Flanders, 1970) or some other observation system appropriate for analyzing student verbal participation might be used. Of course, description of current questioning in the classroom is necessary as a basis for comparison. So, the procedures for collecting and analyzing data are applied immediately. Then, as progress is examined at the times specified, the plans may need to be altered according to the teacher's development.

The one-to-one involvement in planning and monitoring job targets is time consuming. Although personnel to conduct such a program for all teachers is usually limited, it is important to foster teacher development by some systematic procedure. The use of job targets as a professional growth plan, without monitoring by a supervisor or administrator, is effective only when the individual teachers are professionals who are personally motivated. Consequently, school systems may emphasize job targets for beginning teachers, those eligible for tenure, teachers with problems, and perhaps others on a four- or five-year cycle. The use of job targets may become increasingly feasible for school systems as teacher turnover decreases.

School systems have not been very creative in motivating teachers for professional growth. Policy on salary increments may require a minimum of participation in staff development activity, i.e., some schools may not advance a teacher on the salary scale without evidence of professional development. Occasionally, a "master teacher" bonus or step on the salary schedule rewards outstanding effort. A stipend for a particular summer project may be awarded for specific work, such as preparing individualized math packets or planning a science program based on local field trips.

Sergiovanni's (1967) findings about satisfiers for teachers give some clues for motivation. His findings supported Herzberg's motivation-hygiene theory (1976) in regard to teachers. The contributors to job satisfaction—"satisfiers"—are achievement, recognition, and responsibility. When not met, these needs seemed not to contribute to job dissatis-faction. The "dissatisfiers" were different factors, e.g., interpersonal relations with students and peers. Although the importance of achieve-ment, recognition, and responsibility as significant satisfiers for teachers is verbalized by administrators, actual use of the satisfiers is less apparent. Not only can the application of these concepts motivate teachers to pursue professional growth activities, but it can also provide leadership for specif-ic aspects of the staff development program.

TALENT UTILIZATION

Bringing in an expert is usually the first suggestion when planning meetings on specific topics. Often, knowledgeable individuals in the system are ignored. A file of local talent is essential to a well-organized staff development program, since the special skills and interests of indi-vidual teachers provide a convenient and valuable resource. Supervisors should have a talent file and keep it current. In working with different teachers, administrators, and schools, supervisors are in an ideal situation for collecting information about individual proficiency.

Using the talents of the teachers in a system can be a sincere tribute to the expertise of those individuals. This morale booster can enhance the program through a perspective of local conditions and resources. Other teachers in the same system should find the experiences of their colleagues in the local schools and community helpful and challenging. Some exam-ples of local talent follow: one of the counselors may have done a study of conflict resolution; a primary teacher may be successfully using behavior modification with students; a junior high teacher may have used contracts effectively in algebra classes; coping with stress may be the specialty of a high school teacher who has spoken to local service clubs on this topic.

Local teachers can also be used when preparing scripts and producing videotapes for inservice presentations. In Zanesville, Ohio, a series of 20-minute tapes was prepared to focus attention on a variety of teaching strategies. Such a library of tapes is useful for meetings of groups of teachers (a building, department, or grade level) or for individual teachers with a need or interest in the area. Since school equipment is usually available for such production, the library of videotapes can be increased as new ideas, needs, and interests develop. Sometimes students and commu-nity members can be a part of the production team; this situation has excellent potential for good public relations, because information about the staff development program is disseminated.

Closed circuit television is a valuable inservice tool for those schools which are so equipped. Time and energy are conserved when teachers can remain in their own buildings instead of traveling to a central meeting place. Good planning can provide for appropriate follow-up discussions. Such arrangements can use teacher leadership and participation, and the teachers who are involved in this verbal interaction become active learners.

TEACHER CENTERS

Based on the British teacher center, the concept of a specific location for teachers to find study materials, to meet in study groups, and to initiate their own professional activities has materialized for special education teachers in several states. The teacher center is an important resource in staff development. "One of the most promising inservice alternatives" (Bell and Peightely, 1975, p. 17), it brings together professionals who are committed to encouraging continuous growth and renewal among teachers. These centers have been especially helpful to teachers needing teaching materials in classes for students with learning disabilities and for students with other handicaps.

Federal funding in 1976 stimulated the growth of teacher centers. The interest in these centers is illustrated by the Spring 1980 issue of *Action in Teacher Education: The Journal of the Association of Teacher Educators,* which is entirely devoted to teacher centers. Individual school systems, counties, and areas have collected materials for professional development, provided space for group meetings, and assigned personnel to facilitate use of the centers.

Whether these centers should be a function of a school system, a group of schools, teacher associations, a university-school partnership, or some other combination has been questioned, and the financing of such ventures causes delays and conflicts. Bell and Peightely (pp. 18-19) give a taxonomy of teacher center types:

1. Consortium—three or more cooperating institutions or organizations.
2. Partnership—two institutions or organizations.
3. Autonomous—a single controlling unit.
4. Special focus—a center with a primary concern such as individualized instruction, reading, or open education.

If the facility is to be adequately used, there must be a "selling" of a teacher center to the teacher clients. Supervisors and administrators can be instrumental in encouraging its use. Administrative support of teacher centers can foster favorable attitudes and stimulate teacher familiarity with the center according to Zigarmi and Zigarmi (Devaney, 1979, pp. 244-49).

Administrators recognize the following services of teacher centers:

1. Provide teachers with help in problem solving and encourage them to try new approaches in solving classroom problems.
2. Allow teachers to explore and develop materials to use in class.
3. Give teachers contacts so they can share ideas and resources.
4. Provide a source of social-emotional support for users.
5. Organize workshops and college courses for teachers.
6. Provide classroom advisory assistance.
7. Orient new teachers—sometimes also student teachers, substitutes, and paraprofessionals.
8. Help teachers understand the teaching-learning process.
9. Encourage acceptance of responsibility for self-directed professional growth.
10. Give teachers experience in leadership for inservice programs.

Setting a model for teacher center use is an important factor. If the supervisory staff schedules curriculum and textbook committee meetings in the teacher center and uses this facility to house the books and resources needed for the committee's work, then the pattern for coming to the center may be established. A continuing effort is required, if teachers are to learn to use an available teacher center as a resource, for these centers can be a major force in staff development programs.

EVALUATION

Staff development (including individual inservice meetings and also entire programs) must be evaluated. Questionnaires that get immediate reactions to inservice activities can provide valuable insight to help with future meetings. Examples of forms which have been developed for this type of feedback are provided in Figures 7 and 8. However, the real test of effectiveness is whether teacher behavior in the classroom is affected. A program on use of stations for instruction may be well-received by teachers but, unless they then prepare and use stations for some part of their instruction, the inservice cannot be considered effective.

Committees and work groups must be evaluated in terms of both process (formative) and product (summative). As both formative and summative evaluations are made, the participants become more informed about themselves, the group interaction, and the final result of the group activity. As teachers become accustomed to the evaluations, they may learn to view appraisal as an integral part of the growth spiral. More positive feelings of teachers toward evaluation are helpful to the total supervisory process.

Figure 7. Evaluation Form.

Answer Each Question According to this Scale:
- 2–Extremely So
- 1–Very Much
- 0–Somewhat So
- −1–Not So Much
- −2–Not At all

1. Was information presented today useful to you?

   −2   −1   0   1   2

2. Was the topic of this activity a concern that your school may have?

   −2   −1   0   1   2

3. Did the role that each person played seem realistic?

   −2   −1   0   1   2

4. Do you feel that role playing is a good method for presenting this information?

   −2   −1   0   1   2

5. Were you able to draw conclusions from the role play?

   −2   −1   0   1   2

6. Do you feel the teachers in your school would benefit from this activity?

   −2   −1   0   1   2

7. Do you feel the administration of your school would be willing to use this activity in an inservice program?

   −2   −1   0   1   2

Add up your scores and compare them with this scale:

14 – 8	Definitely should be used
7 – 1	Probably should be modified and used
0 – −6	Could be used as a reference or example
−7 – −14	Should not be used

Figure 8. Evaluation of Inservice.

1. How would you rate this inservice? (circle one)

   unsatisfactory   satisfactory   excellent

2. List three positive aspects of this inservice.

   _____

   _____

   _____

3. List any negative aspects.

   _____

   _____

4. Note any suggestions for improvement of this presentation.

   _____

   _____

   _____

5. Comments:

When the group planning for staff development sets up evaluation for both long- and short-term objectives, a basis is provided for further staff development. Data collected in evaluation should be used to indicate appropriate content and procedures for future inservice programs, as well as to appraise staff development in relation to current goals and objectives. Effective teaching requires continuous evaluation of student accomplishments. Whenever objectives are not met, instruction must be recycled and adapted so the objectives can be achieved. Staff development is indeed an instructional program and must be evaluated accordingly. Here, too, when objectives are not accomplished, further opportunities for achieving the designated learning should be planned.

POSITIVE CLIMATE FOR PROFESSIONAL GROWTH

A laboratory approach for inservice was proposed by Harris and Bessent (1969) to promote active learning by teachers. Such participation is in contrast to the passive listening which is often the major activity in staff development programs. The model (Figure 9) for inservice programs developed by Wallace and Smith (1978, p. 123) also emphasizes the teacher as a learner. The identifying of needs, providing appropriate learning environment, using instructional strategies, and promoting interaction are all important aspects of good instruction. In addition, analysis of the classroom climate provides some guidelines for inservice programs.

Every teacher strives to produce a good climate for learning within the classroom. Each student should feel that s/he is an important person who contributes to the group. Instruction is adapted to the individual—starting where the student is, building on strengths and interests, paced to encourage learning, planned to stimulate thinking and promote creative activities and to provide support and assistance whenever needed. Thus, student accomplishments are recognized, shared, and rewarded. Feedback to students and teacher provides continuous evaluation of progress, and this is the basis for individualizing the instructional program.

Figure 9. Model for In-Service Programs.*

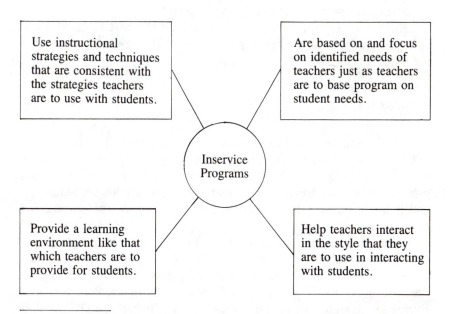

*Adapted from model by D. K. Wallace and E. Smith, in *Breakaway to Multidimensional Approaches: Integrating Curriculum Development and Inservice Education,* (Washington, DC: Association of Teacher Educators, 1978), p. 123.

In translating the "good climate" in the classroom to a "positive climate" for inservice activities, these basic factors should be retained:

1. Start where the individual is.
2. Build on strengths and interests.
3. Pace activities to encourage learning.
4. Stimulate thinking and creative activities.
5. Get the learner actively involved.
6. Provide support and assistance as needed.
7. Recognize and reward accomplishments.
8. Plan toward both short- and long-range goals.
9. Evaluate frequently so individual programs can be modified.

Staff development is specifically geared for professionals. Therefore, the teachers should be participants in the research and its analysis, in establishing objectives, in planning activities, in developing individualized programs, and in evaluation. The responsibility of a professional includes a commitment to continue to learn and grow as a person. Since many teachers today will be continuing in the same system, their educational improvement is increasingly dependent on good inservice programs. Teachers who are here today and here tomorrow must be involved in effective professional growth to provide better educational opportunities for today's students.

SUMMARY

Strong staff development programs are necessary for improvement in today's schools. Effective inservice meetings require appropriate decisions about many factors which are often determined by local facilities and preferences; needs assessment provides a basis for developing both group and individual plans. Individualized programs to promote professional development are frequently a part of a job target program of the school system. Since a professional growth plan involves teacher motivation, the use of teacher talent is a means of capitalizing on the responsibility and recognition important to teachers. Teacher centers have provided an additional resource for encouraging professional improvement of teachers. Evaluation, both formative and summative, is an integral part of any staff development program. Educators are challenged to be more creative in staff development programs, especially in the areas of motivation and evaluation techniques.

REFERENCES

Bell, H., and Peightely, J. *Teacher Centers and Inservice Education.* Bloomington, IN: Phi Delta Kappa Educational Foundation, 1976.

Bloom, B.S., ed. *Taxonomy of Educational Objectives Handbook I: Cognitive Domain.* New York: David McKay Co., Inc., 1956.

Devaney, K., ed. *Building a Teachers' Center.* San Francisco, CA: Teachers' Center Exchange, 1979.

Dillon-Peterson, B., ed. *Staff Development/Organization Development.* Alexandria, VA: Association for Supervision and Curriculum Development, 1981.

Flanders, N.A. *Analyzing Teaching Behaviors.* Reading, MA: Addison Wesley Publishing Co., 1970.

Harris, B.M. *Improving Staff Performance through Inservice Education.* Boston: Allyn and Bacon, Inc., 1980.

Harris, B.M., and Bessent, W. *Inservice Education.* Englewood Cliffs, NJ: Prentice-Hall, Inc., 1969.

Herzberg, F. *The Managerial Choice: To Be Efficient and To Be Human.* Homewood, IL: Dow-Jones-Irwin, 1976.

Howey, K.R.; Bents, R.; and Corrigan, D., eds. *Schoolfocused Inservice: Descriptions and Discussions.* Reston, VA: Association of Teacher Educators, 1981.

Hunkins, F.P. *Questioning Strategies and Techniques.* Boston: Allyn and Bacon, Inc., 1972.

————. *Involving Students in Questioning.* Boston: Allyn and Bacon, Inc., 1976.

King, J.C. "Improving Staff Development Using a Model." *OASCD* 1 (Winter 1978): 18–21.

McFadden, D.N. *Increasing the Effectiveness of Educational Management.* Columbus, OH: School Management Institute and Battelle Memorial Institute, 1970.

Redfern, G.B. *How to Evaluate Teaching: A Performance Objectives Approach.* Worthington, OH: School Management Institute, 1972.

Sanders, N.M. *Classroom Questions: What Kinds?* New York: Harper and Row, 1966.

Sergiovanni, T.J. "Factors which Affect Satisfaction and Dissatisfaction of Teachers." *The Journal of Educational Administration* 5 (May 1967): 66–82.

Taba, H. *Teaching Strategies and Cognitive Functioning in Elementary School Children*. San Francisco, CA: San Francisco State College, 1966.

Wallace, D.K., and Smith, E.B. "Models for Multidimensional Curriculum Development and Inservice Education." In *Breakaway to Multidimensional Approaches* edited by Roy A. Edelfelt and E. Brooks Smith. Washington, D.C.: Association of Teacher Educators, 1978.

Chapter 4
Clinical Supervision

Clinical supervision is widely used today in supervisory programs. This important procedure was first used in the Master of Arts in Teaching (MAT) program at Harvard during the 1950s. Cogan and his colleagues, seeking a more productive approach with student teachers, developed and refined the model of clinical supervision. It was initiated in the preservice program but was soon adapted for inservice education. Cogan described the process in his book *Clinical Supervision;* Goldhammer presented an analysis in his book of the same title. Their steps are basically the same, with some differences in terminology and interpretation. The steps include:
1. Preobservation conference.
2. Observation and collection of data.
3. Analysis of data.
4. Postobservation conference.
5. Postconference evaluation.
The process has been applied to student teachers, interns, and experienced teachers. Although the one-to-one relationship is time consuming, concern with lesson plans and their implementation can result in a more objective observation with a less threatening approach.

PREOBSERVATION CONFERENCE

Observation of a class by a person who is uninformed about the purpose of the class activities often leads to misinterpretation and misunderstanding. A review lesson requires far different teaching strategies from a lesson introducing a unit. The supervisor who is unaware of a teacher's objectives must waste time attempting to figure out what the teacher wants to achieve. Occasionally, the supervisor makes false assumptions about a lesson and does irreparable damage to the working relationship with the teacher. For example, Ms. Johnson is presenting new material to her home economics class, i.e., current developments in nutrition, which is not readily accessible to the class. Mr. Thomas, the principal, who observes this lesson as a supervisor, uses an adaptation of Flanders Interaction Analysis. In the conference following the observation, he suggests that she did not involve the students sufficiently in discussion. Of course, the teacher is upset. Mr. Thomas has criticized without knowing what was happening. Ms. Johnson's lesson was planned to use a lecture approach. Discussion was involved only as an evaluation technique to check on student understanding. Since Mr. Thomas used an observation system which was designed for recording class discussion, Ms. Johnson is resentful and defensive and feels he is unfair.

If a teacher is not familiar with clinical supervision, the supervisor, in the preobservation conference, should explain the purpose, the steps, and the values of this approach. Perhaps a review of this rationale should also be included for teachers who have been exposed to this process previously. The preobservation conference serves to acquaint the supervisor with the lesson plan—objectives, teaching activities, and evaluation. Since objectives determine the kinds of classroom activities and the ways in which student learning can be evaluated, communication between the teacher and supervisor must clarify the classroom situation, explain the relation of this lesson to the unit, and suggest expected student reactions. Plans can be revised or modified quickly if, during the discussion, changes seem desirable.

Information about the students in the class further assists the supervisor. Knowing about mainstreamed students, students with communication problems, foreign students, stutterers, and academic achievement levels should help the observer comprehend the teacher's plan and teaching procedures.

During the preobservation conference, the teacher and supervisor should decide what data need to be collected and a system must be selected or improvised to record the data appropriately. Teachers, who are involved with their students and the teaching process, are often unable to get the facts that they want, e.g., the reaction of individual students, the teacher movement pattern in the class, or wait time after questions. In addition, the supervisor may want specific data. If the teacher has experienced class participation problems, then student involvement—both verbal and nonverbal—may be important information. If improved student behavior is a publicized goal for a school, then the supervisor and teacher will probably agree to take a look at students' activity. The teacher who has expressed his/her interests and preferences should feel more comfortable knowing the kind of information needed and the recording procedures. Since the supervisor will be writing to record classroom activities, this process should not cause the teacher to speculate, "What have I done wrong now?" Such a question might bother a teacher who is being observed without benefit of a preobservation conference.

In summary, this conference gives the supervisor an opportunity to build rapport with the teacher. The teacher provides information to help the supervisor understand the lesson which will be observed, and together, they should decide about data collection. The joint responsibility establishes the base of cooperative effort needed for effective clinical supervision. Figure 10 is a sample of a form used for a preobservation conference. It includes background information under Class Setting and Student Characteristics; the lesson plan under Objectives, Evaluation and Instructional Materials; and collection of data under Supervisory Role (Bellon, 1976, p. 29).

OBSERVATION AND COLLECTION OF DATA

Emphasis on the objectives and the data collected during the observation are not new to supervisors. However, when these two facets of a lesson receive attention, the personal characteristics of a teacher are not threatened. The supervision is individualized, rather than personalized, so the teacher has a feeling that specific teaching behavior is analyzed in relation to a particular lesson.

An observation system is a procedure for recording aspects of classroom activity. Many observation systems have been developed (Simon and Boyer, 1974). Some systems use coding; some involve diagraming or graphing. Systems have been devised for special subject areas (e.g., Moskovitz for foreign language); for particular subjects and grade levels (e.g., Taba for social studies in grades one through six); and for specific teaching strategies (e.g., Flanders for class discussion). Some systems look only at teaching behavior; others look at both teacher and student behavior. The system may record verbal, nonverbal, or both behaviors. It may involve a simple tabulation of a type of behavior or a more complex time sampling of activities. Sometimes, a verbatim transcription is made. Videotape and audiotape also can be used. A repertoire of recording procedures is essential, if an observer wants to be able to adapt quickly to whatever circumstances arise.

Although a supervisor may have an excellent memory, a written system has advantages. The teacher looks at the record as objective data, while an oral recounting without documentation often seems subjective. Emphasis is placed on what happened, so there is less feeling that the teacher is personally threatened. Patterns of teaching can be more easily perceived by both the supervisor and the teacher, when they examine the evidence in black and white.

Information to determine whether objectives were achieved must always be sought, even though this information may be only partially available within the observed time. The effectiveness of a lesson on how to

Figure 10. Preobservation Conference.*

Teacher _____   Observer _____
Subject _____   Date _____

1. *Class Setting:*

   a. What have you and the students been doing the past several lessons?

   b. What is the topic of the lesson that will be observed?

   c. What is the physical setting of the class?

2. *Student Characteristics:*

   a. Are there any prerequisite skills or knowledge needed by the students in order to accomplish the objectives?

   b. Are there any unique characteristics of the students in the class?

3. *Objectives:*

   a. What are your objectives for this lesson?

   b. What will the learner be able to do after your instruction?

4. *Evaluation:*

   a. How will you know if the students have achieved the objectives of the lesson?

5. *Instructional Strategies and Materials:*

   a. What is your role in this lesson?

   b. What do you expect the students to do as far as involvement with you or with each other?

   c. What materials will you use in the lesson?

6. *Supervisory Role:*

   a. What should I focus on while observing your class?

*Source: J.J. Bellon et al. *Classroom Supervision and Instructional Improvement, 2nd ed.* (Dubuque, IA: Kendall/Hunt Publishing Company, 1982), p. 36. Copyright © 1982 by Kendall/Hunt Publishing Company. Reprinted by permission.

plan a descriptive speech can be assessed by student feedback during the class session. But, other valid evidence is the actual speech plans that will be prepared by all students, and these are not available until a later time.

A form used for collection of data by supervisors in a suburban district is provided in Figure 11. It shows an emphasis on objectives. There is space for collecting data on teacher influence in discussion, nonverbal teacher behavior, and the variety of teaching methods. Furthermore, this form provides the possibility of including other materials which may be important to the particular situation. If this form is used in the preobservation conference, the teacher and supervisor must predict the expected behaviors. For example, in a review lesson, the expected student responses might be as high as 20 percent of the student verbalization.

A prepared format of this type allows the supervisor to incorporate decisions made in the preobservation conference. Flexibility can also be demonstrated as the supervisor develops his/her own procedures for mapping teacher movement and student participation. If a supervisor has examined the coding and methods of observation systems, such as the 99 described in *Mirrors of Behavior* (Simon and Boyer, 1974) and the suggestions of Bellon (1976), the supervisor can put together a recording system that s/he is comfortable with. Using his/her own procedures should allow the supervisor to adapt easily to collecting required data.

ANALYSIS OF DATA

This step in the process of clinical supervision is usually done by the supervisor as part of planning the postobservation conference. Here, the supervisor's judgment is involved. How much data should be used as the basis of the conference? In what sequence should the reported facts be presented? If only a portion of the information is deemed advisable, what part should be used? In most situations, a teacher is overwhelmed by a total report—in fact, drowned in a sea of data. When many behaviors are involved, the teacher is apt to be confused about where to start and what to do. Expertise of the supervisor must be exercised in deciding which elements of the data are most important for this specific teacher at this exact stage of professional development. The amount of actual time available for the meeting of the supervisor and the teacher following the observation also creates limitations.

It should be remembered that all materials collected should be available to the teacher. In the process of analyzing data, the supervisor and teacher are scrutinizing collected information to see the overall development of the lesson, to discern any frequently used patterns, and to find evidence of achievement of objectives.

Figure 11. Summary of Objectives, Outcomes, and Teacher Goals.

Teacher _____   Date _____

Class _____

   I.   *OBJECTIVES:*

       EVIDENCE   OF   ACHIEVEMENT   OF EACH OBJECTIVE

  II. *VERBAL BEHAVIOR*

	Category	*%* *Expected*	*%* *Observed*
Teacher Talk			
1.	Accepts Feeling	_____	_____
2.	Praises or Encourages	_____	_____
3.	Accepts or Uses Ideas of Student	_____	_____
4.	Asks Questions	_____	_____
5.	Lectures	_____	_____
6.	Gives Directions	_____	_____
7.	Criticizes or Justifies Authority	_____	_____
Student Talk			
8.	Student Talk-Response	_____	_____
9.	Student Talk-Initiation	_____	_____
10.	Silence or Confusion	_____	_____

 III. *NON-VERBAL BEHAVIOR*

1.	Encouraging	_____	_____
2.	Restricting	_____	_____
3.	Distracting	_____	_____

 IV. *QUESTIONING (percent)*

       Level

1.	Recall (who-what-when-where)	_____	_____
2.	Translation-Interpretation (how-why)	_____	_____
3.	Analytical-Critical evaluation (apply knowledge in a new situation)	_____	_____

		# *Expected*	*#* *Observed*
V. *ACTIVITIES*			
A.	*Variety (number)*	_____	_____
B.	*Individualization*		

       1. Intentions

       2. Outcomes·

For a beginning teacher, data on student behavior may be crucial. An experienced professional may be challenged to explore ways of involving more students in discussion—such a reaction may occur if exact information about numbers of participating students is provided. The teacher in a laboratory situation may be shocked to learn how much time is actually spent "on task" by students who are working on individual projects.

Sometimes, the supervisor will be guided by the teacher's perception of what was important or interesting; in this case, the supervisor allows a mature teacher to provide the focus for the conference and the ensuing plans for professional growth. The supervisor's preparation for such a nondirective conference involves the same survey and summary of data, but the determination of what data to present will be made as the teacher's own interests are revealed in the conference. For example, when Dan Elliott reviews the data collected during observation of his science lesson, he indicates a desire to improve questioning techniques. Pat Dunfee, the elementary supervisor, has copied all his questions as planned in the preceding conference. Mr. Elliott feels that the questions were general and diffuse, he thinks specific questions in an ordered sequence would stimulate more student response, and he wants to develop more skill in using an inquiry method. Dan is an experienced, competent teacher; selection of the target for his development allows him to act as a professional. Together Ms. Dunfee and Mr. Elliott can develop a plan for achieving the goal.

Another model for analysis has been developed by Snyder (1978) based on four variables which Bloom (1976) concludes are significant in quality instruction: cues and directives, reinforcement, participation, and correctives and feedback. These occur in sequence in effective learning situations. Bloom suggests that cues and directives evoke student responses which are followed by reinforcement which leads to participation with correctives and feedback. Data from classroom observation can also be related to each of the four areas, as Snyder has proposed (Goldhammer, Anderson, and Krajewski, pp. 75-76):

CUES AND DIRECTIVES
    Classroom management
    Social-emotional climate
    Body language
    Relationship of program objectives to learning activities
    Student response to cues
    Use of space
REINFORCEMENT
    Motivation strategies
    On-task/off-task behaviors
    Skill maintenance
    Repetition of learning tasks

Verbal reinforcements
Environmental reinforcements
Student response to reinforcement procedures
PARTICIPATION
Teacher-student interaction
Student-student interaction
Levels of thinking tasks
Nature of individual tasks
Nature of group tasks (large and small)
Peer learning tasks
Wait time
Questioning techniques
Student participation in planning
Group roles, tasks, and responsibilities
CORRECTIVES AND FEEDBACK
Selection of program materials
Feedback content
Feedback procedures
Kinds of correctives
Relationship between a learning behavior and feedback
Use of teaching team resources

If the teacher and supervisor work with this or a similar model of effective teaching, the total teaching-learning process is conceptualized. In some other approaches, e.g., microteaching, the emphasis is on a task or skill, and the importance of sequential development may be neglected.

In this analysis phase, the supervisor ordinarily determines priorities. S/he plans a strategy for involving the teacher in a discovery approach for studying the selected data. The strengths of the teacher should be included. If changes of behavior are needed, the task should be manageable, and there should be some reward or recognition for successful change.

POSTOBSERVATION CONFERENCE

The postobservation conference should provide information to the teacher about what occurred in the classroom, and it should develop a basis for improvement of instruction. The feedback, to be useful, should be descriptive rather than evaluative, specific rather than general, and checked to ensure clear communication. The conference should be planned as soon as possible after the observation. Interest in the lesson decreases rapidly if the conference is delayed for a day or two.

The method the supervisor uses in the conference to help the teacher study the data may set a pattern for the teacher to use for self-analysis. One of the purposes of clinical supervision is to encourage professional self-evaluation and to help teachers develop the skills and desire for this type of self-assessment.

A conference climate that is characterized by trust, credibility, and support provides the environment for productive interaction. A trust relationship implies confidentiality. Whatever takes place in the conference or classroom should be restricted information, unless the teacher agrees to share the ideas. Furthermore, the supervisor must follow through on his/her commitment. If the teacher is promised materials, they must be provided or the teacher's trust in the supervisor's word is lost. A supervisor may need to establish credibility. The teacher expects a supervisor to be knowledgeable about content, teaching-learning process, materials, school policies and resources and, if the supervisor is not informed, then s/he should be willing to investigate and get answers for the teacher. Finally, a supportive climate means that the teacher feels the supervisor is positive about the teacher's performance. Although the supervisor must be honest and include information about weaknesses, as well as strengths, an optimistic view about the teacher's prospects for growth should be projected. Concern about the teacher as a person and a helpful attitude contribute to supportiveness.

Although the supervisor may select data and guide the teacher toward the consideration of improving a particular facet of teaching, no prescription for conferences can be given. As Cogan (1973, p. 196) suggests, "the conference defines itself by its context." It should develop as a cooperative interaction with the purpose of professional growth. When this goal is mutually recognized, the potential for productive communication is increased. (Detailed consideration of conference techniques is found in the next chapter, "The Supervisory Conference.")

POSTCONFERENCE EVALUATION

After a plan of action is agreed upon in the postobservation conference, communication between the teacher and supervisor should continue. They need to consider the process of clinical supervision as it has worked for them to determine whether it is constructive. What improvements can these two suggest for the different steps in the process? Has a good relationship developed between them? Are they growing professionally because of their interaction? Is the teacher developing skills in self-analysis? Would the teacher encourage others to use clinical supervision? Would the teacher recommend that his/her colleagues go to this supervisor for assistance? Will this experience have an effect on the classroom of the teacher? These questions can be part of the postconference evaluation.

Information from this phase of clinical supervision should provide a basis to help the supervisor modify his/her supervisory practices. Not only should the techniques of the supervisor be considered, but the values, emotional reactions, and goals should also be discussed. As the supervisor experiences this aspect of clinical supervision, s/he may get a better understanding of the affective dimensions of the teacher's job. The process of clinical supervision can then be recycled. As the two professionals work together, their interaction should reflect insights and improvements from the previous cycle.

ADAPTATIONS OF CLINICAL SUPERVISION

Although clinical supervision began as a cyclical process for working with preservice teachers, it is now also being used for inservice activities. This one-to-one relationship between a supervisor and teacher also has been modified for small group activities. Some of the faculty of the College of Education at Indiana University agreed to work with a group of teachers who volunteered to try a cooperative approach to clinical supervision. The results of their experiments were positive, and others have started similar groups which have found the clinical supervision model a productive way to approach self-renewal and staff development.

From these experiences, certain guidelines were developed. Since not all teachers are secure enough to expose themselves to peer analysis, only mature teachers who want to participate should join a group. The group should be flexible so members could drop out or join as they wish. Administrators should not participate as group members, since their presence inhibits teacher participation. A group of five or six teachers is probably the best size for good interaction. The roles of teacher and group leader should be rotated. Videotaped lessons enable teachers who are scheduled during a lesson to collect data on the lesson. Simulations of the clinical process by the group enable the individuals to recognize the emotional stress experienced when peers observe a lesson, collect data, and help analyze the teaching-learning process. Role playing reveals the importance of using objective data and encouraging the teacher's interpretation of the information. One clever procedure was suggested as a way of determining successful group activity: After the postconference evaluation, would someone volunteer to be the next teacher? No one would expose him/herself to the process unless the group was helpful and supportive.

To meet teacher needs when supervisory services were reduced, one region of the District of Columbia public schools developed a clinical supervision program (Freeman, Palmer, and Ferren, 1980). Almost 400 administrators and teachers were involved in inservice work designed to develop supervisory skills, alternative teaching strategies, and peer supervision techniques. The goal was the improvement of classroom instruction through the improvement of the supervisory process and the use of existing resources. The clinical supervision model was emphasized as it could be adapted to specific settings and to styles of leadership. After four years, the program has become self-sustaining, and improved attitudes toward supervision and confidence in peer supervision are reported.

PROS AND CONS

Clinical supervision is a "thoroughly professional process . . . found infrequently in practice," according to Ben Ebersole, president of the Association for Supervision and Curriculum Development in 1979-80 (Sullivan, 1980, p. v). It is field-based and rests on a colleague relationship between the supervisor and teacher; its goals are instructional improvement and teacher development.

In her summary of research related to clinical supervision, Sullivan (1980) states that general conclusions cannot be made because of the limited quality and quantity of the studies. She suggests that some findings support clinical supervision—evidence seems to validate the model, teacher behavior changes in the desired direction, and teachers grow in self-confidence and self-direction. The process of clinical supervision is humane and democratic, it is based on sound principles of learning, i.e., active involvement and individualization, and the cycle of the model is clearly outlined.

However, clinical supervision considers only the classroom activities of teachers. There are peer relations, parent contacts, curriculum development, extracurricular responsibilities, and other facets of teacher behavior that are ignored in the cycle. In other words, clinical supervision cannot be the only approach a supervisor uses.

The time and personnel required for clinical supervision make it unattainable for some school systems. Programs have been planned that use clinical supervision with specific groups of teachers. In one such program, new teachers are included for three years and then involved every third year; tenured teachers participate in clinical supervision every third year; and a schedule is devised to equalize the number involved each year.

Several supervisors in a suburban district who have successfully used clinical supervision with their teachers contend that they can complete a cycle with a teacher in a two-hour time block. The school system uses clinical supervision in conjunction with other approaches—department meetings, study groups, grade level activities. Needless to say, clinical supervision cannot succeed unless personnel are committed. Both teachers and supervisors must be willing to devote time and effort to this potentially useful activity. The systematic analysis of clinical supervision can provide both a method and a model for cooperative progress toward satisfying outcomes for both the teacher and supervisor.

SUMMARY

Clinical supervision is a systematic process in which a teacher and supervisor cooperatively analyze teaching and work together to improve instruction. The five phases of the cycle include preobservation conference, observation, analysis, postobservation conference, and postconference evaluation. The emphasis throughout is on mutuality and professional development. Objective data are collected and considered in relation to the teaching-learning environment. Clinical supervision, as a part of a supervisory program, provides a humane, participatory framework for professional development.

REFERENCES

Acheson, K.A., and Gall, M.D. *Techniques in the Clinical Supervision of Teachers*. New York: Longman, 1980.

Bellon, J.J., et al. *Classroom Supervision and Instructional Improvement*. Dubuque, IA: Kendall/Hunt Publishing Company, 1976.

Bloom, B.S., ed. *Taxonomy of Educational Objectives Handbook I: Cognitive Domain*. New York: David McKay Co., Inc., 1956.

Cogan, M.L. *Clinical Supervision*. Boston: Houghton Mifflin, 1973.

Freeman, G.; Palmer, R.C.; and Ferren, A.S. "Team Building for Supervisory Support." *Educational Leadership* 37 (4) (January 1980): 356–58.

Goldhammer, R.; Anderson, R.H.; and Krajewski, R.J. *Clinical Supervision*. 2d ed. New York: Holt, Rinehart and Winston, 1980.

Krajewski, R.J., and Anderson, R.H. "Goldhammer's Clinical Supervision a Decade Later." *Educational Leadership* 37 (5) (February 1980): 420–23.

Simon, A., and Boyer, E.G. *Mirrors for Behavior III*. Wyncote, PA: Communication Materials Center, 1974.

Snyder, K.J. *ACT: Administrator-for-Change Training, Module Six*. Lubbock, TX: Pedamorphosis, Inc., 1978.

Sullivan, C.B. *Clinical Supervision: The State of the Art Review*. Alexandria, VA: Association for Supervision and Curriculum Development, 1980.

Chapter 5
The Supervisory
Conference

The supervisory conference is a purposeful meeting of the supervisor with one or more persons. Typically, the conference is between a teacher and a supervisor, following an observation by the supervisor of the teacher in the process of teaching. In real life, the supervisor enters a regular classroom where the students are being taught. In a simulated situation, as in a microteaching laboratory, the supervisor observes a small class being taught a short lesson by a teacher who is often a student in teacher education. In both of these situations, the supervisor must use skills of communication—first, by observing and assessing the teacher and, later, by meeting with that teacher to provide help on a one-to-one basis.

In the following section of this chapter, the coding process and communication networks are explained. These explanations will relate to two environments—the classroom where the observation takes place and the conference site where supervisor-teacher dialog occurs. Different conference styles are discussed, as well as specific suggestions for developing conference skills.

BASIC COMMUNICATION NETWORKS

In some ways, a supervisory conference can be compared to a telephone conversation, as it is described by the phone company in its television commercials. A supervisor can "reach out and touch someone" and, just as a phone call can be either an affirmative or a negative experience, so can a supervisor/teacher conference. The deciding element is not the technology involved in connecting two people, but rather their communication skills. The success of the conference depends on the ability of the people who are sending and receiving messages. In a good conference, a supervisor reaches out, establishes rapport, builds confidence, listens well, asks questions, waits for the teacher's responses, and then works out a plan for improvement with the teacher.

All of these diverse acts are part of the basic communication processes of sending and receiving messages. Both participants are senders and receivers. Coding the numerous verbal exchanges is a method of analysis which clarifies, both to the supervisor and to the teacher, just who says what to whom, and sometimes why.

Supervision requires a study of communication because a supervisor deals with the sending-receiving at two levels: (1) observing communications in the instructional setting, i.e., the teacher sends informational messages to students, students receive the messages and respond; and (2) meeting the teacher in a conference setting and verbalizing these observations so that the classroom data can be analyzed with the teacher.

A supervisor, in observing a lesson, may classify communications under two broad headings: *Macrocommunication* is an interaction which involves the entire classroom. It includes the overall sight and sound of the teacher's explanations and questions, combined with the individual and group responses of the students in the class. *Microcommunication* is a one-to-one communicative relationship. In a classroom, it would pertain to an exchange between the teacher and one specific student. It is a clear-cut example of the sender-to-receiver action.

The simplest sender-receiver action (an example of microcommunication) is coded as follows:

$$S \rightleftharpoons R$$

The message can be both cognitive and affective. For instance, a teacher can communicate with a student by transmitting factual material, as well as by indicating attitudes. An example is, "George, it is important to remember that there are three measures of central tendency: the mean, the median, and the mode."

The verbalization is the initial communication. The teacher walks to the chalkboard and writes the following message:

Measures of Central Tendency
1) Mean
2) Median
3) Mode

The cognitive message on the board constitutes an auxiliary communication which adds different sensory input to foster student retention. As the teacher explains the meanings of mean, median, and mode, s/he may return to the chalkboard and write more information. These communications are primarily cognitive. In order to encourage George to believe he can understand and use this mathematical material, the teacher may follow the explanation with this affective comment: "George, you work with terms like this. A *mean* is just another word for *average,* and you've been figuring out batting averages for your favorite baseball players for a long time."

George says, "Yes, I've got that pretty well figured out now. I know what the mean is. But, I'm not sure that I've caught on to mode. Is it just the grade where the most people have scores?"

The teacher nods and smiles. "Right! That's what mode is. You've got it!"

The communication exchange above could be coded as follows:

$$S \rightleftarrows R$$

The teacher, by using George as a receiver for the information, has brought a personalized tone to the cognitive message. Though George initially accepts the information, the other students are also receivers. The *primary* communication has been between the teacher and George. *Secondary* communication evolves as the other students learn what the teacher has been explaining to George. Bill, another student in the class, might say, "Well, maybe George gets mixed up on the word 'mode,' but as for me, I think 'median' is the hardest. Is it just the middle of a whole bunch of scores, just as though you counted them off?" In this case, the teacher will probably include Bill in further explanations. By expanding eye contact, the teacher can tacitly indicate that other students can inquire about the definitions, and by drawing several people into an open discussion about cognitive material, a teacher builds student understanding.

A supervisor watching this classroom activity has data about the interaction. First, the teacher is using more than one means of communication. The teacher moves from individual to group attention, where the receiver of the communicated messages is encouraged to become a sender. As the communication arrows are drawn back and forth, a supervisor can show that a teacher is doing more than telling the students what to do and what to remember. By varying communication devices, the teacher maintains student attention and develops a vital learning environment. The supervisor can indicate, with the S and R codes, how the sequential teacher and student communications link together, as follows:

$$R^3 \{ S \begin{array}{c} \nearrow R^1 \text{ (George)} \\ \searrow R^2 \text{ (Bill)} \end{array}$$

At the time of the conference, the teacher becomes R and the supervisor becomes S. The ensuing dialog is coded below:

(Supervisor)   (Teacher)

$$S \rightleftharpoons R$$

When a supervisor develops an open relationship with the teacher in the conference circumstance, the communication coding should look like:

(Supervisor)   (Teacher)

$$S \rightleftharpoons R$$

In the coded interactions, note that, even when a receiver sends a communication arrow back to the sender, that individual continues to be coded as a receiver because his/her responses are regarded as reaction to the supervisor's initial message.

A supervisor should have an awareness of the teacher's objectives for the lesson and must be alert to the actual message interchange in the lesson. After studying the complex network of messages in the macrocommunication of the classroom, the supervisor can evaluate the teacher's success in achieving preestablished goals. Skillful identification of the sending-receiving elements aids an instructor in conceptualizing the lesson and providing accurate "feedback."

In the last diagram, showing the coding of communications between supervisor and teacher, there is reciprocal communication which is essential if a meaningful dialog is to result. A wise supervisor will maintain his/her role as sender only for as long as it takes the teacher to react with answers and then finally take over the initiation of comments, eventually turning the supervisor/sender into a receiver of teacher comments.

How is this transferral of roles achieved? By active listening and indirect conference techniques which involve nonverbal encouragement and careful verbal paraphrasing. In the coding messages, there is a simple way of identifying the role transferral. The supervisor, in conference, can actually sketch the S and R arrows on a sheet of paper in clear view of the teacher. If a supervisor draws arrows that show that the comments are all originating with the sender, then there is reason to believe that the supervisor is indulging in a monolog instead of a dialog. Noting this, an astute supervisor will move out of the monolog by asking questions which require expanded answers. From here, it is possible to take an idea from the

teacher, paraphrase it, and wait for further amplification. Thus, a simple
S——→R communication can evolve into the more desirable S⇄R pattern.

CONFERENCE CLIMATE

The conference itself is a relationship. Descriptions of communication lines are provided so that a novice supervisor can more fully interpret an interchange and aid the teacher who has been observed. Some of the main sources of difficulty, however, are ignored if one assumes that the supervisor and teacher arrive tabula rasa for the supervisory experience. In actuality, the participants in a conference have received many communications which predispose them to certain expectations and biases. Teachers are influenced by other teachers in the same building who speak about supervisors and the supervision process. They know that their students are not immune to the tension that a visitor to the classroom imposes. On the other hand, a supervisor seldom arrives in a classroom without hearing comments about the teacher's ability and characteristics, since other supervisors comment openly about problems in a certain school district, in a certain building, and even in a certain teacher's classroom. Teachers and supervisors are human beings first and professionals second; therefore, those who enter the field of supervision should be aware of the multiple influences which impinge on the conference.

The atmosphere of understanding that surrounds the participants in the conference is generally called the conference climate. Figure 12 shows the major human elements which affect the supervisor and teacher as they enter a conference, explaining briefly how message lines reflect human input.

Figure 12. Human Elements Affecting Supervisor and Teacher in Conference.

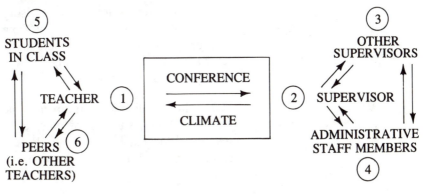

Although category I, in the chart below, represents the supervisory conference, the interactions of the four other categories (II-V) affect the conference climate. If the supervisor is aware that these all have an impact on his/her relationship with the teacher, then the messages from these secondary sources can be recognized and evaluated more critically.

Conference Climate Message Lines

Categories	*Message Lines*	*Description of Messages*
I	1 - 2	Direct communication between teachers and supervisors in the conference setting provides the richest field for a teacher's individual improvement.
II	2 - 3 2 - 4 3 - 2 4 - 2	Communication between one supervisor and another or between a supervisor and an administrative superordinate expands the supervisory linkage to include the entire school system.
III	3 - 4 4 - 3	Communications among supervisors and administrators often precede acts of supervision and/or develop after the conference has taken place.
IV	1 - 5 5 - 1	Before, during, and after a supervisory visit, a teacher gives messages to and receives messages from the students. Usually, these relate to the lesson observed.
	1 - 6 6 - 1	Before and after a formal supervisory visit, most teachers receive input from their peers—usually from teachers in the same area of the school building or in the same academic discipline.
V	5 - 6 6 - 5	In the wider academic environment of the school building, students of other classes, as well as teachers of other classes, express opinions about the supervisory visit.

DIRECT, INDIRECT, AND NONDIRECTIVE APPROACHES

One way of classifying the conference is in accordance with the supervisory approach: direct, indirect, and nondirective. These methods are all used by effective supervisors. Deciding which is appropriate requires an understanding of the situation and the person or persons involved. These styles of conferencing are similar to those in counseling; in fact, there are many similarities between a supervisor and a counselor. Both work with individuals in a helping relationship, where building mutual trust is an essential step. Part of this trust is built on confidentiality; a sure way to destroy a good relationship is by gossiping about personal or professional information revealed in a conference. Listening is an important skill in each job. The ultimate goal in either supervising or counseling an individual is guidance toward an acceptance of responsibility for personal and/or professional development and decisions.

The direct approach is a telling approach, which implies that the supervisor knows and can supply the answers, i.e., that there is one best way. Since teaching is a complex process, there is seldom, if ever, *one* effective way to achieve an educational objective; different teaching styles and a variety of learning styles indicate that there are numerous ways of accomplishing any specific objective. A direct approach encourages a superior-subordinate interaction, where the one who knows informs the uninformed. The dependence which can develop in this type of interplay allows a teacher to rely on the supervisor for decisions, solutions, and suggestions. When unsatisfactory results occur, the teacher can conveniently blame the supervisor.

Ed Meredith, an elementary supervisor in the county office, enjoyed using a direct approach when working with teachers. His family resented the phone calls which interfered with meals and activities at home. In fact, Ed seldom had dinner during the school year without a telephone interruption. One evening, when the Merediths had guests, the meal was ruined by Ed's "emergency" calls. He finally decided to examine his procedures. As a result of his self-analysis, Ed changed his manner of working with teachers. Instead of providing answers as a superordinate, he shifted to the cooperative approach and encouraged teachers to suggest their own solutions. This change was slow and tedious for Ed, since it was quicker and easier to tell the teachers what would solve their problems. Asking questions, getting teachers to suggest possible actions, and then considering results of these alternatives all took time. Furthermore, Ed missed the gratification of seeing his ideas put into operation. Gradually, however, he saw the teachers finding their own ways of handling crises, and the realization that he had stimulated their professional growth provided him

with satisfaction. As a result, his business calls at home decreased notice-
ably, and interruptions at mealtime became a rarity.

There are, however, instances in which a direct supervisory style can
be put to effective use. One example is the supplying of information. If a
teacher needs to know how to get funding from the state department of
public instruction to develop a special mathematics unit involving inventory procedures of local businesses, discussion with the teacher about
where to write for information and how to write grant proposals is inappropriate, if the supervisor can pull a form from the file and give the
teacher specific help. In this instance, the supervisor encourages the
teacher's initiative and facilitates creative efforts by directly providing
assistance.

The welfare and safety of students must always be considered a
priority. When a supervisor becomes aware of unsafe procedures in a
chemistry lab, the condition must be tactfully and directly brought to the
teacher's attention. There is no time for guiding the chemistry teacher to
discover that adequate safety precautions are needed. Recognizing the
importance of the teacher-student relationship, the supervisor should find a
way to speak with the teacher privately, never indicating to the students
any doubts about the teacher's competence.

Sometimes, a supervisor works in many ways with a teacher, but the
teacher's patterns of behavior remain unchanged. In fact, the supervisor
may feel there is no discernible indication that the teacher honestly desires
to improve professionally. In such cases, as a last resort, the supervisor
may try a direct approach, since some individuals respond only to specific
directions or orders. (It is this type of teacher who may develop a dependency on the supervisor.)

Resentment is a typical teacher reaction to a direct supervisory
approach. Since they are not included in planning and decision making,
teachers may feel the supervisor has a lack of confidence in their judgment.
Teachers, as professionals, question the authority and expertise of someone who tells them what to do, and, when they are displeased at being told
what to do, they are apt to defend their own behavior. At this point, they
stop considering alternatives or better procedures. This kind of defensive
behavior precludes professional growth efforts. This type of negative
emotional response can sometimes be modified by the supervisor who uses
a "sell or tell" approach, i.e., by providing careful background, some
direct supervisors can persuade teachers to adopt certain ideas. When
teachers respect the supervisor and his/her skills, this approach may work.

The indirect supervisory style is a discovery approach. Often, a
supervisor decides on a particular area of concern and, by questions and
discussion, guides the teacher to analyze his/her teaching. Through ex-

amination of data collected in the classroom, a teacher and supervisor should decide on a common area for development and cooperatively evolve a plan of action. The teacher and supervisor interact as peers in the process, although the supervisor selects the focus on the basis of objective evidence, understanding of the total situation, and professional judgement. Since the teacher who has been involved in the analysis of data and planning for improvement is putting his/her own ideas into operation, this process eliminates or minimizes teacher defensiveness.

Most educators have developed considerable skill in telling (using the direct approach); the indirect method may require careful practice and conscious effort. Developing good questioning techniques requires commitment. Recording conferences and analyzing them is one technique supervisors can use to recognize their strengths and weaknesses in these skills. Videotaping makes the supervisor aware of the nonverbal, as well as the verbal, interaction. Concern about how one functions in a supervisory conference is the first step toward improvement. Like teachers, supervisors often have a misconception about the amount of advising and directing they do. A periodic check of one's conferences can help an individual develop and maintain a desired conference style.

Although the indirect supervisory technique recognizes the professional experience and preparation of teachers and involves them in the process of examining what happened and investigating other strategies, the process takes time, and the responses from a teacher are somewhat unpredictable. The supervisor cannot have a prearranged outline of activities for the teacher; instead, the conference must be kept flexible so the supervisor can use the teacher's ideas and suggestions. Such "playing by ear" may be uncomfortable for some individuals, because time and uncertainty are considered disadvantages by the supervisor who prefers a structured and carefully timed schedule.

Teacher independence and professional responsibility are desirable outgrowths of an indirect supervisory style. The successful supervisor strives to develop teachers who do not rely on supervision for personal and professional growth. Instead, these teachers are continuously evaluating their teaching, restructuring their activities, keeping abreast of current developments in their subject areas, and expanding their own horizons.

In a nondirective approach, which is appropriate for use with a mature professional, the recognition of a problem or selection of an area for improvement is established by the teacher, and the supervisor's role is that of an active listener—clarifying, reflecting, and summarizing. The supervisor reflects, or mirrors, the verbal and nonverbal messages of the teacher. In these interactions, the teacher is encouraged to sort out ideas, locate a critical area, and plan activities to alleviate problems. The supervisor who uses a nondirective style must be sensitive to the feelings of the teacher. This approach signifies to the teacher an acceptance and support of his/her thinking and knowledge. Such a relationship usually evolves after teachers and supervisors have been working together and building mutual respect.

The supervisor using a nondirective approach must avoid the pitfall of going nowhere in the conference. It is easy to accept teacher ideas but neglect a plan of action. Excellent teachers need the challenge of new experiences, and supervisors should help develop plans for a teacher's professional activity. These plans should be a logical outgrowth of the conference.

An inexperienced teacher, or a teacher with limited background, may be unable to respond to either the indirect or nondirective approach. In essence, the teacher may not be capable of suggesting alternatives because s/he is not aware of other possibilities. Perhaps, the teacher has done little problem solving, because s/he has been protected by a dominating relative or friend. In such circumstances, the supervisor may find a direct approach is the only feasible one. However, the teacher must be encouraged to develop his/her background and problem-solving skills. The supervisor can, in such instances, recommend reading of appropriate professional materials, facilitate visits to other classrooms, arrange for attending professional meetings, and stimulate activities to enrich the teacher's background.

Sometimes, the supervisor finds that the teacher's problem is not related to professional activities. The teacher may, when given an opportunity, want to talk about personal problems. The supervisor, unless trained as a guidance counselor, is limited in the service which s/he can render. Listening may be a valuable aid to the teacher who may simply need to vent ideas and feelings. In this case, the temptation to give advice must be repressed. Besides listening, the supervisor may want to make a referral, i.e., recommend a source of help to the teacher. Most communities have family service or mental health facilities available. Occasionally, the school system itself has personnel to counsel teachers. Information about community resources is useful to the supervisor, not only to make teacher referrals but also to give teachers resources for student help.

Most supervisors use all of the conference approaches—direct, indirect, and nondirective. Effective supervision requires appropriate adaptation to individual cases. Sometimes, the anticipated results are disappointing, and the supervisor must shift from a nondirective to indirect or from an indirect to direct approach. Combining these styles to deal adequately with problems and individuals is a prerequisite for successful interpersonal relationships.

Supervisors need conference skills, and they should consciously work at developing and improving them. A supervisor is sometimes described as a teacher of teachers. As teachers develop unique teaching styles, so supervisors develop unique conference styles. The supervisor, like the teacher, should evaluate results and constantly strive to modify his/her style to attain more effective outcomes.

PURPOSES OF CONFERENCES

Hunter (1980) describes six types of supervisory conferences, five instructional and one evaluative. She categorizes the purposes of instructional conferences as follows:

1. To recognize and explain effective teaching behaviors.
2. To encourage development of a larger repertoire of teaching responses.
3. To identify parts of the teaching which the teacher is dissatisfied with and develop strategies to change them.
4. To discover less effective aspects of teaching not evident to the teacher and develop alternative procedures.
5. To influence continuing growth of outstanding teachers.

Although she feels that all types of conferences can be positive experiences, one with the fourth purpose may have potential for a negative tone. Yet Hunter maintains that "it is a positive experience to have perplexing instructional situations become understandable through interpretation by an observer" (p. 410). She also indicates that such conferences may be a necessary step in working with teachers whose teaching is unsatisfactory (pp. 410-11).

The evaluative conference summarizes a series of instructional conferences and should be anticipated from the results of the previous conferences. Although there is a role conflict between helper and evaluator, many supervisors are expected to function in both roles. Consequently, the supervisor must use objective data and deal honestly and fairly with teachers to create mutual respect and to supervise effectively.

Frequently, the preobservation conference in clinical supervision may not fall into one of Hunter's categories, since its purpose is to inform the supervisor about the teacher's objectives and plans, decide what data should be collected during the observation, and determine how the data should be recorded. Furthermore, the supervisor may confer with several teachers, an administrator, another supervisor, or other individuals concerned with educational programs. Since the purposes of these conferences are varied, they may not readily fall in Hunter's categories either.

CONFERENCE GUIDELINES

Conferences must be fluid and individual; no one format can be prescribed. However, some general guidelines can be suggested to be used and modified in harmony with the occasion. Time and place for the conference are important; a conference following an observation should be scheduled as soon as possible. If several days go by, the teacher and the supervisor may forget the details of the lesson observed. Sufficient time should be available so the conference seems relaxed; however, a short conference held immediately after an observation is preferable to a longer one scheduled a week later.

The physical environment of the conference is also important. No matter how much human warmth is generated by the supervisor, and no matter how open-minded the teacher, the actual setting of the conference can make or break the effectiveness of a meeting. The conferees should meet in a room where they can converse privately and sit comfortably in easy chairs, without a desk or table between them. Good arrangements find the conferees sitting side by side or on either side of a corner of a table or desk, for these are positions for working together. If possible, they should meet in a part of the school building where distracting noises will not interfere with the flow of comments. An empty classroom is better than a pleasant office setting where a phone could interrupt the conference.

Establishing rapport is an important part of setting a friendly climate. A smile and greeting are often sufficient for professional acquaintances. For the first or second conference with a person, more verbal interchange, or ''small talk,'' may seem appropriate. The supervisor must strive to create an accepting atmosphere through sincere inquiries about the teacher's activities and interests.

As the supervisor moves to the primary purpose of the conference—instructional improvement—the teacher's professional strengths should be analyzed, so they can serve as the basis for further professional development. Such an emphasis on the positive creates favorable teacher attitudes. When a supervisor commences work with a teacher, affirmative experiences provide a good base for the helping relationship. Therefore, it is wise to choose a goal attainable within a reasonable time. Perhaps the supervisor can provide some new reading materials or arrange a visit to another class. Such tangible evidence of good intentions promotes positive teacher reactions.

A supervisor should develop good listening skills. Posture, attention, eye contact, verbal and nonverbal reactions are all involved. A good listener sits inclined toward the one speaking, making eye contact, and concentrating on what is said and what the speaker means. The speaker is encouraged to continue by evidence of acceptance and empathy, such as nodding or "I understand." Clarifying questions, paraphrasing, and summarizing are other techniques which may be helpful to both the speaker and the listener. The listener may want to check his/her analysis of the speaker's feelings. Listening techniques (Figure 13) can be developed with practice. A conscious effort is required to check one's use of clarifying questions, neutral responses, reflective comments, and summarizing statements.

Effective listening means developing these techniques and eliminating certain other practices. The supervisor must learn to limit his/her own talking. Interruptions, arguments, emotional reactions, premature judgments, and ridicule will block communication. Silence is not necessarily bad; it may be needed for the supervisor, as well as the teacher, to organize ideas. The supervisor should restrain all tendencies to glance at a clock or watch. Otherwise, the teacher will assume the meeting is lasting too long or that the supervisor is bored by the teacher's comments.

In order to be helpful to a teacher, a supervisor must be specific. A comment about a "good lesson" provides no information about what was effective and which teaching behaviors should be maintained. The teacher, on the other hand, knows exactly what should be continued when s/he hears, "You did a nice job of encouraging participation with your smiling and nodding." The decision that a teacher's questions should be improved is not helpful to the teacher, unless examples and ideas are explored by the teacher and supervisor. If the teacher wants to use open questions, then there should be some substitutions for "Did you enjoy the story?" Appropriate questions should be formulated, e.g., "What did you like about the story?" "How did the author keep your attention?"

Above all, the supervisor should be supportive. Such an attitude conveys to the teacher that s/he is accepted and that the supervisor feels confident that any problems can be solved. This does not mean that the supervisor gives only favorable information; it means that the supervisor is honest, presents data, and helps analyze the situation, even when unsatisfactory results must be faced, and possible procedures for satisfactory outcomes in the future are planned. When the supervisor is a helper, the teacher is treated as a responsible professional who can improve and develop his/her skills.

A good conference needs a summary to review the ideas considered and provide a plan of action. Any recommended action should relate to the purpose of the conference. The plan shows both the teacher and supervisor that something was achieved and that their communication was worthwhile. After both know what is to be done, a time limit should be indicated. Goals and time limits should be put in writing; both the teacher and

Figure 13. Specific Listening Techniques.

This chart gives the key listening techniques, followed by purposes and examples of each. Understanding them is intellectually quite easy, but the problem is using them effectively in relationships with other people. Developing listening skill requires practice, and practice requires repetition and patience.

TYPE	PURPOSES	EXAMPLES
Clarifying	To get at additional facts. To help explore all sides of a problem.	"Can you clarify what you mean?" "Do you mean this . . .?" "Is this the problem as you see it . . .?"
Restating	To check your meaning and interpretation with the person's. To show that you are listening and that you understand what is said. To encourage the person to analyze other aspects of the matter being considered.	"As I understand it, then your plan is. . . ." "This is what you have decided to do and the reasons are. . . ."
Neutral	To convey that you are interested and listening. To encourage the person to continue talking.	"I see." "Uh-huh." "That's very interesting." "I understand." Nodding.
Reflective	To show that you understand how the person feels about what s/he is saying. To help a person to evaluate and temper his/her feelings as expressed by someone else.	"You feel that. . . ." "It was shocking as you saw it." "You felt you didn't get a fair shake."
Summarizing	To bring all the discussion into focus in terms of a summary. To serve as a springboard for further discussion on a new aspect of a problem.	"These are the key ideas you have expressed. . . ." "If I understand how you feel about the situation, you think. . . ."

supervisor should have copies to eliminate future misunderstanding. Supervisors, of course,. must maintain their own record keeping system, which includes keeping files on their teachers.

BAD NEWS CONFERENCES

Few people enjoy the task of conveying bad news. Nevertheless, such tasks must be carried out. Maybe the bad news is job termination, failure to get a promotion, refusal of tenure, or denial of some important request. How can such a disappointing message be conveyed humanely? First of all, it should be accomplished in a face-to-face communication, not in a note in the school mail or through a phone call by the secretary. The time and place should be chosen so the receiver has an opportunity to react in privacy and to recover before facing a classroom of students. A hurried conversation in the hall between classes is inappropriate for relaying bad news. The recipient of the message deserves an opportunity to ask for an explanation, which a supervisor should give fairly and honestly. A climate of respect and sincere concern should be maintained. Whenever possible, the supervisor should express support and extend an optimistic view of the future. For example, Marion Hart did not get the curriculum job she applied for, and the supervisor had the task of telling Marion. Explaining that the new appointee, John Spohn, had more teaching experience at different grade levels was important. If the supervisor felt that Marion could handle a curriculum job, s/he might have commented, "When another curriculum position is open, I'll be glad to recommend you." With this statement, s/he could have provided a positive look toward future prospects.

A person assimilating rejection needs an indication of trust and confidence. Bad news conferences are difficult, but an empathetic supervisor can help a teacher cope with disappointing information.

SUMMARY

The supervisory conference, a purposeful meeting usually between a supervisor and teacher, can be an important contribution to a supervisor's effectiveness. The coding of communication in the classroom facilitates understanding of the teaching, while coding the conference communication helps the supervisor analyze the teacher's involvement. The conference climate is affected by many peripheral communications. When the supervisor becomes aware of these influences, s/he can function with more understanding and success.

Direct, indirect, and nondirective approaches are all used in effective supervision. However, the method should be appropriate for the individuals involved and for the situation. A supervisor should analyze his/her conferences and work toward improving conference techniques. Although conferences are used for different purposes, the supervisor must always consider such key factors as time, place, seating arrangement, listening skills, and the inclusion of a summary. When bad news must be given, the conference should be conducted to help the teacher cope with the disappointment.

REFERENCES

Bebb, A.M.; Low, A.F.; and Waterman, F.T. "The Supervisory Conference as Individualized Teaching." In *Association for Student Teaching Bulletin*. Washington, DC: NEA, 1969.

Boyan, N.J., and Copeland, W.D. *Instructional Supervision Training Program*. Columbus, OH: Charles E. Merrill Publishing Co., 1978.

Carkhuff, R.R. *The Art of Helping*. Amherst, MA: Human Resource Development Press, 1973.

Gazda, G.N., et al. *Human Relations Development*. 2d ed. Boston: Allyn and Bacon, Inc., 1977.

Gordon, T. *Teacher Effectiveness Training*. New York: Peter H. Wyden, 1974.

Hunter, M. "Six Types of Supervisory Conferences." *Educational Leadership* 37 (February 1980): 408–10, 412.

Rogers, C.R., and Coulson, W.R. *Freedom to Learn*. Columbus, OH: Charles E. Merrill Publishing Co., 1969.

Chapter 6
Analysis of Teaching

Teaching is a multifaceted process in which an individual expects to facilitate the learning of others. The process includes finding out what the learner knows, selecting appropriate teaching methods and materials, evaluating student learning, and then either recycling to attain unachieved objectives or progressing to the next concepts to be learned. When this teaching sequence involves numbers of students, a variety of subject areas, and the other organizational responsibilities of a teacher in the school setting (e.g., making out report cards, collecting lunch money, sponsoring extracurricular activities), the job of teaching becomes complex and burdensome. Whenever teaching is described, a question arises: Is it an art or a science? If teaching is a science, then it can be translated into laws that produce predictable results. If teaching is an art, then creativity and intuition, rather than rules and formulas, are called for.

Individuals who enjoy the excitement of interactions with students probably emphasize the art aspect. They often feel their best teaching is done when an unexpected happening or student comment triggers a spontaneous learning experience. Other teachers support the importance of using what is concretely known about learning. They may stress sequencing the steps of a learning task along with appropriate practice and reinforcement. They tend to plan carefully and adhere to their lesson plans. The outcome of science-art arguments usually places teaching somewhere on a continuum between the two. As a practical art, teaching involves judgment, insight, and sensitivity. Recently, Eisner (1978) considered teaching an art and, thus, applied the approach of the connoisseur to classroom appraisal. However, most of the research on teaching has examined procedures and results quantitatively. In fact, the major concern of the researchers was the aspects of teacher and student behavior which can be defined and measured. Most educators agree that good teaching is an art, but they also recommend the application of the principles of teaching and learning. Gage (1978) combined the two viewpoints in a compatible relationship when he wrote *The Scientific Basis of the Art of Teaching*. He noted that, whenever the variables in the teaching situation increase to four or more, ". . . the teacher as artist must step in and make clinical or artistic judgments about the best ways to teach" (p. 20).

WHAT IS EFFECTIVE TEACHING?

For years, the research regarding effective teaching seemed to produce contradictory results. Today, the advances in teacher research provide strong support for the following generalizations about teaching basic skills (Brophy, 1979, pp. 1-2):

1. Teachers do make a difference in how much students learn.
2. Specific teaching behaviors seem to be appropriate in some but not all contexts.
3. Teachers who recognize their role of instructing students spend more time teaching and are more effective than other teachers.
4. Effective teachers maximize time spent in productive activities and minimize time lost in transitions, disciplinary procedures and disruptions. The importance of time on task is a familiar way of referring to this concept of effective teaching.
5. Students taught a structured curriculum achieve more than those taught with individualized learning or discovery approaches.
6. In the primary grades, where basic skills are emphasized, there is more small group instruction, teacher contact with students, praise, drill, and low cognitive level activities than in later grades.

These findings support direct instruction (as described by Rosenshine, in Peterson and Walberg, 1979) as effective for producing learning of basic skills. Direct instruction includes:

1. Focus on academic goals.
2. Extensive content and student involvement.
3. Active monitoring of student progress.
4. Structured activities with immediate feedback.
5. Task oriented but relaxed environment.

As Gage (1978, p. 39) presented inferences for third grade teachers to produce high achievement in reading, he emphasized that teachers should have rules so students could take care of personal needs without asking the teacher. Teachers should move around the room, check student work, and indicate awareness of student behavior. Assignments should be interesting and worthwhile, but students should be able to complete the work on their own. Giving directions should be minimized. A student should be called on before a question is given so the opportunities for answering can be equally distributed. Students who are not strong academically should always give some kind of response to a question; for this, the teacher may need to use creative cues, rephrasing, and questions. Reading group activities should include fast paced drill activities which include feedback to students.

Prescriptive suggestions from research are useful to supervisors. Through these suggestions, teachers can be encouraged and helped in developing a task-oriented climate in which students can master basic skills successfully. The support for organized instruction in teaching skills does not eliminate the possibility of time for creativity and individual student investigation. Good (1979) notes that direct instruction may not be an appropriate approach for developing appreciation, providing enrichment, promoting creativity, or encouraging personal development, but he does stress that some structure is needed for most learning experiences, especially in the primary grades, for low ability students and for students who seem anxious or dependent.

After reviewing the research, Peterson draws the following inference: "If educators want to achieve a wide range of educational objectives and if they want to meet the needs of all students, then neither direct instruction alone nor open-classroom teaching alone is sufficient." (Peterson and Walberg, 1979, p. 67). Some educators propose dividing the school day to provide both approaches for appropriate content, i.e., morning for basic skills with direct instruction, afternoons for other subject areas with open classroom methods. Others recommend that the needs of the student should determine a suitable approach.

The supervisor who is aware of the research implications has a base for discussing the possible outcomes of different methods of teaching. Providing a balance of experiences for students should be considered, along with accomplishing goals in the cognitive, affective, and psychomotor domains. Since the educational scene alters and is affected by social and economic changes, the supervisor should make an effort to be informed about current research findings. There are some general notions about effective teaching which are not consistent with the research profile of the effective teacher, according to Medley (Peterson and Walberg, 1979, pp. 22-23). Although the effective teacher's classroom is orderly and supportive as expected, the class spends considerable time in teacher-directed, total class activity, with low-level cognitive questions and little use of student ideas.

A great deal of research has been done in the lower grades. Studies in upper grades and secondary schools are under way to find factors significant to effective teaching. Higher level questions, more whole class activities, more discussion, more student autonomy, and sustained concentration on activities seem to produce achievement in middle and upper grades. The research in secondary schools (Brophy, 1979) seems to indicate that learning basic skills is a crucial factor. Situations in which such skills are the focus require direct total-group instruction, while classes using the skills in content areas seem to call for other approaches.

BASIS OF ANALYSIS

Analysis of teaching can be based on different ways of looking at teaching. Three common perspectives include teaching skills, educational objectives, and components of the learning process. Regardless of the basis used, the procedure can vary from simple to complex. The data and the method of collection may range from a tabulation of how frequently a particular student is called on to a sophisticated time sampling of coded verbal interaction which is transferred to a matrix for interpretation. The needs of the teacher and the skills of the supervisor are important considerations in determining what and how information will be recorded.

If the emphasis is on teaching skills, tasks, or activities, the categories of teaching behavior are examined. A danger here is that what the teacher does may be more seriously considered than the effect on student learning. Teaching activities have been subdivided in different ways. Some schools may already be using a set of competencies for the evaluation of teaching skills for inservice development. If the school system has never used such programs, the supervisor may want to look at materials such as the Stanford microteaching skills and Weigand's teaching competencies (1971).

Educational objectives put the stress on student learning. These objectives, as stated behaviorally in the lesson plan, should be reasonable for the students and harmonious with the course objectives. The supervisor and teacher can use the data collected to determine achievement of objectives, as well as the effectiveness of the methods and materials. Alternative teaching methods can be considered, whether or not there were unattained objectives. One aspect of objectives which probably should be included is the identification of unanticipated learning. If the students are learning to dislike biology because the teacher expects memorization of details, this aversive effect is important information for the biology teacher.

Since a supervisor must know what the teacher expects to accomplish in a lesson before observation, the objectives for the lesson are part of the analysis. Extensive analysis on this basis could involve the relationship of the lesson objectives to the unit and course objectives, i.e., comparison of short- and long-range goals. Selection of materials and methods, as well as sequencing of activities, might be examined. Dealing with objectives would accentuate planning and implementing the methods to accomplish specific student learning.

When components of the learning process are used as the basis for the analysis of teaching, these may vary according to the learning theory and the terminology of the proponent. Gage (1977) has suggested the following components: motivating, cue-providing, response eliciting, and rewarding. The motivating element stimulates the interest and effort of students. The teacher helps students develop positive attitudes toward learning, expectations of success, and readiness for the particular experience. Cue-providing activities are the learning experiences, such as text materials, films, and lectures. Student involvement in active learning, the component of response eliciting, includes discussion, laboratory experiments, practice, and other participation. Verbal reinforcement, personal satisfaction, group recognition, and grading are some of the rewarding activities in the classroom.

Snyder (1978) adapted the variables Bloom (1982, pp. 115-27) identified as significant in quality learning: As a part of cues and directives, she included such areas as classroom management, climate, and use of space; under reinforcement were such aspects as motivation, repetition, and reinforcement; participation included interactions, group roles, and questioning, as well as other subcategories; correctives and feedback dealt with selection of materials, use of resources, feedback procedures, and other items. (See section on Analysis of Data in Chapter 4 for complete list.) Regardless of the specific components, the supervisor and teacher should view the toal perspective and then work on a certain facet of the teaching process without losing sight of student learning.

The use of a basis for analysis helps both the teacher and supervisor retain a view of the teaching-learning process as a whole. Sometimes, as a piece of teaching activity is isolated, it seems to gain importance beyond reason. The teacher who involves in discussion only those students sitting in front of and to the right of the teacher's desk may be able to involve all students if s/he circulates and helps individuals with problems as students work on assignments. The teacher should be aware of teaching patterns, but a particular behavior must be considered as it relates to overall effectiveness. Retaining a total perspective provides a more balanced approach to professional development.

EXAMINING THE DATA

As data from an observation are studied, the supervisor should look for patterns. Is there a repetition of negative teacher comments to student answers? Is one student criticized and "picked on" by the teacher?

Teachers seem to develop verbal patterns in questioning, responding to students, reinforcing, and controlling students. A teacher's gestures, use of equipment, use of chalkboard, and position and movement in the room often follow a pattern. When a sequence is frequently used, the supervisor must decide whether it should be made evident to the teacher. This decision will be affected by the planning before the observation, priorities for improving instruction, and the effect of the pattern on the teaching-learning process. For instance, the class may resent the emphasis of the teacher who starts questions with "I want you to tell me. . . ." Such wording separates the student and teacher; cooperation and sharing ideas are undermined—often inadvertently. Since such wording may interfere with a supportive climate in the classroom, the supervisor may want to use this data in the conference. On the other hand, if a teacher has used "neat" repeatedly in reinforcing student responses, the supervisor may choose to ignore this wording and deal with data more significant to student learning.

The data collected and the procedure used affect the analysis. If the supervisor makes a seating chart, with a rectangle for every student, and simply indicates each time the teacher speaks to a student and each time the student responds, only the frequency of verbal interaction is recorded. A coding system could be used to indicate questions, correct responses, criticism, or praise. Perhaps capital letters could be used for teacher talk and small letters for student talk:

Teacher Talk	Student Talk
Q-question	q-question
P-praise	r-correct response
C-criticism	x-incorrect or irrelevant answer
D-directions	d-disruptive comments
L-lecture information	

Such coding indicates content, as well as frequency, and provides more information. If the teacher movement is also charted, then data on this nonverbal influence also becomes available. The procedure for recording should be adapted to the information desired in each situation.

Verbatim transcripts provide an extensive record. Some supervisors prefer to use a tape recorder to obtain the verbal interaction while they record other data, such as the nonverbal communication in the classroom or the time on task for individual students.

Verbatim transcripts may be limited to one specific facet of teaching, such as questions. Such limitation enables the supervisor to write only some of the time, giving him/her the opportunity to observe other behaviors.

After the data have been studied for patterns, the supervisor should also look at any critical incidents. Disruptive behavior, student-teacher conflict, student-student confrontation, or student inattention represent negative examples. Critical incidents of a positive nature include cooperative projects, successful problem solving by the group, enjoying an interesting experience, and sharing good feelings. The supervisor who is aware of the long-term effects of these incidents can use them in finding teacher strengths and in locating areas for teacher development. A supervisor may select data relative to a particular incident for the conference so that the teacher and supervisor can explore together the possible causes and implications.

On the whole, examination of the data collected in the observation should include: looking for patterns of teacher behavior, critical incidents, evidence of student attainment of objectives, whether or not the students were learning what was intended, and unanticipated learning. The examination should also be related to the preobservation conference. Teacher concerns should influence study of the data, and the supervisor should plan to provide pertinent information to the teacher.

The outcome of this data examination should be a determination by the supervisor about the major thrust of the postobservation conference. What data have priority? This judgment is made by the supervisor on the basis of his/her knowledge of effective teaching, the teacher, and the students. These decisions about the focus of the conference and the data to be used are important determiners of the helping relationship with the teacher and the professional development plan of the teacher.

FLANDERS INTERACTION ANALYSIS

One rather complex observation system is the Flanders Interaction Analysis. Devised about 25 years ago, it has proven to be an adaptable and flexible procedure for coding verbal interaction in a class discussion. It has ten categories—seven for teacher talk, two for student talk, and one for silence or confusion. (See Figure 14.) The number of categories can be increased, e.g., Asks Questions can be subdivided into kinds of questions. If the teacher wants to know whether open or closed questions were used, this can be indicated by 4a and 4c. The kind of thinking required by the student could also be indicated by a subscript, as follows:

> 4a question requiring recall
> 4b convergent question
> 4c divergent question
> 4d evaluation question

Figure 14. Summary of Categories for Interaction Analysis.*

Teacher Talk	Indirect Influence	1. Accepts Feeling: Accepts and clarifies the feeling tone of the students in a nonthreatening manner. Feelings may be positive or negative. Predicting and recalling feeling are included. 2. Praises or Encourages: Praises or encourages student action or behavior. Jokes that release tension, not at the expense of another individual, nodding head, or saying "uh-huh?" or "go on" are included. 3. Accepts or Uses Ideas of Student: Clarifies, builds, or develops ideas or suggestions by a student. As teacher brings more of his/her own ideas into play, shift to category five. 4. Asks Questions: Asks a question about content or procedure with the intent that a student answer.
	Direct Influence	5. Lectures: Gives facts or opinions about content or procedures. Expresses his/her own ideas. Asks rhetorical questions. 6. Gives Directions: Gives directions, commands, or orders with which a student is expected to comply. 7. Criticizes or Justifies Authority: Makes statements intended to change student behavior from nonacceptable to acceptable pattern. Bawls someone out. States why the teacher is doing what s/he is doing. Uses extreme self-reference.
	Student Talk	8. Student Talk-Response: Talk by students in response to teacher. Teacher initiates the contact or solicits student statement. 9. Student Talk-Initiation: Talk by students, which they initiate. If "calling on" student is only to indicate who may talk next, observer must decide whether student wanted to talk. If s/he did, use this category.
		10. Silence or Confusion: Pause, short periods of silence, and periods of confusion in which communication cannot be understood by the observer.

* Source: E. J. Amidon and N. A. Flanders, *The Role of the Teacher in the Classroom* (Minneapolis, MN: Paul S. Amidon & Associates, Inc., 1963), p. 12. There is NO scale implied by the numbers in this figure. Each number is classificatory; it designates a particular kind of communication event. To write these numbers down during observation is to enumerate, not to judge a position on a scale.

Nonverbal behavior can be included in the category system: 1-9 can be used for verbal behavior with concurring nonverbal messages, and 11-19 can be used for verbal behavior which conflicts with the nonverbal message. One of the recommended procedures requires that the observer record, at three-second intervals, the verbal activity in the class discussion. Of course, learning the categories and practice with the system are needed to develop this proficiency. The data are then transferred to a matrix which shows some sequential relationships and patterns. The end result is an objective description of what happened in the discussion. Although there is no model for effective discussion, this system can provide a teacher with an accurate picture of what has occurred. Data can be compared to what the teacher expected or what the teacher perceived. Teacher perceptions of how much teacher talk, criticism, and positive reinforcement are used have often been quite inaccurate. Since observation of class discussions is an important and useful technique, a supervisor may want to master this system. (More detailed information about this system is available in Flanders' *Analyzing Teacher Behavior.)*

SPAULDING'S COPING ANALYSIS SCHEDULE

Another observation system is the Coping Analysis Schedule for Educational Settings (CASES), devised by Spaulding and developed as a behavior modification approach with students. The categories (Figure 15) describe student behavior from aggressive and dangerous though acceptable social behavior to extreme withdrawal. The student is observed in three school settings for about ten minutes in each setting, and the student's behavior is recorded every three seconds. The summation of categories provides information for classifying the student. Student styles A–F are defined by Spaulding in relation to the frequency of behaviors 1–13, as below:

Style A–aggressive, annoying	3% or more in categories 1, 2, 3b
Style B–passive aggressive	10% or more in categories 4, 5b, 6b
Style C–dependent, withdrawn	15% or more in categories 9b, 11, 12, 13
Style D–gregarious, peer dependent	15% or more in categories 7b, 8b, 9b
Style E–obedient, conforming	80% or more in categories 5a, 7a, 9a, 10
Style F–responsible, productive	85% or more in categories 3a, 5a, 6a, 7a, 8a

Figure 15. A Coping Analysis Schedule for Educational Settings (CASES).*

(Brief Form for Quick References).

1. *Aggressive Behavior:*
   Direct attack: grabbing, pushing, hitting, pulling, kicking, namecalling; destroying property: smashing, tearing, breaking.
2. *Negative (Inappropriate) Attention-Getting Behavior:*
   Annoying, bothering, whining, loud talking (unnecessarily), attention getting aversive noise-making, belittling, criticizing.
3. *Manipulating, Controlling, and Directing Others:*
   Manipulating, bossing, commanding, directing, enforcing rules, conniving, wheedling, controlling.
4. *Resisting:*
   Resisting, delaying; passive aggressive behavior; pretending to conform, conforming to the letter but not the spirit; defensive checking.
5. *Self-Directed Activity:*
   Productive working; reading, writing, constructing with interest; self-directed dramatic play (with high involvement).
6. *Paying Close Attention; Thinking, Pondering:*
   Listening attentively, watching carefully; concentrating on a story being told, a film being watched, a record played; thinking, pondering, reflecting.
7. *Integrative Sharing and Helping:*
   Contributing ideas, interests, materials, helping; responding by showing feelings (laughing, smiling, etc.) in audience situations; initiating conversation.
8. *Integrative Social Interaction:*
   Mutual give and take, cooperative behavior, integrative social behavior; studying or working together where participants are on a par.
9. *Integrative Seeking and Receiving Support, Assistance and Information:*
   Bidding or asking teachers or significant peers for help, support, sympathy, affection, etc., being helped; receiving assistance.
10. *Following Directions Passively and Submissively:*
    Doing assigned work without enthusiasm or great interest; submitting to requests; answering directed questions; waiting for instructions as directed.
11. *Observing Passively:*
    Visual wandering with short fixations; watching others work; checking on noises or movements; checking on activities of adults or peers.
12. *Responding to Internal Stimuli:*
    Daydreaming; sleeping; rocking or fidgeting (not in transaction with external stimuli).

* Source: R. L. Spaulding, *Classroom Behavior Analysis and Treatment* (Durham, NC: Duke University, 1968), p. 3–4. Copyright © 1968 by Robert L. Spaulding. Reprinted by permission.

Figure 15. A Coping Analysis Schedule for Educational Settings (CASES) (cont'd).

---

13. *Physical Withdrawal or Passive Avoidance:*
Moving away; hiding: avoiding transactions by movement away or around; physical wandering avoiding involvement in activities.

Note: Categories 3, 5, 6, 7, 8, and 9 are further coded as *a* or *b* in structured settings to indicate appropriate or inappropriate timing or location of activity (based on the teacher's expectations for the setting). Example: 5a would be recorded when a child was painting during art period (when painting was one of the expected activities). Painting during "story time" or in an academic setting would normally be coded 5b. The code *b* represents behaving in a certain coping category at the "wrong" time or place. What is "right" or "wrong" is based on the values and goals of the teacher or authority responsible in a given situation.

A child might be sharing with another child in an integrative manner (7) some bit of information the teacher regarded as highly inappropriate. It would be coded as 7b since it was an integrative act of sharing occuring at the "wrong" time in the "wrong" place, from the point of view of the teacher.

The treatment schedule for style A starts with a very structured plan with no choices. (See Figure 16.) The plan is devised to eliminate the worst aggressive behavior and reinforce acceptable social behavior. The goal is to apply the treatment and gradually help the individual to develop more acceptable classroom behavior. The student is reclassified and is put on a new treatment schedule as behavior changes. Treatment schedules are available for each of the student styles.

A supervisor may find this observation system helpful in a situation where a teacher needs specific help in beginning a program with a disruptive student. Often, a system for recording student behavior is needed by a teacher, but this information is hard to obtain because of the teacher's responsibility for the total group of students. (Complete information about using CASES can be found in Spaulding's *Classroom Behavior Analysis and Treatment*.)

STUDENT FEEDBACK

Another source of information which can be helpful in analyzing teacher influence is student feedback. This information can be displayed simply, as in Figure 17. Very young students can express their reactions to a school situation by checking happy or sad faces. Of course, more detailed

Figure 16. Treatment Schedule.*

Style A

Aggressive
Annoying, bothering
Dominative, controlling
Resistant

CASES 1, 2, 3b
3%[1] or more in *any*
social setting

Treatment Schedule[1]

1. Set strict, narrow limits (set specific routine to follow). Give no choices, set specific concrete academic tasks.
2. Assign to specific work station (to work alone).
3. Instruct individually or in groups of 6 or fewer.
4. Supervise closely (do not leave child unattended).
5. Punish *all* unacceptable behavior immediately by social isolation (time-out from reinforcement).
6. Reinforce *all* emerging desirable behavior (100% schedule).
7. Ignore visual wandering (11) and daydreaming (12).

Special CASES Classification and Treatment
(For Style A)

Isolate	Ignore	Reinforce
Cases 1, 2, 3b	Cases 4, 5b, 6b, 7b, 8b, 9b, 11, 12, 13	Cases 3a, 5a, 7a, 8a, 9a, 10

[1]Use this treatment when Style A behavior is predominant (above 3%) during baseline observations extending a minimum of 5 days in a given setting. Discontinue this treatment when Style A behavior remains below 3% for 10 days in the settings observed. Then shift to the treatment for the style currently predominant.

* Source: R. L. Spaulding, *Classroom Behavior Analysis and Treatment* (Durham, NC: Duke University. 1968), p. 15. Copyright © 1968 by Robert L. Spaulding. Reprinted by permission.

Figure 17. Young Student Feedback.

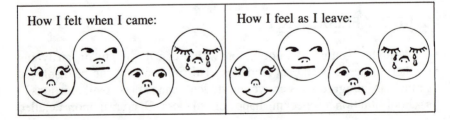

information can be obtained from older students. A sample form used with high school students is given in Figure 18.

Students can provide valuable information, when they mark such forms anonymously and when they are convinced that their honest reactions can be useful to the teachers in future planning. Their responses should be interpreted as an indication of the general impression of the teacher. Helpful ideas can come from the general picture. Extreme reactions, unless they are marked by a number of students, can be disregarded.

Teachers should be encouraged to use student feedback. Supervisors can sometimes assist in the interpretation of the results. Since some teachers are very skeptical about the use of student evaluation, the supervisor may encourage use of student feedback and proceed cautiously.

One sophisticated approach is the Tuckman Student Feedback Form (Figure 19). It uses the semantic differential format, and the quantification of its four dimensions of classroom climate—creativity, dynamism, organized demeanor, and warmth and acceptance—is unique. (See Figure 20.) Statistical analysis of these dimensions provides a basis for some interesting comparisons (Hyman, 1975).

The scores alone are meaningless. Either the teacher or the supervisor, or the two together, indicate expectations or perceptions. These figures can then be compared with student perceptions, probably the mean or median of the group. Comparisons might include teacher expectation to student perceptions, teacher perception to student perceptions, supervisor perception to student perceptions, or teacher perception to teacher expectation. Discrepancies could be investigated by examining specific items. Discussion of marked differences could result in thoughtful consideration of teaching behavior and plans for follow-up action.

For example, when the mean of students on organized demeanor is 21 and the teacher's perception of the same dimension is 39, there should be an examination of the items involved. Does the teacher seem to the students to be uncertain, "on the run," preoccupied, capricious, disorganized, erratic, flighty? Specific descriptors used by the teacher and students which differ greatly should be located. Then, the teaching behavior should be examined to find why students have this impression. Students can often explain why they chose descriptors. When these actions are specified, the teacher can decide what changes are desirable. A supervisor can be helpful in planning changes and checking to see whether they are incorporated. It is hoped that later use of the Tuckman Teacher Feedback Form will show more consistency between the students and teacher.

This instrument is obviously prepared for use by older students. However, a teacher who is interested could modify the vocabulary and adapt it for use with younger students.

Figure 18. High School Student Feedback.

Circle the appropriate number:

1. Does your teacher show enthusiasm for teaching this course?
   Very Little   1   2   3   4   5   Very Great

2. To what degree is the teacher prepared for class?
   Never Well   Always Well
     Prepared   1   2   3   4   5   Prepared

3. To what degree are you aware of what is expected of you in this course?
   Nearly Always   Almost Always
     Confused   1   2   3   4   5   Aware

4. Considering everything, how would you rate this teacher?
   Very Bad   1   2   3   4   5   Very Good

5. To what degree do you feel the teacher is willing to give you personal help with your work?
   Extremely Unwilling 1   2   3   4   5   Extremely Willing

6. To what degree is the teacher fair in grading?
   Very Unfair   1   2   3   4   5   Very Fair

7. How frequently does the teacher encourage or permit discussion and disagreement?
   Hardly Ever   1   2   3   4   5   Nearly Always

8. To what extent does the teacher organize the subject matter of the course clearly?
   Nearly Always   Nearly Always
     Disorganized   1   2   3   4   5   Organized

9. How much concern or interest does the teacher show for students as persons?
   Very Little Interest 1   2   3   4   5   Very Great Interest

10. To what extent has your knowledge, understanding, or skill increased as a result of this course?
    Very Little Increase 1   2   3   4   5   Increased Greatly

11. Has your teacher motivated you to do related work beyond what is assigned?
    None   1   2   3   4   5   Much

Figure 19. Tuckman Teacher Feedback Form.*

Person Observed _____ Observer _____

Date _____   Time _____

1. Original	— — — — — — —	Conventional
2. Patient	— — — — — — —	Impatient
3. Cold	— — — — — — —	Warm
4. Hostile	— — — — — — —	Amiable
5. Creative	— — — — — — —	Routinized
6. Inhibited	— — — — — — —	Uninhibited
7. Inconoclastic	— — — — — — —	Ritualistic
8. Gentle	— — — — — — —	Harsh
9. Unfair	— — — — — — —	Fair
10. Capricious	— — — — — — —	Purposeful
11. Cautious	— — — — — — —	Experimenting
12. Disorganized	— — — — — — —	Organized
13. Unfriendly	— — — — — — .—	Sociable
14. Resourceful	— — — — — — —	Uncertain
15. Reserved	— — — — — — —	Outspoken
16. Imaginative	— — — — — —— —	Exacting
17. Erratic	— — — — — — —	Systematic
18. Aggressive	— — — — — — —	Passive
19. Accepting (People)	— — — — — — —	Critical
20. Quiet	— — — — — — —	Bubbly
21. Outgoing	— — — — — — —	Withdrawn
22. In Control	— — — — — — —	On The Run
23. Flighty	— — — — — — —	Conscientious
24. Dominant	— — — — — — —	Submissive
25. Observant	— — — — — — —	Preoccupied
26. Introverted	— — — — — — —	Extroverted
27. Assertive	— — — — — —— —	Soft-Spoken
28. Timid	— — — — — — —	Adventurous

*From the book *School Administrator's Handbook of Teacher Supervision and Evaluation Methods* by Ronald T. Hyman. Copyright © 1975 by Prentice-Hall, Inc. Published by Prentice-Hall, Inc., Englewood Cliffs, NJ 07632. [pp. 43–46]

Figure 20. Tuckman Teacher Feedback Form—Summary Sheet.*

Person Observed _____ Observer _____

Date _____   Time _____

A. Item Scoring Procedure Summary

1. Place an "X" on one of the seven dashes between each pair of adjectives.

2. Above the first set of dashes on the sheet of 28 items write the numbers 7-6-5-4-3-2-1. This will give a number value to each of the seven spaces between the 28 pairs of adjectives.

3. Determine the number value for the first pair, Original-Conventional. Write it into the formula given below on the appropriate line under Item 1.

4. For example, if you place an "x" on the second dash next to "Original" in Item 1, then write the number "6" on the dash under Item 1 in the Summary Formula below. Do the same for each of the 28 items. Plug each value into the formula.

5. Compute the score for each of the four dimensions in the Summary Formula below.

B. Summary Formula & Score for the Four Dimensions of Classroom Climate

　I. Creativity
　　Item (1+ 5+ 7+16) − (6+11+28) + 18
　　　　(+ + +) − (+ +) + 18 = ____
　II. Dynamism (Dominance & Energy)
　　Item (18+21+24+27) − (15+20+26) + 18
　　　　(+ + +) − (+ +) + 18 = ____
　III. Organized Demeanor (Organization & Control)
　　Item (14+22+25) − (10+12+17+23) + 26
　　　　(+ +) − (+ + +) + 26 = ____
　IV. Warmth & Acceptance
　　Item (2+ 8+19) − (3+ 4+ 9+13) + 26
　　　　(+ +19) − (+ + +) + 26 ____

*From the book *School Administrator's Handbook of Teacher Supervision and Evaluation Methods* by Ronald T. Hyman. Copyright © 1975 by Prentice-Hall, Inc. Published by Prentice-Hall, Inc., Englewood Cliffs, NJ 07632. [pp. 43–46]

SUMMARY

Teaching is a complex process which seems to combine a scientific base with an art. Any analysis of teaching should consider current research on teaching. The direct approach seems to be strongly supported as effective for teaching the basic skills. Teaching skills, behavioral objectives, and components of learning may be used to analyze teaching.

Analysis of teaching requires that the supervisor and teacher together examine data to find evidence of attaining objectives. Looking for teaching patterns is important, and critical incidents must also be considered. Observation systems may provide their own procedures for analysis, e.g., Flanders Interaction Analysis and Spaulding's Coping Analysis Schedule for Educational Settings. In addition, student feedback can provide useful information about teaching. The ultimate purpose of such in-depth study is to plan cooperatively for professional development which results in instructional improvement.

REFERENCES

Bloom, B.S. *Human Characteristics and School Learning*. New York: McGraw-Hill, 1976.

Brophy, J.E. "Advances in Teacher Research." *Journal of Classroom Interaction* 15 (1) (Winter 1979): 1–7.

Eisner, E.W. "The Impoverished Mind." *Educational Leadership* 35 (8) (May 1979): 615–23.

Flanders, N.A. *Analyzing Teaching Behavior*. Reading, MA: Addison-Wesley Publishing Co., 1970.

Gage, N.L. *The Scientific Basis of the Art of Teaching*. New York: Teachers College Press, 1978.

———. "Toward A Cognitive Theory of Teaching." In *Learning and Instruction,* edited by M.C. Wittrock, pp. 603–09. Berkeley, CA: McCutchan Publishing Corporation, 1977.

Good, T.L. "Teacher Effectiveness in the Elementary School." *Journal of Teacher Education* 30 (2) (March–April 1979): 52–64.

Hyman, R.T. *School Administrator's Handbook of Teacher Supervision and Evaluation Methods*. Englewood Cliffs, NJ: Prentice-Hall, Inc., 1975.

Levin, T., and Long, R. *Effective Instruction*. Alexandria, VA: The Association for Supervision and Curriculum Development, 1981.

Peterson, P.L., and Walberg, H.J., eds. *Research on Teaching*. Berkeley, CA: McCutchan Publishing Corporation, 1979.

Snyder, K.J. *ACT Administrator-for-Change Training, Module Six*. Lubbock, TX: Pedamorphosis, Inc., 1978.

Spaulding, R.L. *Classroom Behavior Analysis and Treatment*. Durham, NC: Duke University, 1968.

Weigand, J.E., ed. *Developing Teaching Competencies*. Englewood Cliffs, NJ: Prentice-Hall, Inc., 1971.

Chapter 7
Curriculum Skills

Supervisory responsibilities in the area of curriculum are varied, but a general description of the supervisor's role in curriculum is that of facilitator. The development of curriculum requires planning and organization, with input from various sources. Printing and distributing curriculum materials precedes any implementation of plans; inservice activities to prepare teachers to use the curriculum increase its potential value. Supervisors can contribute in all these steps.

Supervisors should not be responsible for the actual writing of curriculum. If a new curriculum is to be introduced, it must be the product of teachers. Curriculum written by supervisors is generally unused and laid aside by teachers. Curriculum is defined in various ways. Some educators feel that curriculum is the answer to the question, "What do schools teach?" Lewis and Miel define curriculum as "a set of intentions about opportunities for engagement of persons-to-be-educated with other persons and things (all bearers of information, processes, techniques and values) in certain arrangements of time and space" (1972, p. 27). Sergiovanni and Starratt use the following definition of curriculum: ". . . that which the student is supposed to encounter, study, practice and master" (1979, p. 234). The obvious planning and intended outcomes implied in the concept suggest the importance of texts and other materials, e.g., programs for individualized instruction. In the selection of these instructional aids, supervisory personnel can often help organize committees and secure the books and materials to be examined.

MODELS FOR CURRICULUM DEVELOPMENT

Tyler (1950, pp. 1-2) suggested four basic questions concerning curriculum and instruction:
1. What educational purposes should the school seek to attain?
2. What educational experiences can be provided that are likely to attain these purposes?
3. How can these educational experiences be effectively organized?
4. How can we determine whether purposes are being attained?

This model puts emphasis on the objectives which become the basis for selecting materials, for devising learning activities, and for developing evaluation procedures. The supervisor, observing a lesson in the clinical supervision pattern, becomes involved with this model. Although Tyler's model is pervasive, and provides a rational procedure for dealing with curriculum, there are other models. Taba (1972) presented a seven-step model: diagnosing needs, formulating objectives, selecting content, organizing content, selecting learning experiences, organizing learning experiences, and determining what and how to evaluate. Other extensions of Tyler's model put greater emphasis on values and modifications for use in instructional technology; these adaptations establish the value of the basic concept. The supervisor working with curriculum development should be aware of and use them to help structure appropriate activities.

The model prepared by the Ohio State Department of Education (1980, p. 6) is part of a publication that assists districts to develop graded courses of study which have been required by state law since 1957. The course of study is an official statement, general in nature, which prescribes what is to be taught; it is a broad definition of the educational program. A curriculum guide, on the other hand, is specific, containing suggestions about methods, materials, and instructional aids. A course of study communicates what is to be taught in a given area of study for a particular grade or specified grades and is a document approved by the board of education; the curriculum guide contains recommendations for teachers and serves as a reference for teachers. The former is directive; the latter is suggestive.

The Ohio model for curriculum development (Figure 21) starts with the philosophy and goals of the district which are then translated into program goals. These goals are put into terms appropriate to the subject area, and content is planned according to grade level. This in turn becomes the course of study. Further consideration of how to teach the content and what materials to use can be organized into curriculum guides. Inservice activities are needed to orient teachers to the new program. Hopefully, these inservice programs will involve local teachers whose work is represented in the course of study and curriculum guides. Effective educational programs depend on teacher actions: the program evolves from effective teacher practices (input) and is put into operation by teachers (implementation) as they plan units and lessons for their own classroom use. Supervisors must work with teachers to ensure the use of these materials, which may be put on a shelf to collect dust unless someone specifically encourages teachers to put the plans into action. Of course, student evaluation is a part of the teachers' plans. The continuous process of curriculum development requires a needs assessment or evaluation phase, which cycles the district into another philosophy and goals study.

Figure 21. Model for Curriculum Development.*

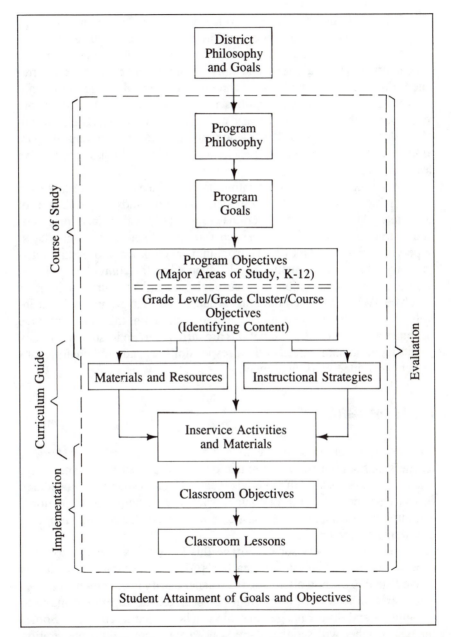

*Source: State of Ohio Department of Education. *Course of Study Development: A Process Model* (Columbus, OH, 1980), p. 6. Copyright © 1980 by Ohio Department of Education. Reprinted by permission.

TEXTBOOK SELECTION

Schools frequently have a cycle for selecting textbooks, perhaps every five or six years. Since curriculum should be adjusted to meet changing conditions, a curriculum study is usually scheduled on a similar time interval. This way, texts and curriculum are kept current and interrelated. Figure 22 is a sample plan for reviewing curriculum. The thoroughness of the study, and expectations for revision of the curriculum, are suggested by the type of study: basic major, major, or minor. The traditional academic subjects—math, science, social studies, and English—are emphasized, while vocational, aesthetic, and physical education receive less attention.

In the six-year cycle, the continuing committee has a major task each year: (1) needs assessment, (2) graded course of study, (3) selection of materials, (4) inservice, (5) criterion testing, or (6) evaluation of programs and instructional materials. With such a structure to guide the committees, supervisory personnel may find curriculum development proceeding satisfactorily. However, in many schools, even when the committee action is well-defined, group action may be neglected unless a critical issue is involved. Whenever a community group or teacher group becomes involved in a controversial matter related to curriculum, then the committee becomes active. But, these situations are infrequent, and a supervisor may need to remind committees of their responsibilities and prod chairpersons to get committee work underway.

PILOT PROGRAMS

Ideally, pilot programs are always developing in a school system, as teachers and administrators originate or find ideas that they want to try. These ideas may deal with materials (such as local resources), procedures (such as mastery learning), or content (such as environmental protection). The supervisor can support and assist a teacher who has a sound proposal and wants to implement it.

How can a supervisor encourage this kind of creativity? First, the supervisor should listen to the teacher's ideas. Questions asked in this active listening session often help the teacher clarify his/her own ideas. As s/he views an idea from a different perspective, the supervisor may see advantages and disadvantages that the teacher failed to consider. Sometimes, a teacher will see that there is need for more careful preparation before an idea can become operational. Hopefully, the teacher will make this decision, but sometimes, an administrator or supervisor must indicate

Figure 22. Textbook-Curriculum Cycle and Committee Structure.*

6-Year Cycle—K-12 Studies

1980-81	*	Science
1981-82	*	Social Science
1982-83	+	Home Economics
	+	Industrial Arts
	0	Physical Education
	+	Health
1983-84	+	Business Education
	0	Driver Education
	0	Art
	+	Music
	+	Foreign Language
1984-85	*	Language Arts
		Reading
		Writing
		Spelling
		Literature
		Grammar
		Speech
		Journalism
1985-86	*	Math

This will be a repeating cycle.

Type Textbook-Curriculum Study	Release Time	# on Committee
* Basic Major Study 1 Elementary and 1 Secondary Committee	1 Full Day 3 Half Days	36
+ Major Study 1 Committe	1 Full Day 1 Half Day	12
0 Minor Study 1 Committee	2 Half Days	12
All committees will operate on a continuing basis–study and recommend every 6 years and meet 3 times each of the other 5 years.	1 Half Day	12 or 18

*Source: Jackson Local School District, Stark County, OH.

the need for more specific plans before a pilot program can be undertaken. Unless the framework for an experiment is constructed carefully, and the materials, activities, and processes are prepared in advance, the chances for success are slight. In other words, a pilot program should not be undertaken until the plan has been evaluated, supplies are available, and arrangements are feasible. For example, a teacher may be qualified and want to teach scuba diving. The course may be appropriate for the "mini-courses" scheduled during the activity period, and a group of interested students may have secured the equipment needed. But, if there is no swimming pool available, the plan must be abandoned.

Helping the teacher adapt an idea to the specific situation is another supervisory service. The students, parents, school, and community must be recognized as part of the total scene. When the plans for the experiment have been worked out with the administrator, then others who are involved should be informed about the project, its rationale, and possible results.

Before outdoor education became an integral part of one school's curriculum, certain classes tested the proposed program. A sixth-grade class was the pilot group. The teacher, of course, was enthusiastic about outdoor education; Ms. Toliver had always included field trips and hiking in her science program. She had been active on the committee which proposed a week at a nearby camp for all sixth graders. The committee prepared a curriculum guide, with plans for developing lessons in language arts, social studies, math, science, art, and music. A proposal for providing food, recreation, and parental supervision was approved by the administration. The students and their parents were involved in decisions about the transportation, financing, supervision of the students, and the general program. The science supervisor, physical education teacher, art teacher, and music teacher participated in planning activities and scheduled their participation in the program. Such cooperative effort made the experience both memorable and valuable. The pilot program provided a base for modifying the camping curriculum for other sixth-grade groups.

Collecting data to evaluate the pilot program is essential. Here again, the supervisor helps plan for effective evaluation. Occasionally, the analysis of data requires procedures for which the supervisor is not prepared. In such instances, the supervisor may want to secure competent assistance.

A pilot program may be undertaken as a result of interest in a new program or new materials prepared by a group of specialists, a publishing company, or a department of education. In these cases, supervisors may need to find teachers who will cooperate and try the experimental program. Volunteers should be sought. In almost every school, there are a few teachers who want to try new approaches. When these teachers are involved, they show renewed interest which can stimulate student learning.

Enlisting teachers who do not want to get involved often results in resistance and inadequate testing of the program.

If a school system encourages teachers and administrators to test new ideas, there will be an interest in different ways of teaching and new content areas. Collected data from each test need to be evaluated. Sometimes, results merit further investigation, i.e., continuing and enlarging the experimental group. Other times, the results are enlightening and may be shared so that teachers can modify their teaching activities. If results are favorable and the curricular offerings need to be changed, the experimental program may be implemented as part of the curriculum. Supervisors can contribute to curricular development by helping teachers to develop and test ideas.

Pilot programs will not always be incorporated into the course of study. If the pilot program does not work out successfully, the teacher must be recognized favorably—as someone who is willing to try a new approach—rather than considered a failure. Unless supervisors provide support for teachers who take risks, there is little motivation for their developing or helping with exciting new programs.

TOTAL PERSPECTIVE

Often, as curriculum is developed, it is viewed as bits and pieces. Primary teachers work on their area, as do the intermediate grade teachers. Middle school curriculum is considered as a unit, and high school courses are planned as separate entities. The total scope and sequence organized for a content area often require supervisory assistance, as well as insistence. More effective teaching is possible when teachers are aware of the total picture—skills, concepts, and attitudes; progression from simple to complex; review; repetition; and the introduction of new materials. Curriculum development which emphasizes continuous progress can be facilitated by an appropriate charge to a curriculum committee, by a careful selection of committee members to represent all levels, and by support and information supplied from the supervisory staff.

A balanced curriculum is needed to provide learning experiences in all areas. When a school's financial support decreases, fine arts courses seem to be eliminated first. Leisure time has increased for the population as a result of the shorter work week and longer retirement expectancy, and the quality of life is recognized as a factor which must be considered in educational planning. Since aesthetic education relates to the quality of life and to worthy leisure activities, perhaps the supervisory staff can provide some leadership in reaching a more equitable curricular balance.

The push toward basics and the rise of interest in vocational offerings have caused further imbalance. Student competencies have also affected curriculum. School systems have concentrated efforts on deciding what content areas should be included, and they have established competency levels. This kind of planning frequently neglects talented students. Enrichment opportunities and programs which are challenging must continually be available in a good school system. Accountability has many interpretations, but emphasis on accountability for basic skills can certainly set limits for potential learning. A curriculum suitable for today's school must consider broad and futuristic goals.

Supervisory personnel can assist by obtaining input for curricular ideas from teachers. In classroom observations and school visits, a supervisor can collect suggestions about what and how content should be taught. In addition, these teacher contacts provide an opportunity for the supervisor to interpret the curriculum.

Successful implementation of a new program is often dependent upon how effectively the teachers are prepared to use it. The preparation must be both cognitive and affective, i.e., teachers must understand the content of the new program and its rationale, and they must also feel comfortable teaching it. Too many times, new materials are given to teachers without adequate explanations. The expectation is that they are ready to go forth and teach. The uncertainty of dealing with different concepts, often presented in a new format, makes many teachers uneasy. A series of inservice meetings may be needed. Before actual classroom use, teachers might work with the content and methods in role playing and group discussions. Such activities familiarize the teacher with the terms, concepts, procedures, and possible problem areas. Continuing inservice, along with supervisory encouragement, may result in more adequate use of both curriculum guides and courses of study.

Teachers who are new to a system may require special orientation to the curriculum. Sometimes, principals provide this experience for new teachers in the building; but, frequently, the newcomer is simply handed the textbook and course of study. Supervisors can assist these teachers in getting acquainted with and using the materials. Helping a new teacher get a good start can be a real contribution to the school.

CONTROVERSIAL ISSUES

The supervisor may become involved in community concern about controversial issues. There is increased pressure on schools from conservative groups, and censorship is having an effect on the curriculum. The "radical right" seems to be influencing what is taught; although this group is a minority, it is active and vocal (Aarons, 1979). Some school libraries have books with words and phrases inked out; certain books and magazines have been completely removed from other school libraries.

Should teachers avoid controversial issues? Sex, drugs, and divergent language are a part of the modern world. Surely, avoiding topics offensive to certain community factions is unfair to students. What stance, then, should a supervisor take in regard to such materials and topics? The supervisor should help teachers prepare for community reaction to sensitive issues. S/he can help teachers interpret opposition as a matter of principle, not as a personal attack. Parents can be involved in needs assessment and basic planning, but the course of study and curriculum guides require professional preparation. Teachers should maintain an open professional approach based on the rationale that curriculum is important, valuable, and appropriate. Parents should be informed about the curriculum; inviting them to examine books and audiovisual aids is usually desirable. Schools should encourage constructive criticism from parents and offer alternative programs for students whose parents object to specified lessons. When the school communicates with the community, parents know what is going on at school, and they are less disturbed by gossip and rumors.

Supervisors should remind teachers of the importance of presenting different points of view on issues. Communities change continually, a phenomenon which means different concerns and values; teachers should expect different responses from year to year. The fact that fewer community members have children in school should stimulate educators to find ways of involving adults in school activities—in adult education classes, in the roles of tutors, in resource relationships. Interaction between school age students and older citizens can be mutually beneficial and satisfying.

While supporting teachers, a supervisor should help them avoid making foolish assignments in a classroom. Asking high school students to play the roles of homosexuals in a marriage is a totally inappropriate teaching strategy for a class in a conservative midwestern town—even though this situation actually happened. The supervisor may want to help inexperienced teachers plan their activities in some of the critical areas. The education goal is, of course, providing students with information so they can use problem-solving approaches to reach reasonable solutions.

One conflict which may frustrate supervisory personnel arises when a humanistic curriculum is instituted under a coercive administrator. Since teachers, in the classroom, implement the leadership style they experience, humaneness in content is undermined by the contrasting climate of the school. When the leader fails to recognize these incompatible elements, supervisors must work with teachers to stress any commonalities, such as recognition and use of talent or planning based on objectives. Effective teaching is best facilitated when the curriculum and the school leadership style have similar basic values.

SUMMARY

Supervisory responsibilities include assistance in curriculum development, for instructional improvement is achieved by instituting better curriculum. While a curriculum guide provides specific suggestions, the general course of study is a prescriptive document. One of the steps in the continuous process of curriculum development is textbook selection. Pilot programs can be used to test ideas which seem promising for curriculum progress.

Because a supervisor can view the total perspective in curriculum, s/he can coordinate the programs in scope and sequence, K through 12. A balanced curriculum is needed so that there is opportunity for aesthetic education, as well as academic, vocational, and physical education. Implementation of curriculum requires appropriate inservice activities. Supervisors can effectively help teachers understand new programs and use them. Supervisors can help teachers deal with controversial issues by encouraging communication with the community and by reminding teachers of the importance of presenting different points of view.

REFERENCES

Aarons, S. "Book Burning in the Heartlands." *Saturday Review* (21) (July 1979): 24–26, 28–29.

Davis, O. L., Jr., ed. *Perspective on Curriculum Development 1776–1976*. Washington, DC: Association for Supervision and Curriculum Development, 1976.

Eisner, E. W. "Future Priorities for Curriculum Reform." *Educational Leadership* 37 (6) (March 1980): 453–56.

English, F. W., and Kaufman, R. A. *Needs Assessment: A Focus for Curriculum Development*. Washington, DC: Association for Supervision and Curriculum Development, 1975.

Foshay, A. W., ed. *Considered Action for Curriculum Improvement*. Alexandria, VA: Association for Supervision and Curriculum Development, 1980.

Frazier, A. *Adventuring, Mastering, Associating*. Washington, DC: Association for Supervision and Curriculum Development, 1976.

Lewis, A. J., and Miel, A. *Supervision for Improved Instruction*. Belmont, CA: Wadsworth Publishing, 1972.

Molnar, A., and Zahorik, J. A., eds. *Curriculum Theory*. Washington, DC: Association for Supervision and Curriculum Development, 1977.

Sergiovanni, T. J., and Starratt, R. J. *Supervision: Human Perspectives*. 2d ed. New York: McGraw-Hill Book Co., 1979.

State of Ohio Department of Education. *Course of Study Development: A Process Model*. Columbus, OH: Department of Education, 1980.

Taba, H. *Curriculum Development, Theory and Practice*. New York: Harcourt, Brace and World, Inc., 1962.

Tyler, R. W. *Basic Principles of Curriculum and Instruction*. Chicago: University of Chicago Press, 1950.

Wiles, K., and Lovell, J. T. *Supervision for Better Schools*. 4th ed. Englewood Cliffs, NJ: Prentice-Hall, Inc., 1975.

Chapter 8
Alternate Strategies

Since different kinds of responsibilities are assigned to supervisors, a variety of supervisory tools is needed. Some supervisors may find that one of these methodological tools is sufficient, e.g., clinical supervision may be the one approach used in a school system. Most supervisors find that an eclectic approach is best, since it permits the choice of an appropriate tool. These choices include microteaching, staff development, clinical supervision, conferences, analysis of teaching, and curriculum development, as developed in the preceding chapters. There are still other strategies, and some of these will be suggested here.

Generally, educational supervisors need well-stocked tool kits to achieve the instructional improvement they are seeking. In fact, supervisors in any enterprise need to develop tools to fulfill the responsibilities which Dorsey (1980) describes: "(a) getting the job done promptly, efficiently and well . . .; (b) knowing what was going on in the work force (perceiving what is really there, hearing what is really said and conceptualizing what must be dealt with); and (c) developing people to the limit of their ability." This description—with the change of "work force" to "professional staff"—could be applied to supervisors in schools, since it emphasizes the human factors which are so important.

The number of supervisees with whom a supervisor works may prohibit a continuing one-to-one relationship. Numbers, along with time constraints, may force the use of group activities. The group process, of course, contributes uniquely to professional growth. One may expect certain outcomes, such as sensitivity to responses of other persons, awareness of interaction patterns within a group, identification of roles, and recognition of group productivity. Teachers can appreciate the time required for problem solving by a group, as well as the personal commitment developed by participation. A combination of individual and group procedures may prove effective for many supervisors.

COUNSELING

Clinical supervision is a relationship between a teacher and supervisor which deals with a lesson or lessons. Mosher and Purpel (1972, pp. 126 -27) recommend ego counseling as a one-to-one relationship which some supervisors may find useful. This technique focuses on self-appraisal, relationship of actions to objectives, consideration of obstacles, and the development of new ways of thinking and acting as a teacher. Instead of considering the lesson, as in clinical supervision, the conferences in ego counseling deal with a problem in reality, e.g., the discrepancy between professional expectations and achievement. A revised model is rehearsed and tested in the later stages of the process.

An experienced elementary teacher who enjoyed an unusually cooperative class last year now has a fourth-grade group of children that is easily distracted and academically uninterested. William Hall, the teacher, is puzzled about his lack of success with these children. Why are they progressing so slowly? What should he do to motivate them? Why does he spend so much time on behavior problems? Last year, he seldom spoke to the students about respect for others and common courtesy. He realizes that he is searching for new ways to punish—and he has always advocated using a positive approach. What has happened to his teaching skill? Is he burned out? Is he in a rut? Should he look for another job? What is happening to his professional philosophy? The timing is right for ego counseling. A supervisor who has known Bill Hall as a successful teacher can be helpful in decreasing the discrepancy between Bill's expectations and the reality. The analysis of the problem can lead to a restructuring of objectives which are suitable for these students, based on their unique levels of achievement, aptitudes, and interests. In addition, an examination of the learning styles of the individual students and an adaptation of teaching methods may produce more effective results. With revised goals and better teaching-learning situations, the discrepancies which Hall perceives can be decreased. Furthermore, in the process, Hall has probably reached a better understanding of himself and his skills and revamped his professional philosophy.

Although many supervisors may not feel qualified for such counseling, others have specifically prepared themselves for it. If a supervisor feels unqualified and discovers a situation which requires a counselor, referral to counseling professionals is appropriate. Supervisors should be aware of local agencies and qualified personnel so that they can suggest suitable resources. A supervisor who does not choose to develop skills as a counselor should not feel deficient, if s/he has other strategies for fulfilling essential supervisory responsibilities.

One warning in ego counseling: Limit the field to professional problems. If a teacher has been involved in a traumatic divorce, his/her teaching behavior may be affected. However, the supervisor must restrict consideration of the divorce action to the effect on the teacher's professional activities. The supervisor who becomes involved in personal counseling of supervisees may spend excessive amounts of time in nonsupervisory activities. The supervisor must learn to draw the line between ego counseling and personal counseling. Another danger of personal involvement is the possible destruction of a professional relationship. When a supervisor knows the intimate details of a supervisee's personal life, the supervisee may feel self-conscious about having divulged such personal information, and their working together professionally may be severely hampered in the days ahead.

Once again, the importance of listening skills for a supervisor should be recognized. Often, the supervisee needs an opportunity to verbalize a problem. The supervisor—by clarifying questions, paraphrasing, and summarizing—can provide a supportive environment. Listening to professional problems is one service that all supervisors must be prepared to perform. Frequently, the supervisee analyzes and solves, or at least sees possible solutions to, the problem during the process of talking.

VALUE CLARIFICATION

Value clarification is a technique for encouraging thought about what one considers important and why that concept is valued. It includes questioning choices, making forced choices, self-analysis of behavior, ranking ideas, and expressing opinions. Improvement of instruction should result when the relationship between teaching behavior in the classroom and values is studied. As a teacher analyzes his/her own teaching as an overt indication of values, new insight about harmony and control of one's own behavior should emerge. Instead of sporadic reactions, the teacher has a rational basis for decisions and action. The cognitive assessment of values provides the teacher with the beginning of a personal philosophy of education.

Value clarification is recommended as a teaching procedure and value development is recommended as a supervisory strategy. Zahorik (1978) argues that teacher behaviors should be a meaningful and consistent whole to have a maximum impact on students. When teachers examine and clarify their values, they will choose teaching behaviors that are appropriate, and they will employ strategies more effectively. A value position can bring consistency and commitment to teacher behavior. The focus of value development supervision should be the basic elements of education, such as students, curriculum, teaching, and learning. Value clarification activities could be undertaken in conference or in group settings.

The assumption is sometimes made that teachers in a geographical area, who are similar in educational background and socioeconomic status, will have the same values. Such a similarity does not exist.

In a study that used items from the Rokeach Value Scale, graduate students in educational supervision in an urban university in the Midwest were to arrange the following 18 terminal values according to importance in their lives—one for the most important, two for next in importance, down to 18 for least important (Phillips, 1972, pp. 7-8):

A comfortable life (a prosperous life)
An exciting life (a stimulating, active life)
A sense of accomplishment (lasting contribution)
A world at peace (free of war and conflict)
A world of beauty (beauty of nature and the arts)
Equality (brotherhood, equal opportunity for all)
Family security (taking care of loved ones)
Freedom (independence, free choice)
Happiness (contentedness)
Inner harmony (freedom from inner conflict)
Mature love (sexual and spiritual intimacy)
National security (protection from attack)
Pleasure (an enjoyable, leisurely life)
Salvation (saved, eternal life)
Self-respect (self-esteem)
Social recognition (respect, admiration)
True friendship (close companionship)
Wisdom (a mature understanding of life)

Every entry on the Rokeach Scale was chosen as the first, second, or third most important value in the lives of the 350 participating students. The most frequently selected items in the top three were inner harmony and self-respect; family security and happiness were next in frequency. The most apparent disagreement centered on salvation—76 students selected it as first in importance in their value system and 75 rated salvation as 18 or lowest in influence in their lives. National security was most frequently rated in the bottom three as least important. A world of beauty and social recognition were next in frequency as the lowest three in importance. Every item which was rated as part of the top three by some was rated as part of the bottom three by others. One person indicated self-respect as 17. Other items which were put in the lowest three positions by less than four percent of the subjects included: a sense of accomplishment, family security, freedom, inner harmony, mature love, true friendship, and wisdom. In other words, most subjects ranked these concepts as more important to them.

The fact that values are different for a group of people with similar educational, professional, and socioeconomic experiences is significant for supervisors. Values are determined by many factors, such as culture, social class, religion, political affiliation, sex concepts, personality factors, and experiences. The supervisor who recognizes what a teacher values can work more effectively with that teacher. If social recognition is important to a teacher, then appropriate rewards can be provided—rewards which would not be as effective for teachers who do not value such recognition.

Value clarification activities can be developed around student motivation, educational goals, learning processes, humane education, and similar topics. Many such activities are available in the following sources: *Values Clarification* by Simon, Howe and Kirschenbaum, *More Values Clarification* by Simon and Clark, *Value Exploration Through Role Playing* by Hawley, *Value Clarification as Learning Process* by Hall, and *The Teacher's I-View* by Curwin and Fuhrmann. A sample activity for ranking the 12 qualities of an ideal classroom is provided in Figure 23. This ranking encourages the analysis of values. The translation of values into teaching

Figure 23. Values in the Classroom.*

Below are 12 qualities that might be displayed in various ways in a classroom. In your ideal classroom how would you rank them? Place a "1" next to the quality you most value in a classroom, a "2" next to the second most important, and so on through "12," which will represent the quality you value least in relation to the others. When you have finished, list three examples from your class today which show you value your first and second choices. What can you do to improve the atmosphere of your classroom so that it more nearly approximates your ideal? Compare your rankings with the rankings of others.

_____ Freedom	_____ Orderliness
_____ Self-direction	_____ Creativity
_____ Quiet	_____ Respect
_____ Laughter	_____ Equality
_____ Concentration	_____ Fairness
_____ Purposefulness	_____ Love

*Adapted from R.L. Curwin and B.S. Fuhrmann, *The Teacher's I-View* (mimeographed, 1972), p. 29.

behavior is enhanced by the different interpretations. If teachers share their ideas, the interaction provides opportunities to consider the thinking of others. Value development strategies in supervision require both individual and group activities to attain the desired results.

PEER SUPERVISION

Inflation affects school budgets which, in turn, eliminate supervisory personnel. These cutbacks have forced some educators to recognize a need to organize specific structures to encourage alternate means of professional growth. Like all human beings, teachers do not remain at the same professional level; they either improve by developing new skills, interests, and activities or they decline. More than an inspirational speech at the beginning of the school year and work on a textbook selection committee are required for a teacher to feel professionally renewed. A specific focus on improvement of instruction can be achieved through peer supervision.

The school system in Washington, DC, when working with university personnel, undertook a program to prepare a cadre of administrators and teachers for clinical supervision. In this funded project, individuals provided leadership for cooperative efforts and participated in training colleagues in the skills of clinical supervision. Conferencing, collecting observational data, analyzing data, problem solving, and providing support were included skills. Whether instructional improvement was approached on a one-to-one basis, or in a small group setting, these trained educators were on-site resources for their peers. The success of this program, evolving from the needs and ideas of participants, was attributed to the commitment of those involved. Freeman, Palmer, and Ferren (1980, p. 358) have concluded that "there is clearly a renewed sense of commitment to the potential of supervision and confidence in the merits of peer supervision."

A study in a rural elementary school investigated the effect of peer observation teams on teacher attitude toward supervision. The staff was trained in the use of the clinical supervision cycle and two observation instruments. Teachers were organized into triads to work as teams over a five-month period. Teacher attitudes toward supervision significantly improved. The findings reinforce the idea that teachers feel more positively toward supervision when they help select the purposes and procedures, when supervision is help rather than evaluation, and when the focus is on teacher-perceived problems. Thus, the peer observation team is recommended as a catalyst for changing teacher opinion or as a "low-cost substitute" for traditional supervision (Ellis, Smith, and Abbott, 1979).

Some department heads have been able to develop effective peer supervision programs. The department as a whole can function as a unit seeking new teaching strategies, new materials, and new structure. Members are encouraged to attend professional meetings and then share new ideas and experiences with the group. Tests and learning materials are developed together. Individual teachers invite peers to observe lessons and help analyze the teaching-learning process. With these strategies, a helping relationship is cultivated. Building a group commitment to an effective educational program demands cooperation and leadership. Teachers must be open and trusting to work for departmental goals. Such an effort is based on the assumption that teachers can provide motivation and opportunities for their own professional growth.

Other groups of teachers have successfully used clinical supervision to improve their teaching. (See the Adaptations of Clinical Supervision in Chapter 4.) An effective teaching clinic, a term applied to the process of clinical supervision with group involvement, usually has six or seven teachers who want to improve and increase their teaching skills. These individuals must be mature and willing to risk exposure of their lesson plans and teaching to group study. The teachers learn from each other by examining lesson plans, observing, and analyzing, as well as by the analysis of their own lessons. It should be noted that, although the clinical supervision model may be useful, it is not essential for peer supervision.

The "buddy system" is a form of peer supervision that has been used for many years. A teacher new to a system is paired with an experienced teacher. The newcomer can get information and help from the buddy, who is a resource about grading, scheduling audiovisual aids, lunchroom duty, attending extracurricular activities, and other pertinent information. If these assignments are made wisely, i.e., the two are compatible, the relationship can be mutually beneficial. The best orientation to a school is often provided by the buddy of the new teacher, who may introduce new materials and ideas about teaching.

Some educators feel that teachers cannot profit from peer supervision. A determination to be positive and a reluctance to talk honestly about weakness or failure are cited as reasons why many teachers will be subjective and unable to treat data with necessary objectivity. Not all teachers can cope with peer analysis, but the process is a valid alternative for some.

PROFESSIONAL READING

When supervisory personnel have too many duties and supervisees, one route to stimulating teacher growth may be the reading of professional literature. A professional library in a school may be nice; but, unless teachers read the materials, it is a waste. Some supervisors regularly duplicate and send pertinent journal articles to potential leaders in each school, e.g., a teacher selected from the English department at the middle school and another at the high school will be sent copies of a current article on how to improve student writing. Research results which relate to particular subject areas also can be disseminated and creative teachers can be encouraged to try new ideas. Without follow-up by the supervisor or principal, the readings may be ignored. Wilhelms (1973, p. 39) has suggested that conversational opportunities can be used to convey the message "that we are competent partners in a professional enterprise." Such opportunities include meetings in the hall, lunch room contacts, and encounters in the teacher's lounge, where concepts from the articles can be casually discussed.

Teachers working on specific committees must be provided with appropriate and current information. Any publications about schools and learning that are discussed in the media should be available to teachers. In fact, newsletters from supervisors should include reviews of such literature. Since teachers can prepare these reviews, both the literature and the reviewer receive recognition. Supervisors must be familiar with current educational publications, and, if possible, they should make extensive use of this resource to promote instructional improvement.

SUMMARY

Most supervisors use a variety of strategies in working with teachers; individual contacts, small group activities, and large group meetings are usually included. In addition to microteaching, clinical supervision, analysis of teaching, supervisory conferences, staff development, and curriculum development, many supervisors can also use counseling, value clarification, peer supervision, and professional reading as techniques for helping teachers improve their instructional activities.

Ego counseling is concerned with teachers' professional problems, such as the discrepancy between expectation and reality. Some supervisors with training in counseling will use this approach; others will refer teachers to outside counseling services. Value clarification procedures may be used by supervisors to help the teacher find a basis for consistent teaching behavior. Peer supervision has been effective for professional development in several school situations. A clinical supervision model may be adapted for group application, but other group programs and one-to-one relationships, like the buddy system, may also be used. Sharing professional materials is another way teachers can be stimulated to improve instruction. If the supervisor has numerous alternatives for working with teachers, appropriate techniques can be selected as needed.

REFERENCES

Curwin, R.L., and Fuhrmann, B.S. *The Teacher's I-View.* Mimeographed, 1972.

Dorsey, J. "On Management," *Sky* 9 (10) (October 1980): 34, 37.

Ellis, E.C.; Smith, J.T.; and Abbott, W.H., Jr. "Peer Observation: A Means for Supervisory Acceptance." *Educational Leadership* 36 (6) (March 1979): 423–26.

Freeman, G.; Palmer, R.C.; and Ferren, A.S. "Team Building for Supervisory Support." *Educational Leadership* 37 (4) (January 1980): 356–58.

Hall, B.P. *Value Clarification as Learning Process.* New York: Paulist Press, 1973.

Hawley, R.C. *Value Exploration through Role Playing.* New York: Hart Publishing Co., 1975.

Mosher, R.L., and Purpel, D.E. *Supervision: The Reluctant Profession.* Boston: Houghton Mifflin Co., 1972.

Phillips, J.A., Jr., ed. *Developing Value Constructs in Schooling; Inquiry into Process and Product.* Worthington, OH: Ohio Association for Curriculum and Supervision Development, 1972.

Raths, L.E.; Hamrin, M.; and Simon, S.B. *Values and Teaching.* Columbus, OH: Charles E. Merrill Books, Inc., 1966.

Simon, S.B., and Clark, J. *More Values Clarification.* San Diego, CA: Pennant Press, 1975.

Simon, S.B.; Howe, L.W.; and Kirschenbaum, H. *Values Clarification.* New York: Hart Publishing Co., 1972.

Wilhelms, F.T. *Supervision in a New Key* Washington, DC: Association for Supervision and Curriculum Development, 1973.

Zahorik, J.A. "Supervision as Value Development." *Educational Leadership* 35 (8) (May 1973): 667–69.

Using Management Skills

Chapter 9
Organizational Process

Management is the skill that draws powerful forces together and disperses them into a multitude of areas to effect change, progress, and improvement. From a military standpoint, it is often described as strategic action. From an industrial standpoint, it is usually considered a process of the administrative structure which occurs within and for the structure itself. Educators who think management activities are of primary importance usually draw on both military and industrial patterns. A school does not produce a tangible, salable product, nor does it maneuver actual attacks against anything except ignorance. But, the processes within a system which are organized for efficient movement are indeed management processes, and they must be seriously considered by supervisors.

The hierarchy in a school system is easily recognized. Administrative policies are ordinarily activated through this chain of command. The supervisors, however, may find themselves outside the line positions. The school superintendent delegates authority to assistants, deputies, directors, coordinators, principals, and assistant principals. However, supervisors, considered to be in staff positions, are often assigned to several schools and work in cooperation with principals, but the designation of their authority is sometimes vague. This poorly defined area of responsibility may complicate their relationships.

Supervisors should be familiar with the stated missions, goals, and philosophies of their school systems. These statements, adopted by the board of education, are available in the central office and ordinarily are distributed to newly hired school personnel. If these documents are not available, a newly appointed supervisor should inquire about how and where to obtain them. Often included in such materials is a structural model which shows the interrelationships of various offices and gives a clear indication of who's who in a particular school situation. The model indicates where the institution's official power base lies, and it is a quick way for new personnel to ascertain the importance of the individuals who fill designated positions. In a democratic society, the model will show where the real power of each system originates—with the people via the elected board of education.

Some people entering a school system, exposed to a management structure for the first time, may feel that institutional hierarchy is denigrating to the individual. This reaction is unfortunate and may limit the effectiveness of the newly appointed employee if s/he decides to "buck the system" or work outside of the chain of command. If individuals understand the institutional procedures, they can work for change within the structure, even though the process may be slow and frustrating. Most plans which are put into action without institutional backing will flounder, because the management structure is where planned cooperation develops and where economic backing can be obtained.

In fact, an obligation for efficient delegation of both funds and responsibilities justifies a tightly organized school structure. Since supervisors need access to both of these elements, they must know the structure and follow the protocol for introducing new ideas and activities. Unless the administration has built a nomothetic structure (an organization maximizing institutional roles and goals) which is impervious to suggestions from below, most systems provide some procedure whereby teachers, supervisors, and other personnel can express their opinions, feed them to top management, share them horizontally with peers, and process them to others in the system.

ORGANIZATIONAL THEORIES

Much has been written about organizational theory. Schools and supervision in the schools have been influenced by these ideas. In the early twentieth century, the scientific management concepts of Frederick Taylor influenced a movement for efficiency in the schools (March and Simon, 1961). Supervisors were a part of this scientific approach to find the best way of teaching and managing learning.

Supervisors should be aware of these theories so they can understand the basic concepts involved. Such knowledge enables them to analyze the functioning of their school system, to see where they fit in, and to understand how they can work effectively within the system. Furthermore, the dysfunctions of the organization can be recognized and perhaps remedied or modified appropriately. (Only brief reference is made here to organizational theories, but supervisors can broaden their backgrounds by further investigation.)

Organizations are defined as social units which seek attainment of specific goals. Max Weber (1947) described bureaucracy as an ideal type of organization. Characteristics of bureaucratic organizations include division of labor, hierarchy of authority, written policies and regulations, impersonal basis for interaction, and longevity of administrative careers.

Bureaucracy provides stability, efficiency, and orderliness; however, it is rigid and impersonal, often stifling creativity and perpetuating separate, rather than common, interests. Problems arise in the bureaucracy when unintended results occur. In the enforcement of rigid behavior patterns, for instance, individuals in the organization may become dissatisfied, resistant, and even militant. Dress codes in schools have sometimes caused such reactions among faculty and students. Because professionals are involved in education, some theorists have advocated a professional model which provides for adaptiveness, specialization, and job satisfaction for the members of the organization (Sergiovanni, 1979, pp. 53-54).

Another way of studying an organization is by viewing it as a social system. Getzels and Guba (1957) developed a conceptual model depicting the interaction of the institution and the human element. The nomothetic dimension relates to the institution as defined by the roles and role expectations which are designed to achieve institutional goals. The ideographic dimension starts with the individuals who seek goals according to their personalities and need dispositions. These dimensions interact constantly; organizational effectiveness is achieved by institutional conformity; and individual efficiency is reached by an individual's conformity. When the organizational goals and individual goals are similar, decisions are simplified. However, disparity between the goals of the institution and the individuals within the institution creates conflict. Role expectations are another source of misunderstanding. Supervisors are often caught in the conflict between the role expectations of teachers and those of principals. Teachers are seeking a helping relationship with the supervisor, while the principal wants the supervisor to get the teacher to "shape up." If the supervisor recognizes these conflicting expectations, s/he can strive to clarify supervisory responsibilities and to create a better environment for cooperation.

ORGANIZATIONAL CLIMATE

The climate of a school is subjective; it deals with an impression or feeling that teachers and students have for the school. Climate is determined by the organizational structure, leadership, and reactions of the people in the organization, as well as the values, motivation, and performance of the teachers.

Miles (1965) described organizational health as consisting of 10 dimensions: goal focus, communication adequacy, optimal power equalization, resource utilization, cohesiveness, morale, innovativeness, autonomy, adaptation, and problem-solving adequacy. These dimensions are interdependent and interacting. For example, if personnel is used effectively, members feel they are important to the enterprise, and the morale of the group is high. When the school is a healthy organization, the supervisor can serve as a facilitator for professional development and improvement of instruction. Otherwise, the supervisor's effort is needed to improve relationships within the school before any progress can be made in the teaching-learning process.

The four management systems proposed by Likert (1967) describe school climate. In this approach, effective work groups are important for group decision making, maintaining high performance goals consistent with those of the school, working with other school groups in overlapping and linking structures, and building feelings of personal worth in the group members. Likert's four management systems are included in a survey instrument which can be used to show member perceptions of the climate, as well as the management, desired. Characteristics of organizations in the profile include leadership processes, motivational forces, communication processes, interaction-influence processes, decision-making processes, goal setting, control processes, performance goals, and training. Table 1 shows these items and their descriptions regarding leadership. Such information can help supervisors and administrators assess their own behavior in relation to the functioning of the organization, and the appraisal can give a supervisor some insight into improving supervisory activities.

SUPERVISORY CONTACTS IN THE ORGANIZATION

A supervisor's organizational connections are almost exclusively tied to three management directions: up, down, or across. A supervisor can be identified with three categories of professionals: superordinates, peers, and teachers. If the individual is a full-time supervisor, the superordinates are usually at the central office. The individual supervisor often has an office and receives assignments at headquarters near the superintendent and the board of education offices. A supervisor's superordinates are the board, the superintendent, and, in some larger systems, a director. Peers are other supervisors who function in different schools, in different subject areas, for special projects, or at different school levels. These peers can provide a support system for and give helpful professional suggestions to the supervisor who feels alienated from the teachers. The clients are ordinarily limited to the group of teachers being supervised. If the term subordinate is used for the supervisees, the reference is a categorical one, limited only to the relationship developed between a supervisor and a teacher for the teacher's self-improvement. The teacher does not report to or defer to a supervisor. In most situations, the supervisor is not in an authority position to determine termination or promotion.

Knowledge of the school hierarchy is a necessity for a supervisor. Perhaps no other member of the school system works with a system, and expedites changes and improvement through the system, more than a supervisor. Yet, in many ways, no member of a system is as free of organizational structure as the supervisor. Usually, s/he functions near, but not in, a specific organizational framework. The bond between the supervisor and the principal is surely one of the most ambivalent in the school system. By most standards, in any given school, the principal is the one who is the decision maker. Yet, a principal can profit immeasurably when a supervisor assists a teacher who is having problems. The responsibility for the instructional program in a school belongs to the principal, but few administrators have time to do everything involved in carrying out that responsibility. Most principals need assistance and consider supervisory services a definite asset. Providing help to a new teacher in lesson planning and classroom management can be time consuming, yet such professional aid is essential if that teacher is to become a contributing member of the staff. The principal-supervisor team can strengthen a school by providing for the growth of teachers and supporting professional activities.

A principal has responsibilities to each teacher in the school building. If a supervisor makes a suggestion that appears to be inadvisable, too expensive, badly timed, or in conflict with a previously established school policy, the principal can veto the supervisor's plan. Thus, the supervisor must develop good working relations with the principal, as well as promote trust and a helping relationship with teachers. Because principals consider their buildings private territory, the supervisor must realize the importance of friendly contact. Administrators must be informed about the plans and goals which are evolved by the teacher and supervisor. When a supervisor is aware of the sensitivity regarding someone coming into a school, s/he can and should be especially careful about maintaining confidentiality and professional behavior.

Conflicting points of view and different activities often put the supervisor in stressful situations. A supervisor may be placed in the role of delaying a movement toward reorganization at one school, while hoping for a restrained, well-devised plan to develop. At the same time, the supervisor may be cast in the role of accelerating a movement toward badly needed change in another school, working toward the eradication of outmoded, nonproductive methods. A supervisor must not only know the organizational structures, but s/he must work within them daily, as they are the framework of both conservative and liberal action. Supervisors need to describe the school system's design to new teachers, so that the teachers can function acceptably within this framework.

Table 1. Profile of Organizational Characteristics.*

Organizational variable	System 1	System 2	System 3	System 4	Item No.
1. Leadership processes used a. Extent to which superiors have confidence and trust in subordinates	Have no confidence and trust in subordinates	Have condescending confidence and trust, such as master has in servant	Substantial but not complete confidence and trust; still wishes to keep control of decision	Complete confidence and trust in all matters	1
b. Extent to which subordinates, in turn, have confidence and trust in superiors	Have no confidence and trust in superiors	Have subservient confidence and trust, such as servant has in master	Substantial but not complete confidence and trust	Complete confidence and trust	2
c. Extent to which superiors display supportive behavior toward others	Display no supportive behavior or virtually none	Display supportive behavior in condescending manner and situations only	Display supportive behavior quite generally	Display supportive behavior fully and in all situations	3

*Source: R. Likert, *The Human Organization: Its Management and Values* (New York: McGraw-Hill Book Co., 1967), pp. 197-98. Copyright © 1967 by McGraw Hill Book Company. Reprinted by permission.

Table 1. Profile of Organizational Characteristics (cont'd).

Organizational variable	System 1	System 2	System 3	System 4	Item No.
d. Extent to which superiors behave so that subordinates feel free to discuss important things about their jobs with their immediate superiors	Subordinates do not feel at all free to discuss things about the job with their superior	Subordinates do not feel very free to discuss things about the job with their superior	Subordinates feel rather free to discuss things about the job with their superior	Subordinates feel completely free to discuss things about the job with their superior	4
e. Extent to which immediate superior in solving job problems generally tries to get subordinates' ideas and opinions and make constructive use of them	Seldom gets ideas and opinions of subordinates in solving job problems	Sometimes gets ideas and opinions of subordinates in solving job problems	Usually gets ideas and opinions and usually tries to make constructive use of them	Always gets ideas and opinions and always tries to make constructive use of them	5

A fortunate supervisor is one who has strong backing from superordinates in the central office. With administrative understanding, a supervisor can act on the behalf of teachers with widely varying needs and plans, yet still not create confusion in the hierarchy.

SUPERVISORY TASKS IN THE ORGANIZATION

Fayol (1949), an early management analyst, described assignments usually fulfilled by administrators, stating that they consist primarily of planning, organizing, commanding, coordinating, and controlling. In modern schools, few supervisors function with an overall sense of control, and supervisors do not have the authority to command anyone to do anything. But planning, organizing, and coordinating are high on the list of functions in which supervisors may assist administrators. Since these processes must be compatible with legally stated policies, supervisors must first know the policies and second, must operate within the bounds set by them.

To some extent, planning requires a prognostication about the future of the school system itself, and it requires that the individual teachers are being supervised and guided. Awareness of change agentry is essential. But, even before considering the rather specific skill of the change agent, supervisors must have the courage of their own convictions. They should have confidence in their own analyses of future needs, so there can be a nonhesitant, forward motion. The supervisor, as an acknowledged professional, plans on the basis of pertinent information and in conjunction with those who will be affected. The philosophical base of such plans must be faith in the democratic system and the educability of individuals.

Organizing is an important process of administration in which supervisors are directly involved. It should take into consideration the best ways to guide people into productivity so their energies are used advantageously. Before an organizational pattern can be set into motion, an awareness of both human and material potential should be considered.

Coordinating, as a supervisory skill, usually relates to the encouragement of human production so there is organizational harmony. This necessitates an awareness of both the macrostructure of, and the numerous microstructures within, the school system. For example, a supervisor should arrive at a particular school building knowing, in general, the school system's expectations for that site. Then, a supervisor should build an atmosphere of cooperation with the principal. The principal, functioning as expected by the central office, will have established patterns of operations within the policy bounds of the system. But, beyond this framework, where much of the supervisory action takes place, almost every cluster of teachers who function together will have their own micro-structure, which is as firmly a part of their organizational understanding as the system policies. In fact, some teachers will be functioning very efficiently, fully understanding their peer group activities, even when they have only a vague conception of the institutional philosophy implemented by the central office.

When teachers seem to be in conflict with school policy, the supervisor may have a difficult task—aligning the group with institutional standards without alienating the members. Here, human relations skills—sensitivity, timing, and communication—are put to use.

In the organizational control that a supervisor maintains, s/he can keep a guiding hand on teachers, with tact and with indirect action. It may be essential to point a teacher in a new direction to help build new goals, new methods, and new attitudes. The teacher who is disregarding curriculum may be doing a disservice to students who will be handicapped by the lack of sequence in their school experiences. Throughout these major or minor changes, a supervisor should consider the teacher's own preferences and inclinations, since only in this way will the teacher move ahead willingly and productively.

The managerial skills which a supervisor must exert within an organization are complex and numerous. In many ways, a supervisor is indeed a figurative Hydra, with several heads, all facing different directions, considering several situations at the same time. Even when most supervisor-teacher relationships seem pleasant and constructive, a supervisor should approach every day with anticipation of unexpected problems and curiosity about new situations which may need supervisory attention. The supervisor is in an interesting position, because, as circumstances change, there are new problems.

SUPERVISORY COMMITMENT TO THE ORGANIZATION

In facing the surprising array of human problems, an educational supervisor has the most subtle set of responsibilities of supervisors in a myriad of fields. An industrial supervisor can assess the skills of supervisees by looking at the products of their work. An army officer in a supervisory position can measure progress by the victory or defeat of the troops in action. But, an educational supervisor, hoping to improve the teaching-learning environment for students, has a nebulous set of things and people to assess. Tests indicate how well students have learned, but the basic learning that will be internalized by young people in a reservoir of beliefs, attitudes, skills, and knowledge cannot be evaluated easily or immediately. Without hard data to indicate effectiveness, these supervisors must continue to seek new procedures for evaluating teaching and alternative ways of improving instruction.

Educational supervisors must accept the professional requirement of continuous learning. Peter Drucker wrote:

> The productivity of people requires . . . continuous learning. It requires that people are constantly challenged to think through what they can do to improve what they are already doing. It requires adoption in the West of the specific Japanese Zen concept of learning: that one learns in order to do better what one already knows how to do well. To be sure, this presupposes enough psychological security in the work group so that people are not afraid of working themselves, or their colleagues and neighbors on the next machine or in the next office, out of a job. But above all, it requires willingness to ask employees systematically and to listen to their answers. It requires acceptance of the fact that the person who does the job is likely to know more about it than the person who supervises (1980, pp. 24-25).

Educational supervisors can benefit by adapting these ideas to their work. Listening to teachers and recognizing their expertise will contribute to the learning of supervisors.

Commitment to the organization can be demonstrated by supervisors in many ways:

1. A supervisor should strive to develop an atmosphere of trust among people in the institution, because no organizational structure will last without mutual good will.
2. A supervisor should have the willingness to delegate responsibility, since this is an expression of faith in another person's ability to achieve within the organizational framework.
3. A supervisor should accelerate positive action among groups committed to working together, if s/he fosters enjoyment on the job. The ability to laugh at one's self can open the way to a sharing atmosphere—necessary as groups or individuals work together productively and happily.
4. A supervisor should strive for consistency in behavior. Because of the plurality of tasks a supervisor performs, maintenance of harmonious actions requires a value basis for decisions.
5. A supervisor should facilitate communication, particularly input from teachers to superordinates. Vertical communication upward is often neglected in an organization.
6. A supervisor should maintain a continuing awareness of the whole person as s/he deals with teachers, principals, or anyone else in the organization. Members of an institution often feel insignificant, if they view themselves on a low rung of the success ladder. Supervisors can contribute to the mental health of a supervisee by

acknowledging the individual's personal attributes as interesting, unique, and worthwhile. Positive reinforcement—encouragement and support—can be used effectively by supervisors.

SUMMARY

Educational supervisors can function more productively when they understand the structure of the organization and their place in this structure. Organizational theories are helpful in developing basic concepts. The Weber bureaucracy model has strengths and weaknesses; it can be modified for professional institutions. The social interaction approach of Getzels and Guba and an analysis of school climate enable one to study specific aspects of an institution.

A supervisor's contacts within an institution are with superordinates, teachers, and peers. Some of the institutional functions performed by supervisors include planning, coordinating, and controlling. Within these complex contacts and tasks, supervisors must nurture good interpersonal relationships as they demonstrate institutional commitment. They can facilitate the improvement of instruction through the use of the organizational structure.

REFERENCES

Campbell, R., et al. *Introduction to Educational Administration*. 4th ed. Boston: Allyn and Bacon, Inc., 1971.

Drucker, P.E. *Managing in Turbulent Times*. New York: Harper and Row, 1980.

Fayol, H. *General and Industrial Management*. London: Pitman and Sons, 1949.

Getzels, J.W., and Guba, E.G. "Social Behavior and Administrative Behavior." *The School Review* 65 (1957): 423–42.

Killen, K. *Management: A Middle-Management Approach*. Boston: Houghton Mifflin Co., 1977.

Leeper, R., ed. *Supervision: Emerging Profession*. Washington, DC: Association for Supervision and Curriculum Development, NEA, 1969.

Likert, R. *The Human Organization: Its Management and Value*. New York: McGraw-Hill, 1967.

———. *New Patterns of Management*. New York: McGraw Hill, 1961.

March, J., and Simon, H.A. *Organizations*. New York: John Wiley and Sons, Inc., 1961.

Miles, M. "Planned Change and Organizational Health: Figure and Ground." In *Change Processes in the Public Schools,* pp. 11–34. Eugene, OR: Center for the Advanced Study of Educational Administration, 1965.

Sergiovanni, T.J., and Starratt, R.J. *Supervision: Human Perspectives*. 2d ed. New York: McGraw-Hill, 1979.

Weber, Max. *Theory of Social and Economic Organizations*. Translated by A.M. Henderson and T. Parsons. New York: Oxford, 1947.

Chapter 10
Leadership

Leadership involves complex interactions between leaders and followers. It is behavior that influences individuals to move toward the attainment of goals. Leadership can be direct, so that those being led are aware of the forces which incite the action, or it can be indirect, with the primary influence being exerted by an unidentified or secondary source.

Direct and indirect leadership are found in the following positions:

1. Spearhead Leadership—with the leadership stating the goal and moving identifiably to the forefront, sometimes emphasizing leadership by example. This kind of leadership is typified by a football coach who determines the courses of action and teaches the ways to achieve them through plays selected and taught in his/her own manner. These actions are deployed by a quarterback who calls the plays and leads the way to the opponents' goal post.

2. Companion Leadership—with the leader often identified as an initiator of action, but with the peer relationship so consistently maintained that only close analysis reveals the human source of group guidance. The companion leader usually stays with the group through a sequence of changes or actions. This kind of leadership is most evident in a gathering of young people who are playing together but who wait for the leader to decide on the game, choose the directions, or signal approval of suggested gang activities.

3. Shepherd Leadership—with the leader exerting influence from a position behind the group. In many ways, this position has the most subtle influence and force of all. Nominal leadership can be assigned to someone else who is physically out in front of the group, and only close observation will indicate the real source of leadership. The leader's position is fluid, moving from one position to another and from one level of dominance to another. Leadership forces can gain or lose power and, sometimes, become inactive for periods. Such flexibility can be an intentional development. Motivational force applied by a leader is often an initial

exertion of influence which is removed after the mobilized individuals gain momentum. When a gathering of people shows evidence of producing its own leadership, the initiating leader who hopes to develop other leaders may retract his/her leadership influence so the new leaders may function.

Supervisors should recognize that they will use these different positions in their work—mixing and matching as situations demand. Frequently, a supervisor is in the shepherd position with a supervisee. Though clearly affecting the supervisee's professional behavior, a supervisor may guide his/her client toward a goal in such a way that the supervisee feels in complete control of the situation. This interaction maintains good supervisee self-concept and is often a desirable pattern for a supervisor. Supervisors should realize that some teachers will not respond to the subtle shepherd action. The collegial approach, or a companion leadership position, is probably the next alternative to use with a supervisee. Supervisors use spearhead leadership, or a modification of it, infrequently with individual supervisees, but this dominant pattern of action is sometimes effective with sizeable gatherings. For example, spearhead action is effective when several dozen teachers need an explanation of a new teaching method and a special inservice program has been set up. Even when meeting with a large group, such as a general PTA meeting, supervisors often find that spearhead action is acceptable because, for the most part, human beings are willing to follow a well-intentioned, forward-moving leader, if s/he does not attempt to expand the leadership force beyond appropriate limits.

The three designations of leadership may appear to be in contrast with one another, but there are common qualities maintained in each position. One visible quality in all three is communication. In fact, the mode of selected supervisory communication is usually the clue which can point to the type of leadership employed. The leadership positions are shown in Figure 24. The leader in the spearhead position (L^1), the leader in the companion position (L^2), and the leader in the shepherd position (L^3) provide impetus for leadership from three different vantage points. Without effective expressions and explanations, the L-figure (leader) would be indistinguishable from the other members of the group.

Consistently throughout the process of activating leadership, there is a crosscurrent of plural movement. Customarily, the leader exerts personal influence to channel these movements in a single direction. Effective leadership does not restrain individual expression among members; instead, the combined impetus of individuals creates the forward motion which is guided by a leader. Authentic leadership is experienced when several individuals share an interest or concern in an ultimate goal. Often, the goal has been determined separately and has been the raison d'être for the

Figure 24. Leadership Positions.

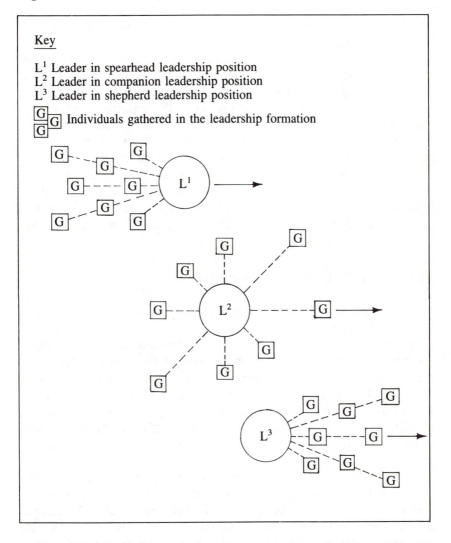

ingathering of individuals. The leadership force is still in a similar pattern when the leader imposes the goal, as well as the means of achieving it.

In an educational milieu, when a number of teachers have gathered to share a mutual concern, a supervisor is frequently in the position of facilitator. In this role, the actual decision-making skills are secondary to the skill of producing a coalescence of other people's ideas. Bringing seemingly disparate ideas together and effecting a compatible merger require that a supervisor sort through suggestions and discard irrelevant ideas without offending the offerors. A successful demonstration of the leadership role produces a synthesis of suggestions and a plan of action which is not just politically acceptable, but which may implement the mutual concern of the teachers.

In these instances, supervisors must develop the skills which can move group members toward an honest solution to their problem, instead of just providing a forum for the members to express their dissatisfactions or criticisms. Mere venting of opinions is usually ineffective in providing any genuine problem-solving result; instead, participants usually settle for a gratification which is purely emotional and is a form of expressing the idea that misery loves company. These activities are not goal-oriented—they focus on the intracommunication activities of the group members. Activity which is not goal-oriented is a circular motion which seldom brings solutions or even inadvertent progress toward alleviating a problem. A leader should be able to use the information presented and direct group effort toward formulating possible solutions.

RESEARCH RELATED TO LEADERSHIP

For years, people have been fascinated by the phenomenon of leadership, and they have speculated on what makes a good leader, why a group rejects an individual leader, how effective leaders can be selected, and other similar questions. Research to answer these questions has been carried out in many fields, including sociology, business, psychology, and education. Educators have long been interested in these results and their implications, but the many studies to determine the characteristics of effective leaders have led to the conclusion that no characteristics are consistently found. Thus, research efforts turned to the study of leadership styles.

One of the pioneer studies on leadership was done by Lewin, Lippitt, and White (1939). Groups of boys worked under leaders using different leadership styles—autocratic, democratic, and laissez-faire. The group achievement and climate varied under the different styles. Production in the groups with autocratic leaders was slightly higher than in groups with democratic leadership, but aggression, discontent, and dependency were higher also. Boys with democratic leaders were more motivated, original, and group oriented; their work was of better quality. Groups with laissez-faire leaders were least productive and motivated; they operated with a great amount of fooling around and discontent. Other studies have indicated similar results: autocratic and democratic (or participatory) leadership styles produce different achievements and climates in group situations (Alfonso, Firth, and Neville, 1975, pp. 51-52).

One of the most interesting aspects of leadership is that no leader exists without followers; when leaders are considered, the followers cannot be forgotten. The leader-follower relationship is a complex, changing interaction. One crucial factor in the relationship is the leader's overall regard for people. McGregor (1960) proposed two management philosophies which he called Theory X and Theory Y. In Theory X, there are some assumptions about human behavior:

1. Individuals are by nature lazy and work as little as possible.
2. Individuals dislike responsibility, have little ambition, and want to be told what to do.
3. Individuals are selfish and unconcerned about organizational needs.
4. Individuals are stupid and can be easily misled.

On the other hand, the assumptions about people for Theory Y include the following:

1. Individuals are by nature active and want to be involved.
2. Individuals can handle responsibility when given the opportunity.
3. Individuals are concerned about organizational goals and will work to achieve them.
4. Individuals are self-directed, creative, and self-actualizing.

In his study of business organizations, McGregor saw both Theory X and Theory Y implemented. Theory X emphasized punishment, manipulation, and control; Theory Y encouraged human development and challenged individual participation. Organizational leaders who accept the philosophy of Theory X will behave in a completely different pattern from leaders who accept Theory Y. In education, although practice sometimes seems to indicate suspicion and mistrust, the goals demand that supervisors subscribe to and pursue Theory Y assumptions. .

Motivation is a concern of those who are interested in the study of changing behavior. Maslow's theory (1954) classifies needs and arranges them in a hierarchy of prepotency. There are five levels which an individual can experience. As one level is fairly well-satisfied, the needs at the next higher level begin to emerge and affect the person's behavior to motivate him/her. A gratified need is not a motivator. The five levels are somewhat overlapping, but a person is not influenced by the needs of a particular level until the needs of lower levels have been reasonably supplied. The first level is physiological needs—food, water, rest, exercise, and protection from the elements. Safety needs—the next higher level—include protection against danger, threat, and deprivation. Social needs, which represent needs for belonging, acceptance, giving and receiving friendship, and love, are the third level. The ego needs, the fourth level, relate to self-confidence, independence, achievement, competence, status, recognition, appreciation, and respect. The highest level is the need for self-actualization. This is a level that few individuals actually satisfy. Although many persons have fulfilling experiences in some areas of life, only a limited number of individuals gratify the need for realizing their full potential. One interpretation of this level includes becoming a contributing member of a larger unit, i.e., using one's talents in a helping relationship in the community. Such an altruistic commitment may be appropriate in the culture of a democratic society.

Supervisors who work with teachers must be aware of their different needs. Motivating teachers to change behavior is one of the continuing responsibilities and challenges of supervision. Studies of motivation factors have produced some helpful conclusions. Herzberg and his associates (1959) developed the motivation-hygiene theory. They found that removing the dissatisfactions of workers did not result in satisfaction and motivation, since the factors associated with satisfaction and motivation are different factors from those producing dissatisfaction (hygiene factors). The hygienic factors associated with lower order needs are found in the work environment—salary, interpersonal relations, supervision, company policy, and working conditions. The motivators, in contrast, stimulate performance; they are found in the work itself and are associated with higher order needs. They include achievement, recognition, the work itself, responsibility, and advancement.

Sergiovanni (1967), in a study involving teachers, found that achievement and recognition are the most potent motivators. Significant hygiene factors causing teacher dissatisfactions include interpersonal relations with students and peers, school policy and administration, supervision, and incidents in the teachers' personal lives. Later, Sergiovanni and Starratt (1979, pp. 169-70) suggested that some teachers are more interested in hygienic factors than motivational factors. Supervisors can encourage these teachers to function professionally, but the failure to develop motivators within a school system results in the waste of human resources.

DIMENSIONS OF LEADERSHIP

Supervisors are concerned with leadership in at least two ways. They act as leaders in numerous educational groups—inservice sessions, committees, parent meetings, professional activities—and they strive to develop leaders among teachers. Encouraging teacher leadership requires that the supervisor model effective behavior and teach appropriate skills, along with providing opportunities for teachers to serve as leaders. Supervisors should be aware of the research on leadership effectiveness and the current theories so they can select an appropriate leadership style.

Two dimensions that appear in descriptions of leadership /managerial behavior are concern for production (task orientation) and concern for people (relations orientation). Reddin (1970) used these dimensions and suggested indicators for each combination in four styles of leadership:

RELATED STYLE
Low task concern

High people concern

Leader listens, accepts, trusts, advises, encourages

SEPARATED STYLE
Low task concern

Low people concern

Leader examines, measures, administers, controls, maintains

INTEGRATED STYLE
High task concern

High people concern

Leader interacts, motivates, integrates, participates, innovates

DEDICATED STYLE
High task concern

Low people concern

Leader organizes, initiates, directs, completes, evaluates effectiveness

Another dimension of effectiveness is added in Reddin's 3D Theory of Leadership. For example, a dedicated supervisor working with a curriculum committee that is interested in and works to develop an appropriate course of study will find the committee helpful in completing the job. (See Figure 25.) In this situation, the leader is considered a benevolent autocrat. However, if the committee lacks interest and impetus to get to work, the supervisor may come across as a harsh task master—an autocrat.

Figure 25. Effective and Ineffective Expression of Leadership Style.*

When used inappropriately	Basic Styles	When used appropriately
Compromiser ◄———	INTEGRATED ———	► Executive
Deserter ◄———	SEPARATED ———	► Bureaucrat
Autocrat ◄———	DEDICATED ———	► Benevolent autocrat
Missionary ◄———	RELATED ———	► Developer
Less effective		More effective

*Source: From *Management Effectiveness* by W.J. Redding, p. 40. Copyright © 1970 by McGraw-Hill. Used with the permission of McGraw-Hill Book Company.

Reddin assumes that no one best style of leadership exists, but that his four basic styles—related, integrated, separated, and dedicated—can be applied in appropriate situations. The same style that is effective in one situation may be ineffective in another.

Contingency theories of leadership are more complex than the best style theories, because situational variables are considered in the analysis. Fiedler (1967) included leader-member relations, task structuring and position power as major variables in the determination of whether a situation is favorable or unfavorable to the leader. Vroom (Sergiovanni and Starratt, 1979, pp. 123-28) emphasized participation of subordinates in decision making. Hackaby (1980) suggested other factors which may be considered in studying leadership, including the maturity of the followers, expectation of followers, behavior of followers, institutional role of the leader, previous role incumbent, specialization of task, formal and informal organizational structure, and climate of the organization. Supervisors should be aware of these many influences as they affect relationships within the schools.

When a supervisor has sufficient opportunity to plan for leadership, s/he may consciously want to appraise the situation. After determining the task and the implications of accomplishing the task, the leader should examine the group. How mature is the group? One consideration is the education and experience of the group. Usually, the teachers who have more education and experience will facilitate group action. A leader must recognize, however, that a mature participant in a study group on teacher effectiveness training may not function on the same level in a committee planning a public relations campaign for a school levy. The members' interest in the job to be done will affect their behavior, since interest is often reflected in involvement, a requisite for the mature group. The achievement motivation, i.e., the drive to do an excellent job, must also be evaluated, as should the potential for controversy over issues and the amount of responsibility which the followers demonstrate. With such information about the followers, the leader can judge which of the leadership styles is appropriate. Unfortunately, a supervisor may find that planning for specific leadership situations is difficult because of time constraints and the unpredictability of group membership. Yet, if a supervisor is aware of all the factors involved, s/he may be able to analyze on-going group activities and modify his/her behavior accordingly.

GROUP PROCEDURES

Group dynamics encompasses group procedures and group roles. It provides opportunity for efficient problem solving, and it can be a vital method of teaching. The purpose of such group activity is individual growth. Educational supervision necessarily uses group dynamics because of the potential of group processes in achieving professional development. Mathematically, the whole is the sum of its parts but, in group procedures, the interaction among group members extends a group beyond the sum of its individuals.

In chronological order, the developmental stages of a group achieved by leadership can be structured as follows:

1. The Gathering Period

   Gathered individuals convene with some concerns. Although, in a school system, the overall atmosphere reflects a desire for better teaching, there are nonetheless people with divergent needs who meet together as part of a gathering. Examples of situations which may have brought about the gathering include: (a) faculty interested in mini-courses for activity periods; (b) groups of teachers discussing textbook adoption; (c) combined school/community groups seeing the need to work together to achieve passage of a school levy; (d) combined teacher/parent groups exchanging ideas about interdisciplinary programs in a middle school; and (e) teachers interested in Gordon's TET (Teachers' Effectiveness Training).

2. The Transformation Period

   During this period, gathered individuals begin to merge their opinions and share ideas. There is sometimes vociferous exchange among the individuals. While the differences are brought to light, similarities also become evident. Pressure is on the leader to maintain the group and define its task. Achieving these goals may require three stages:

   a. Stage one

   In this stage, a leader should strive to establish a workable structure, with regard to setting up the goals to be achieved and the commitment of all individuals. Usually, if the leadership has functioned well in the gathering period, a certain rapport will have developed. If rapport seems slow in building, a leader should exert influence to structure a working rapport until person-to-person respect and affection develop among the gathered individuals. The most urgent need at this stage is unity of purpose.

   b. Stage two

   This is the stage where the group begins to gel, i.e., individuals merge to put effort toward the common cause. The mood of the crowd indicates that things are beginning to hold together. A sentence, a word, or an idea expressed to the whole may get the same response as it would if expressed to a unit of the whole. From a communications vantage point, certain phrases will be commonly used. Humor may also develop in the group. A leader should note that, when the group disperses, the breaking away of individuals will occur slowly. The group is coalescing and individuals may remark that they feel excited about the prospects ahead.

c. Stage three

At this stage, mature individuals will be inclined to move immediately into group action. A leader will be able to recognize these individuals and assign responsibilities to them to facilitate group action. Specific task sharing will be discussed. When motivated individuals show signs of being able to move ahead, a confident leader should encourage this independence. In most cases, these new leaders in the gathering will have arrived with a reservoir of experience. In stage three, this potential force will become active. If helpers are needed to supply information or guidance, one of these new leaders will take the initiative to contact the resource person, explain the situation, and request aid. An immediate report to the gathering is a logical and helpful development.

3. The Formation of a Working Group

The actual formation of a group marks a notable achievement. No longer is the gathering just a physical assemblage of individuals; instead, most of the divergent personal opinions are integrated into a group goal—an achievement which requires the combined efforts of all members. At this point, the leader is in a position of delegating responsibilities and explaining how and when the goal may be reached. The goal itself is not a remote, idealistic attainment, but a clearly defined point towards which they are working. For example, if a group of parents, teachers, students, and community members had gathered to discuss the passage of a school levy, there would have been several expressed ideas about the success of the venture at the outset. But, at this third stage, when the group has formed, each individual would know that s/he should personally contact 20 neighbors, make 30 telephone calls, sign two letters to the editor of the local newspaper, and attend at least three neighborhood kaffee klatches to promote the passage of the levy. Those who make posters would know how many they are responsible for producing. The group delivering signs to homeowners to put in their front yards would know which streets, what areas, and how many signs to take.

In short, the group is now a functioning whole. The leader does not stop action after the working group is moving. Instead, a leader maintains a connection with each subleader's activity and with the total progress toward the goal. The leader should remain active in coordinating efforts to complete the task.

Since the process of group development may be considered linear, the progressive steps are illustrated in Figure 26. In this figure, the individuals who constitute a gathering are graphed in separate boxes, indicating that each person arrived with his/her own set of ideas and plans. Their coming together indicates that the unified action has a good chance of succeeding, with the assistance of effective leadership.

The second period, identified as the transformation period, has three interior stages which are adaptable and flexible, responding to the guidance of the leader. Sometimes, these stages are insignificant. If the supervisor is working with a group of primary teachers to select a reading series, the task has been established. The teachers are acquainted with each other and have worked together previously. Stages one and two will converge and these individuals can probably move into unified group action, stage three, at their first meeting. Often, a new group will require at least three or four sessions to reach an action stage.

The third and final stage in development of an effective communal project is the unifying of many individuals into one single functioning unit, the group. By the time the group has formed functioning sub-groups, the goal is usually clearly understood; the many jobs necessary to reach the goal have been clearly defined, and the work has begun. The group must cooperate to the completion of the task and achieve the agreed-upon goal.

Figure 26. Process of Group Development.

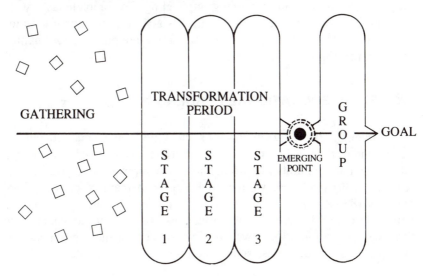

Otherwise, individual members of the group will feel that the completion of their own individual tasks will mark an end to their contributions. A leader with the confidence of group members will indicate that members may take on further assignments, help others, finish up unexpected tasks, and polish their initial achievements. As members of the group, nobody is finished till the goal is reached. The shared singular purpose of many people is indicated in the diagram by the arrow which extends through all of the designated stages which require leadership skills.

All gatherings do not develop into effective groups; some never get beyond the assembly point. Other gatherings of individuals get into the transformation period—sharing ideas and developing rapport—but fail to produce commitment to a common cause. Sometimes, leaders feel guilty when the number of persons decreases. Self-selection of participants may be essential to the evolving of a functioning group. Whenever individuals interact and emerge as a working group which accomplishes a desired goal, there is shared satisfaction. Whether or not they are successful, all experiences with gatherings of individuals can be used as learning experiences for the leader and participants.

Likert (1961) indicated that many highly effective work groups function in industry and government, where both maintenance and task functions must be carried out. One classification system for role functions is presented in Figure 27. The roles and responsibilities assumed by different group members change as relationships change and as they are needed. In an effective group, nonfunctional behavior is minimal. As shown in the figure, some roles are useful in both task and maintenance functions. Maintenance roles generally include encouraging, helping, setting standards, following, and interpreting group feeling. To complete tasks well, some of the necessary roles include initiating activity, seeking information and opinion, giving information and opinion, elaborating, coordinating, and summarizing.

WOMEN AS EDUCATIONAL LEADERS

Although affirmative action laws and Title IX have encouraged sex equity, there still exists a great disparity between the number of women in education and the number of women in leadership roles in education. As Rosser (1980) indicated, women make up 66 percent of public school teachers (83 percent elementary and 47 percent secondary), but they constitute only 13 percent of the principals (18 percent elementary and three percent secondary). Fewer than one percent of the superintendents and three percent of the assistant superintendents are female.

Figure 27. Role Functions in a Group.*

A. Task Roles (selecting and carrying out a group task)
   1. Initiating Activity: Proposing solutions, organizing material.
   2. Seeking Information: Requesting clarification, information, etc.
   3. Seeking Opinion: Looking for others' feelings, values, ideas.
   4. Giving Information: Offering facts, generalizations, experiences.
   5. Giving Opinion: Stating an opinion or belief.
   6. Elaborating: Clarifying, giving examples, developing meanings.
   7. Coordinating: Showing relationships, pulling together.
   8. Summarizing: Assembling related ideas, restating suggestions.
B. Group Building and Maintenance Roles
   1. Encouraging: Being warm, friendly, responsive, and accepting.
   2. Gatekeeping: Helping another make a contribution.
   3. Standard Setting: Expressing procedures for group to follow.
   4. Following: Being an audience, going along with the group.
   5. Expressing Group Feeling: Describing group reactions to ideas.
C. Both Group Task and Maintenance Roles
   1. Evaluating: Measuring accomplishments, comparing decisions.
   2. Diagnosing: Seeing difficulties, next steps to take, etc.
   3. Testing for Consensus: Sending up trial balloon on closure.
   4. Mediating: Making compromise solutions, harmonizing.
   5. Relieving Tension: Draining off negative feeling, jesting.
D. Types of Nonfunctional Behavior
   1. Being Aggressive: Criticizing, blaming, deflating others.
   2. Blocking: Introducing tangent, unrelated personal experiences.
   3. Self-Confessing: Using group as personal sounding board.
   4. Competing: Talking the most, playing the most roles, etc.
   5. Seeking Sympathy: Disparaging one's ideas to gain support.
   6. Special Pleading: Relating all to one's own pet concerns.
   7. Horsing Around: Clowning, joking, mimicking, disrupting.
   8. Seeking Recognition: Calling attention to self.
   9. Withdrawal: Being indifferent and passive, wandering from the subject.

Persons using this classification scheme should be careful to avoid blaming any person who appears to fall into the "nonfunctional behavior" area. It is probably more useful to regard such behavior as a symptom of the group's inability to satisfy the needs of individuals within it, i.e., rather than look to individuals as the source of nonfunctional behavior, look to the processes of the group itself.

*Source: This classification system was developed by Morton Deutsch. In *Group Dynamics: Research and Theory,* by D. Cartwright and A. Zander. Evanston, IL: Row Peterson & Co., 1960.

Although research shows the competence of women administrators, sex role stereotyping is a barrier. School boards and hiring administrators tend to consider discipline and authority as areas that males can handle better.

Both men and women in education must become more aware of the limiting effect of stereotypical thinking. Many actions which result in inequities are neither deliberate nor malicious; individuals simply behave in patterns which they have never analyzed. Often, they are surprised to know what messages about females are transmitted by their behavior, e.g., referring to female educators as "girls," while recognizing the inappropriateness of "boys" as a term for male colleagues. Sensitivity to stereotypical behavior is the first step. The ultimate goal is that a person, male or female, is evaluated for hiring, promotion, or termination on the basis of his/her qualifications and performance.

Women who are interested in careers in educational administration must participate in training programs and develop the competencies needed in management. Social skills and attitudes which are part of team sports, i.e., competing, cooperating, setting goals, planning, winning, losing, and accepting criticism, also seem important for success (Atkinson, 1981, p. 312). Female candidates for administrative positions must visibly interact with administrators, gain visibility, and demonstrate administrative skills. In other words, a woman aspiring to become an educational leader must take an active role in making a transition to the administrative level. Although change in organizations is slow, the persistence and success of women leaders can encourage sex equity in educational leadership.

SUMMARY

Leadership is a complex interaction between leaders and followers. The leader's position is flexible and varies in relation to direct or indirect influence. Research indicates that group achievement and climate vary in accordance with the leader's style, which is affected by the leader's assumptions about people. Motivation is important to supervisors who aspire to change teacher behavior, and Maslow's hierarchy of needs and the motivation-hygiene theory have implications for supervisory activities.

Two major dimensions of leadership are the concern for people and the concern for tasks. These factors are used to determine styles of leadership. Maturity of the group and participation in leadership are examples of situational influences which may be included in an analysis to select an appropriate leadership style.

Group process is important in supervision. The evolving of a gathering of individuals into a working group is an interesting process which supervisors often facilitate. Roles assumed by group members are varied and changing; both tasks and maintenance roles are required. The members of effective work groups fill these roles as they are needed. Supervisors who are aware of leadership factors and group dynamics should be able to analyze their situations and plan wisely.

REFERENCES

Alfonso, R.J.; Firth, G.R.; and Neville, R.F. *Instructional Supervision: A Behavior System*. Boston: Allyn and Bacon, Inc., 1975.

Atkinson, J.A. "Women in School Administration: A Review of the Research." *Review of Educational Research* 51 (3) (Fall 1981): 311–43.

Burns, J. "Two Excerpts from Leadership." *Educational Leadership* (6) (March 1979): 380–83.

Cartwright, D., and Zander, A. *Group Dynamics: Research and Theory*. Evanston, IL: Row, Peterson, and Co., 1960.

Cawelti, G. "Which Leadership Style—From the Head or Heart?" *Educational Leadership* 36 (6) (March 1979): 374–78.

Fiedler, F.E. *A Theory of Leadership Effectiveness*. New York: McGraw-Hill, 1967.

Hackaby, W.O. "Integrating Style and Purpose in Leadership." *Educational Leadership* 37 (6) (May 1980).

Herzberg, F.; Mausner, B.; and Snyderman, B. *The Motivation to Work*. New York: Wiley, 1959.

Lewin, K.; Lippitt, R.; and White, R. "Patterns of Aggressive Behavior in Experimentally Created 'Social Climate'." *Journal of Social Psychology* 10 (1939): 371–99.

Likert, R. *New Patterns of Management*. New York: McGraw-Hill, 1961.

Maslow, A.H. *Motivation and Personality*. New York: Harper and Row, 1954.

McGregor, D. *The Human Side of Enterprise*. New York: McGraw-Hill, 1960.

Reddin, W.J. *Managerial Effectiveness*. New York: McGraw-Hill, 1970.

Rosser, P. "Women Fight 'Old Boys' for School Administration Jobs." *Learning* 8 (March 1980): 31–34.

Sergiovanni, T.J. "Factors Which Affect Satisfaction and Dissatisfaction of Teachers." *The Journal of Educational Administration* 5 (1) (1967): 66–82.

————. "Is Leadership the Next Great Training Robbery?" *Educational Leadership* 36 (6) (March 1979): 388–90, 392–94.

Sergiovanni, T.J., and Starratt, R.J. *Supervision: Human Perspectives*. 2d ed. New York: McGraw-Hill, 1979.

Weingast, D. "Shared Leadership—'The Damn Thing Works'." *Educational Leadership* 37 (6) (March 1980): 502–04, 506.

Chapter 11
Coping with Conflict and Stress

Stress has become one of the most common problems in today's world. Almost everyone claims to recognize symptoms of stress in others, as well as in one's self. Increasing numbers of books, pamphlets, and periodicals dealing with stress and stress management are available. Educators have indicated that mental and physical stress is causing teachers to leave the profession or to remain in the classroom exhausted and depressed. Teacher "burnout" increased in frequency in the 70s and the National Education Association in July 1980 expressed concern about teacher stress leading to burnout in a resolution urging recognition, prevention, and treatment of stress-related problems.

Supervisors also experience stress, and they should learn to cope with it so that it becomes a positive force. Stress is useful in many ways—it motivates, stimulates, excites, and adds emotional pleasure to experiences. However, intense and persistent stress can be a debilitating influence—leading to illness, inefficiency in work, and unhappiness.

Supervisory staff members must be aware of coping mechanisms to maintain personal health and to help supervisees. Two of the major areas in which stress can be created are conflict situations and time pressures.

CONFLICT

Conflict in school situations is a normal state of affairs. Unanimity among teachers, administrators, students, parents, and community members seldom exists. Differences are often ignored because, as Feitler and Redburn (1979) explain, most persons prefer to avoid conflict or dealing with differences, rather than using confrontation and/or conflict management. Avoidance of persons and situations perceived as threatening can sharply reduce opportunities for open communication. In essence, this withdrawal reduces educational opportunities, since better ways of dealing with differences are not sought.

Conflict, long considered a destructive force, can be used to over-come inertia and stimulate growth. An organization in which the leader has surrounded him/herself with "yes" persons is limited. Progress is con-fined by the leader's experience and ideas, rather than expanded by the variety of thoughts of several individuals and by the interactions produced in discussion of different viewpoints. Usually, heterogeneous groups are more productive than homogeneous groups, because the diversity provides a broader base of information and skills. In the last decade, ways have been investigated for dealing constructively with conflict in personal, family, business, organizational, and political contexts.

Conflict is neither good nor bad, right nor wrong. The people in-volved in conflict interpret the situations, i.e., meanings are assigned by the individuals as they view the conflict and react according to their perceptions. Although a few people seem to enjoy a good fight, most individuals find conflict threatening. Since teachers usually can perform their jobs without the involvement of others, their differences are often disregarded. In fact, admission of conflict with a colleague may earn a teacher a reputation of "hard to get along with" and "disagreeable."

Conflict with students, of course, receives more attention. Teachers and administrators are vitally concerned about discipline. Classroom man-agement techniques focus on routines to minimize conflict by providing students with an understanding of what is expected and what the conse-quences are for failure to comply. Student confrontations are an acknowl-edged source of stress for teachers. Activities to develop skills in conflict resolution with students can provide teachers with skills they can use in other types of conflict situations. Workshops and inservice programs on discipline encourage teachers to explore a number of strategies for han-dling conflicts with students and to select and implement those strategies which seem appropriate and feasible. A recommended attack for dealing with types of conflict follows:

1. Know your usual responses to conflict.
2. Explore possible ways of handling such situations.
3. Select strategies that appeal to you as workable and prepare to try them.
4. Investigate ways of preventing and decreasing conflict. Develop skills in these areas also.

CONFLICTS IN STUDENT TEACHING

Student teaching, long recognized as a valuable experience in the preparation of teachers, can create conflicts. Ideally, the public school and the college or university work together to create an environment that fosters personal and professional growth for the student teacher. Realistically, the involvement of numerous individuals and several institutions constitutes a potential source for problems. Conflicts may arise because of personalities, roles and responsibilities, procedures, and philosophies.

The supervising or cooperating teacher in the public school may want to work with a novice in the teaching profession, yet s/he may still experience feelings of jealousy as his/her students respond to the student teacher and turn to the newcomer for help. Although some teachers work well with students, they are unable to work well with student teachers. Even a well-organized professional may be unable to cope with the stress involved in watching a novice perform teaching tasks. One factor which contributes to a teacher's discomfort is the concern for student progress. Other times, the supervising teacher may lack tolerance for inexperience or for implementing new and different strategies. The student teacher who is required to follow a cooperating teacher's style of teaching may feel stifled, and s/he may fail to develop an appreciation for different teaching and learning styles.

Occasionally, a supervising teacher seems to favor the "sink or swim" view of student teaching. When the student teacher arrives, the teacher may turn over the classroom with a comment like "I'll be in the teacher's lounge if you need any help." Student teaching should be a gradual transfer of responsibilities to the student teacher, and such a transition requires collaborative efforts. The student teacher and teacher need to plan, evaluate, and recycle the teaching activities. Only by observing the student teacher can the teacher contribute to an analysis of what transpired and to a proposal for improvement.

On the other end of the continuum is the teacher who gives the student teacher no opportunity to plan and carry out activities independently. In this case, the supervising teacher is always in the classroom, always prescribing what should be done and how it should be accomplished. Along with guidance from the cooperating teacher, student teachers need some freedom to experiment, and conflicts may arise over scheduling the assignment of responsibilities to the student teacher.

Classroom teachers have sometimes given student teachers the impression that what was learned in college classes is useless and that the "real world" of the classroom requires a more practical approach. Cooperative efforts between public schools and colleges have decreased such attitudes; however, the student teacher may find him/herself caught between the classroom teacher and the college supervisor—the representative from the college or university who oversees the activities of the student teacher. A supervising teacher has daily contact with the student teacher, while a college supervisor's visits are generally on a weekly basis. The roles of the two must be well-defined: the cooperating teacher should deal with students, curriculum, school policies, and day-to-day activities; the college supervisor should be concerned with course requirements, overall development of teaching skills, and general coordination of the program. Conflicts may develop if either supervisor ignores the role boundaries.

Without open communication, misunderstandings can occur. For example, Jim Malone explained to his college supervisor that his supervising teacher would not allow him to try role playing in social studies class. Jim felt this technique would help the students gain a new insight into the legislative process. The college supervisor might have concluded that the supervising teacher was limiting Jim's development. But, when the supervising teacher was included in the discussion, the college supervisor learned that the idea for role playing was a sudden inspiration, not a part of the lesson plan, and it had not been considered in regard to time required or student readiness. The three-way communication provided a beginning for the student teacher's use of carefully planned role playing.

Principals and supervisors in the public school may be involved with student teachers through assigning them or through supervisory activities. Since the student teaching experience involves different people from various backgrounds, the potential for conflict is great. Awareness of the attitudes of the persons involved and active efforts to prevent and decrease conflict are important. In addition, better communication and planning are recommended.

CONFLICT HANDLING MODES

One way of diagnosing one's own style of dealing with conflict is to take a test, i.e., use an appropriate instrument. One such instrument is the Thomas-Kilmann Conflict Mode Instrument (Thomas and Kilmann, 1974). This assessment instrument uses a two-dimensional model. The extent to which a person tries to satisfy personal concerns is called assertiveness, while the extent to which the person tries to satisfy the concern of other individuals is cooperativeness. These dimensions produce five conflict-handling modes: avoiding, competing, collaborating, accommodating, and compromising. The Conflict Management Survey (Teleometrics Int'l., 1973) also uses a two-dimensional model; concern for personal goals and concern for relationships are the two axes. The styles in this instrument are labelled 9/9 synergistic style, 5/5 compromise style, 1/9 yield-lose style, 9/1 win-lose style, and 1/1 lose-leave style. (See the next section for a more detailed description of these conflict-handling modes.)

Collision of the personal goals of individuals in an interdependent relationship is one description of conflict. These collisions may involve incompatible goals, goals which require resources limited in supply, goals which are attainable by different and disputed means, and value differences. Some examples of conflicts which arise over personal goals follow: John Smith, a senior, cannot play in the band concert at Fremont High and take his English test at the same time—here, the goals of the band director and English teacher are incompatible. The limited budget for the math department means that either equipment for the math lab or books for the library can be purchased. Although enrichment opportunities for students are endorsed by both Ms. Leiter and Mr. Porter, she wants the lab equipped and he favors library materials. Although the goal desired is the same, the means for attaining this end is disputed. Value conflicts may arise over the grading of mainstreamed students: A teacher in the "regular" classroom grades by group comparison, while the special education teacher grades on individual progress and student potential.

RELATIONSHIPS

The interpersonal context of conflict may involve two individuals, small groups, or confrontation between groups. If the relationship involved in the conflict is considered important and worth maintaining, the person will react differently from the individual who considers the relationship unimportant. Feelings about relationships are revealed in behaviors employed in managing conflict.

There are five similar responses (modes or styles) for reacting to conflict in the Thomas-Kilmann Conflict Mode Instrument and the Conflict Management Survey:

1. 9/9 synergistic style—or collaborating mode—attaches importance to personal goals and relationships simultaneously. It assumes that all goals must be recognized and satisfied. Problem solving is the general approach; acceptance of feelings and tolerance for differences are in evidence. There is an attempt to work together to find solutions that are mutually acceptable. This response implies an open investigation to develop creative alternatives.

2. 5/5 compromise style—or compromising mode—is an attempt to find an expedient, acceptable solution which satisfies everyone partially. The parties involved win a little and lose a little. It may be considered persuasive and manipulative since concessions are exchanged to find a middle ground position. *Often,* it is a temporary settlement.

3. 1/9 yield-lose style—or accommodating mode—is unassertive and cooperative. It appeases others by neglecting one's own con-

cerns; self-sacrifice and submission to the goals of another protect the relationship. It implies that it is better to ignore differences than to risk combat.

4. 9/1 win-lose style—or competing mode—is assertive and uncooperative. It uses whatever power is available to gain one's own goals. Losing implies a loss of status and lack of competence. Aggressive, inflexible, dogmatic, and unreasonable behavior is characteristic of this response. Coercion and suppression may be employed.

5. 1/1 lose-leave style—or avoiding mode—protects the individual from the struggle which s/he feels can not be won. Noninvolvement results by withdrawing, postponing, or ignoring the differences. Impersonal tolerance is the approach, but frustration and hostility may result for the user.

Each of the conflict-management styles has an appropriate use. All persons are capable of all these responses, but individuals seem to find some modes more useful than others. The preferred style, plus backup styles, allows for flexibility in responding to conflict management. Anyone dissatisfied with his/her conflict management can undertake a program to change those behaviors. Research findings suggest that an ideal ordering of style to produce more constructive effects is: the synergistic or collaborating, the compromise, the yield-lose or accommodating, the win-lose or competing, and the lose-leave or avoiding (Teleometrics Int'l., 1973, p. 6).

After an analysis of one's own pattern of behavior in conflict, the next step should be a consideration of other styles. If these reactions seem more constructive, then the person should consciously plan to build some new responses to potential conflict situations. Actual use of the behavior should be implemented, and the results should be analyzed. Unless a different style for conflict management is intentionally prepared, the usual pattern of reaction will probably be maintained—often detrimentally.

Specific reading on handling conflict can be helpful in increasing an awareness of the factors which create conflict situations; in addition, strategies for encouraging communication and providing acceptable expression for strong emotions should be developed by supervisory personnel. Teachers and students should have ways of indicating their concerns— surveys, gripe sessions, grievance procedures, and advisory groups. Violence must be discouraged as a means of conflict management; people can disagree without becoming unpleasant or hostile. Instead, people should be encouraged to examine their areas of agreement. Even in conflict situations, there is more agreement than disagreement. A mature person should be able to discuss ideas without implying that the person who disagrees with the proposal dislikes the proponent. Dealing with conflict constructively can improve educational opportunities, personal satisfaction, and group processes. According to Nebgen (1979, p. 27), ''Proper handling of the inevitable conflict situations that arise can bring about group cohesiveness and unity and contribute to overall performance, stability and effectiveness of the school organization.''

TIME MANAGEMENT

Time for educators often is measured by bells—time to start school, class periods, lunch time, and the end of school. The bell signaling the close of school usually does not conclude the activities of teachers, administrators, and supervisors. Paper grading, planning, problems, extracurricular responsibilities, and public relations activities demand time and effort. Attention to the sensible use of time is essential for individual efficiency in professional and nonprofessional pursuits. Most educators feel that they do not have enough time to perform all the tasks they are expected to do.

Time management is not a means of saving time. Individuals use time according to priorities, plans, and procedures. The efficient use of time means that important work gets done and the individual also engages in activities chosen for fun and pleasure. If time is considered a scarce resource, its management becomes important; time is too valuable to be wasted.

Individuals must determine when they are most productive. This time should be used for important decisions and activities. Some people are at their peaks when they first arrive at school; others are still waking up. Save routine jobs like phone calls or sorting materials for the low activity times.

Individuals must also determine how they spend their time. One way of doing this is by keeping a daily log for a week, recording all activities, interruptions, phone calls, meetings, travel, conferences, and the time required for each. After studying the records, summarize the time spent on major responsibilities and decide whether time is being used efficiently. If not, rescheduling is necessary. Some flexibility must be built in, but, generally the schedule should be kept. Lists can be helpful, especially if the priorities for the day are recorded as reminders of what to do.

Establishing priorities is essential. One classification system that can be used groups activities as important-urgent, important-not urgent, urgent-not important, and not urgent-not important. The important-urgent tasks must be done. However, there is danger that the urgent ones may displace the important-not urgent ones. Delegating routine tasks should allow an individual to put more emphasis on important responsibilities.

An organized desk and files facilitate efficiency. Materials needed can be located quickly, and persons are not distracted by clutter in their work spaces. When a systematic procedure is arranged, the routing of messages and materials can be handled with minimum effort.

Meetings can take an unbelievable amount of time. When attending a meeting, a supervisor can sometimes schedule the time for the activities that s/he is concerned with. For example, if a supervisor is explaining to an elementary school faculty the new procedure for curriculum revision, there is no need for the supervisor to be present for the entire session. The explanation might be planned as the first agenda item, then the supervisor can leave when the job is completed. Agendas for meetings are essential; they provide a plan for the session and also ensure that the meeting is purposeful. A meeting is unnecessary if the message can be written or delivered via telephone.

Conferences or meetings in an office can become prolonged, unless they are terminated graciously. Sometimes, the supervisor can simply get up and move toward the door to close a conference. An appointment may be scheduled at the time a meeting should conclude, so the supervisor has a reason for finishing promptly. A stand-up conference is usually short. This technique of standing is particularly useful if the visitor has interrupted a supervisor's work, and s/he needs to return to it. When going to see another person, the visitor controls the time spent, so the place for the meeting should be considered.

Is time wasted because attention is elsewhere? Everyone has experienced some unintentional mistakes like pouring coffee on cereal or discarding a bill and saving junk mail. Often, such behavior indicates that actions are done without thinking, when a person is preoccupied with a problem or more interesting ideas. To counteract such waste of time and effort at work, an individual should change positions, perhaps move to another seat. Regular checking of perceptions and summarizing what has been said or done also helps one maintain focus.

Are unpleasant tasks postponed? Sometimes, a person can find a dozen little jobs to do before starting to write a report or before setting up an appointment for a conference with a teacher who has shown no improvement. Comfortable things are selected, while aversive tasks are avoided. Verbalization is another way to postpone. Self-discipline in this area can improve time use. An unpleasant job is a worry until it is done, and it can often interfere with effective functioning.

Is it possible to say no when additional responsibilities are not desired? Many individuals find refusals difficult; however, saying no is easier when one can suggest an alternative. An individual should say no and then give an explanation for declining. Practice in this negative response makes it easier to resist other requests.

Helpful tips for organizing efficient use of time can be found in many publications. One such procedure is to avoid handling papers more than once. If a message requires an answer, write the reply immediately. File the information that is for future use, rather than putting it into another pile to be filed later. Make a periodic check on whether there is duplication of effort; if there is replication, eliminate it. When a job seems unbelievably large, divide it into portions and do a section at a time. Such apportionment is a part of the long- and short-term planning which should be done to achieve the objectives set for the year. Finally, keep a notebook or card so ideas can be jotted down. Many valuable thoughts are lost because they are not recorded for later consideration.

Time management is one of the coping skills in controlling stress. Since personal values are a major factor in establishing priorities and selecting activities, each individual must determine his/her own time use. After all, people do what they choose to do.

STRESS

Stress is a perception of circumstances that places a demand on an individual. Stress can be positive or negative, depending on whether the person feels that s/he can handle the situation adequately. Dr. Hans Selye (1976), a pioneer in research and writing about stress, wrote that *how* the person interprets a situation is important. Stress can stimulate and challenge—for instance, a jogger running well in a race—or it can intimidate and immobilize—for example, an actor who is a victim of stage fright. A moderate amount of stress is helpful, but excessive, persistent stress lowers resistance to disease, narrows a person's perceptual field, leads to rigidity in cognitive processes, impairs efficiency, lowers resistance to other stressors (causes of stress), and speeds aging. Areas of stress include all aspects of experience—societal, institutional, personal, and interpersonal.

Persistent and intense stress builds tensions which threaten the health of an individual. Stress is frequently an invisible phenomenon with aftereffects that can become problems that need to be treated by medical doctors. Whenever possible, preventive measures should be provided by fellow educators, particularly by supervisors. Although a diagnosis of debilitating stress cannot be made, a supervisor can often recognize a stress situation which might cause teacher tension, and s/he can work at eradicating the conditions. Stressful circumstances can also be damaging to efficiency. Rather than waiting to see how upset or bothered a teacher will become, the supervisor should take immediate action to treat the situation—a procedure usually much less expensive in time and energy than the eventual treating of the teacher.

Frustrations, conflict, and pressures are all stressful. They trigger the physiological responses that prepare the body to handle an emergency. Increased heartbeat and faster breathing are two identifiable physical reactions which prepare a person for "fight or flight" as a means of dealing with the situation. When stress is controlled and planned for, it can be pleasurable and motivating.

Teachers and other educators experience many conditions which are potential causes of stress. Some of these stressors include:

1. Professional Isolation

   This circumstance occurs when an educator works alone and cannot compare progress with a peer. The situation affects an educator's sense of financial security also, because s/he may not have a way outlined for the review of job performance. The result is uncertainty about actual success and inability to predict commendation or criticism from superiors. The teacher working with immature students may have little or no opportunity to interact with adults. In schools where there is a time and place for peers to converse, teachers often feel pressed to grade papers, prepare lessons, and write reports, activities which further isolate the individual teacher.

2. Heavy Teaching Responsibility

   In times of economic crunch, some school systems are cutting corners by filling classrooms with larger groups of students. Whereas a teacher might be able to teach a class of 20 or 25 without undue stress, s/he might suffer from tension when the enrollment is expanded to 30 or 40. Unfortunately, extra assignments also seem to mount at the same time, for the same reason— budget. As the staff decreases, teaching assignments become more varied. More preparations are required. The elementary teacher, who now has more students in class, must also teach physical education and art, since the number of special subject teachers has been decreased or eliminated. In secondary schools, the math teacher has four or five preparations, instead of the previously assigned three. Larger class size means that fewer sections of a class are needed; instead of four algebra classes, only three are scheduled.

3. Competitive and Compulsive Habits

   Observers of stress in teachers point out that, when over-used, the best qualities can become teacher traps, causing anxiety which can lead to inefficiency and ill health. Some of these qualities are outgrowths of conscientiousness and may include zealous grading of papers on the day an exam was given, developing projects for above-average students who need creative opportunities, staying after class to discuss questions or projects with students, or volunteering for work on committees which seem important for the school. Taken individually, each of the areas of activity is laudable. But, some teachers overload their schedules with activities which are apt to diminish efficiency and cause dissatisfaction.

4. Lack of Recreational Activities
   Despite a cultural tendency toward leisure-time activities, teachers often ignore the development of their own sports and hobbies—sometimes simultaneously with recommending such activities for their students. Whereas participation in a sport might provide an outlet for tension, many teachers ignore the playing fields, jogging tracks, and tennis courts. Perhaps a lack of coordination and skill deters some educators whose efforts have been devoted to academic work.

ASSISTANCE FOR STRESSFUL SITUATIONS

What can a supervisor do to help teachers overcome stressful situations? As members of an educational system, supervisors have the unique opportunity to provide assistance. First, a supervisor should provide conference time to a teacher who feels isolated—whether or not there is overt indication of stress. The importance of the individual teacher in the school organization can be emphasized, and the supervisor can be an active listener as the teacher expresses his/her sense of isolation. Also, these teachers can be deliberately involved in inservice activities. If further counseling is needed, the supervisor may want to refer the teacher to other professionals.

If a teacher feels overloaded with teaching responsibilities, a supervisor can conduct a private assessment of the teacher's work schedule and decide how accurately the teacher is describing his/her own schedule. If a schedule appears to be onerous to the teacher but appears to be reasonable to the supervisor, it is the supervisor's responsibility to work with the teacher, developing more efficient work habits. Often, however, the supervisor's analysis of the situation will concur with the teacher's. In that case, the supervisor has a twofold job: helping the teacher become more efficient and selective in fulfilling assignments and seeking a more reasonable work load allocation for the teacher. In the economic crunch when classes are bigger, there is no quick, easy solution. But, an unfair distribution of responsibilities can often be adjusted by working cooperatively with the principal of the building where the teacher works.

Overcrowded schedules are visible clues that an individual is taking on more jobs than s/he can efficiently handle. A supervisor can work with this type of teacher by actually dealing with the items which are written on a weekly or monthly calendar of events. This process puts attention on the schedule, rather than on the teacher. Supervisors can spot an overloaded schedule by noting the number of hours which are filled by appointments— sometimes drawing an accurate conclusion about the teacher by the frequency of meetings, without even noting the where, when, or with whom elements of the engagement book. By inviting the teacher to share observations and opinions, a supervisor can usually discover which engagements are stressful for the teacher. By rearranging or setting priorities for activities, a breakthrough toward a more workable schedule can be achieved in a single conference. A supervisor might explain how quality contacts are more important than quantity contacts with students, parents, and other teachers. By accepting this point of view, most teachers can slash excess appointments, shorten their working days, and diminish some of the stressors.

When a teacher is reluctant to delete elements of his/her schedule, the supervisor may have to provide alternatives. For example, if a teacher seems unable to eliminate 4:30 p.m. appointments with students who want to take make-up exams after basketball practice, the teacher needs help in establishing a schedule which can provide a reasonable balance of activities. Often, a teacher can be convinced that his/her performance on the following day can be more effective when the late-afternoon appointments are eliminated. Personal development through new recreational activities can be the key. Late afternoons can become times of exercising, relaxing, and enjoying life—ultimate assets in building teacher confidence and efficiency. The values of walking, reading, painting, having a cup of coffee with a friend, arriving at home in time to greet the family, and finding time to go to the library for a book of fiction should be emphasized. In this way, supervisors can tie in suggestions for combating compulsive work habits with the development of new hobbies.

Physical activity is especially useful in coping with stress. Swimming, jogging, walking, calisthenics, and bicycling can all be pursued individually or with others. These kinds of exercise may appeal to teachers who want to avoid competitive sports. Not only does an individual build muscle tone and cardiovascular conditioning in physical activities, but an outgoing person will be able to meet new friends while pursuing worthwhile hobbies. There is no question that an individual needs both work and play to balance life experiences.

A supervisor can suggest several possible ways of dealing with stress and hope that at least one of the suggestions will be accepted and tried by a supervisee. Furthermore, a supervisor should try to ascertain if a teacher is reluctant to share problems with a family member or friend. In this case, the supervisor can often describe the benefit of being open with at least one person—sharing problems, fears, ideas, and using the confidante as a sounding board for both personal and professional opinions. Problems become more manageable when a person talks things out and shares with a close friend, lover, spouse, or family member. Surprisingly, a supervisee given this kind of suggestion may abandon his/her determination to be strong and silent. In the past few decades, personal sharing has been accepted as a necessary, helpful human activity. From the days of Sigmund Freud to the modern times of Thomas Gordon, the positive effects of verbalizing and being helped by those who receive the shared confidences have been recognized. Awareness and verbalization are progressive steps toward plans for coping. Supervisors truly work toward the improvement of learning when they exert themselves to help teachers eliminate negative stress from their lives.

SUGGESTIONS FOR COPING WITH STRESS

Although coping with stress is a complex task which must be adapted for each individual, a few basic suggestions may be useful to the supervisor in maintaining a happy, successful life and in helping others cope with the pressure of the contemporary world:

1. Plan so work can be completed. Anticipate situations that will arise and consider possible ways of dealing with them. Such preparation allows one to be self-confident and to feel in control.

   The supervisor should run a time analysis of his/her schedule. Educators function by the calendar and by the clock. Sometimes an overload of activities and appointments can cause one to "blow a fuse." In most cases, in-depth time analyses by outside helpers are not necessary for teachers or supervisors, since the fulfillment of assignments is a skill learned by most educators.

2. Recognize and accept limits. When an individual knows him/ herself, strengths can be utilized. But, the pacing of activities is necessary to adjust to physical and emotional limits. Getting adequate sleep and rest is essential. Proper nutrition also affects physical responses. Taking care of oneself is basic to stress management.

   Stress inventories can be taken by an individual who feels tense but has no idea of the cause. Sometimes just the introspection and self-awareness required to take a personal inventory can prove to be therapeutic, as well as diagnostic. If an educator pinpoints a situation regularly associated with inner tension, then the burden lies on that person to remedy the situation. Sometimes, a direct communication related to the stress-inducing situation must be scheduled with individuals. Other times, the stress-afflicted individual can quietly extricate him/herself from the tense circumstances. Although this action sounds difficult to do ("What do you want me to do—quit?" or "How do I tell the boss he bugs me?"), an individual who has found how debilitating stress can become should realize that action is necessary.

3. <u>Have fun.</u> Laughter makes people feel better. A balance in life includes a contrast between seriousness and humor. An individual should do what s/he enjoys doing. Latent hobbies or sports may be activated. Pleasurable activities should be done for their own sake, with no guilt feelings. Happiness requires such pursuits.

4. <u>Be positive.</u> Since perception is such a significant part of dealing with stress, a positive point of view is helpful. Such a perspective eliminates many fears and threats as the good aspects of persons and situations are sought. The emphasis is on the useful, helpful, cheerful, desirable, and constructive. One should tolerate and forgive instead of holding a grudge. Accept what cannot be changed. Destructive remarks and actions are curbed as the supervisor finds ways to encourage and build.

5. <u>Get regular physical exercise.</u> The body can work off tensions with such exertion. A scheduled program of physical activities contributes to health, and it also provides a way of getting rid of frustrations. Exercise groups, participation in sports, or individual physical activities should be scheduled regularly, probably a minimum of three times a week. Business and industry provide facilities for their employees to get physical exercise; educators should use school facilities for their own welfare.

6. <u>Learn to relax.</u> Quiet time can allow a person to escape from a hectic environment for a brief, restful interlude. Occasionally, one needs to get away from problems mentally. New, exotic activities are sometimes effective with people who either do not or feel they cannot respond satisfactorily to familiar people, familiar hobbies, or everyday activities designed to lessen inner tension. At present, there are opportunities to join Transcendental Meditation groups, relaxation classes, Transactional Analysis activities, meditation groups of both religious and secular nature, and Oriental exercise classes, such as Tai Chi.

7. Talk out troubles. Establish a regular time each week to have a sharing relationship with someone whose presence proves to be continually supportive. Give the appointment the same respect given a medical or dental appointment: It will benefit health and well being!

The suggestions above are some of the antidotes recommended for stress management. All of these are made with the assumption that the educator is in a normal state of health. If the tension or stress has persisted over a long period, causing evident harm to health, then the first step in treating the problem should be an appointment with a doctor. A supervisor can often help teachers by encouraging them to be aware of their physical and mental conditions. They may need reminders about what activities are essential for happy and successful living.

SUMMARY

Conflict and time pressures are two factors which contribute to stress for many educators. Individuals are better able to cope with conflict when they are aware of their preferred style of conflict management, have considered and developed alternate modes of handling differences, and are actively using procedures for preventing conflict situations. Teachers, administrators, and supervisors must recognize that conflict is a part of life. The school environment involving different personalities and group interests is a fertile ground for the collision of goals of teachers, student teachers, students, administrators, parents, and community groups.

Efficient time use can be planned. Analysis of a carefully kept record of how time was spent for a week can be helpful. Setting priorities and organizing to eliminate unnecessary effort often give a teacher or supervisor opportunities for the necessary "fun" activities. Delegating and routinizing procedures should promote efficiency. Self-discipline is required to establish and maintain a reasonable schedule, but a person is amply rewarded as s/he gets the work done without stressful time pressures.

Stress can be both a positive and negative factor for an educator. There are many potentially stressful experiences in the educational environment. A supervisor should be familiar with stress management techniques to maintain his/her own happiness and efficiency and to assist others in coping with stress.

REFERENCES

Benson, H. *The Relaxation Response*. New York: Morrow, 1975.

Blue Cross Association. *Stress*. Blue Print for Health, vol. 25, no. 1. Chicago: Blue Cross Association, 1974.

Davis, F. "How to Live With Stress—and Thrive." *Woman's Day* (May 22, 1979): 76,78,80.

Dugan, G. F. "Time Management and the Educational Administrator." Akron, OH, March 1979. (Typewritten.)

Eric Clearinghouse on Educational Management. "Managing Conflict," Research Action Brief, no. 3, October, 1978.

Feitler, F. C., and Redburn, F. S. *"Coping with Conflict: Even the Winners Are Losers."* Youngstown State University, OH, January 1979. (Mimeographed.)

Martin, P. *"Organizing Yourself for Success."* Kiwanis Magazine (March 1980): 22–24.

Matezynski, T., and Rogus, J. "A Principal's Checklist for Streamlining Routine Program Maintenance." *Bulletin of the National Association of Secondary School Principals* (March 1978): 49–56.

McQuaide, W., and Aikman, A. *Stress.* New York: E. P. Dutton and Company, 1974.

Monet, A., and Lazarus, R. S., eds. *Stress and Coping: An Anthology.* New York: Columbia University Press, 1977.

Negben, M. K. "Coping with Conflict in Educational Circles," *Thrust* 9 (2) (November 1979): 25–27.

Richelson, G. *Burnout.* New York: Doubleday, 1980.

Selye, H. *The Stress of Life.* New York: McGraw-Hill, 1976.

Teleometrics Int'l. *How to Interpret Your Scores from the Conflict Management Survey.* The Woodlands, TX: 1973.

Thomas, K. W., and Kilmann, R. H. *Thomas Kilmann Conflict Mode Instrument.* Tuxedo, NY: Xicom, Inc., 1974.

Chapter 12
Evaluation

Today's world is attuned to evaluation. Business and industry have recognized the importance of evaluation; customer response is one aspect of evaluation. On the desk in a motel room, the customer often finds an evaluation form. Department stores periodically request information from customers about their satisfaction or dissatisfaction with the service and merchandise. Frequently, restaurants provide customers opportunity to fill out appraisal forms, since management wants information about the customers' perceptions of food and service. The amount of business may increase or decrease; such indications of customer reactions are easily recognized. However, the reasons for customers' behavior can be determined more accurately if records of their reactions are secured. Without customer feedback, a business may not have a basis for desirable changes. If customers are pleased with the quality of food, but find the waiters and waitresses lacking in courtesy, a program for improvement can be planned appropriately.

The reasons for evaluation vary. In business, the purpose is often to improve a product or process. The data collected in an appraisal can be significant for any decision making related to the situation. Sometimes, evaluation is for specific approval or certification, such as the health department's checking of a restaurant to see if it conforms to prescribed criteria. Other purposes of appraisal include an accurate description of the current status, a consideration of resources and their adequacy, the location of strength and weakness, and knowledge of the effects of a program or activity.

In education, the emphasis on accountability has increased general awareness of the importance of evaluation. Accountability for specific accomplishments must be determined by some type of evaluation. If, for example, a supervisor is accountable for implementation of a new language arts curriculum in grades one through six, the question is whether or not the new course of study for these grades has been put to use. An evaluation of what is being taught must be made before the question can be answered. Procedures must be developed to determine what is being taught, and this content must be compared to the new curriculum. Such information is required before the supervisor's accomplishments can be judged.

THE SUPERVISOR AND EVALUATION

Educational supervision is concerned with evaluation in several areas, including curriculum, materials, teachers, supervisory program, and self. Evaluation is a continuous process; in every educational activity, evaluation is an essential part of the cycle. In an inservice project dealing with controversial issues, the teacher committee working with the supervisor determines the objectives for the series of sessions. On the basis of the objectives, activities are planned. After the meetings are begun, formative evaluation is done, i.e., progress toward the goals is assessed. If the results show anticipated development of participants, all is well. However, when there seems to be little or no headway made toward the objectives, modification of plans is needed. When the series is terminated, there is a final, or summative, evaluation. If the objectives have not been attained, then a reorganization and new procedures may be required. If the objectives have been achieved, then there is a recycling of activities to achieve more sophisticated or different objectives.

Evaluative procedures should be preplanned. To ensure effective evaluation, purposes should be specified. In curriculum evaluation, information should be collected to determine whether or not requisite skills for competency are effectively taught. Another purpose for evaluating curriculum might be to check inclusion of current concepts in the content area, e.g., nutrition information provided should reflect the newest developments. In addition to the why question, an evaluation plan also should specify what, who, how, and when. What is to be evaluated must be related to the purpose; who evaluates and how the data are collected should be decided in the planning stages. To get as complete a picture as possible, a number of sources and a variety of instruments should be used. In evaluating a supervisory program, teachers, supervisors, and administrators should be involved, so they can provide data from different viewpoints. Checklists, anecdotal reports, questionnaires, logs, and specific observational data about teaching behavior can all be useful in assessing a program. To ensure objectivity and a fresh point of view, some projects should be evaluated by outside resource persons. Whenever appraisal precedes a decision about a controversial issue, the use of an outside evaluator, in addition to local talent, should be investigated.

Timing should also be planned. In any continuous process like evaluation, the purpose and the anticipated use of the results must be considered in determining deadlines. An assessment of materials should be scheduled so that those selected can be ordered and available for use during the next school year.

A part of planning that is often neglected is the interpretation and reporting of results. Assessment activities are useless, unless the results are used. For example, if a supervisor examines his/her log of activities to classify the work engaged in and to get an objective view of time use, this procedure becomes a mere exercise unless the supervisor compares results to the job description and to the priorities evidenced in the objectives for the school year. These comparisons for self-evaluation require individual effort and planning.

In some situations, reports of evaluation findings, and the resulting recommendations, should be prepared for official use and sometimes for wider dissemination to school personnel and/or to the community. The evaluation plan should provide for such reports, including information about who is responsible for tasks, such as assembling the information, interpreting results, writing the document or documents, and dispersing them to the appropriate persons. When such ideas are a part of the initial plans, there is a better delineation of the process, i.e., the purpose and procedures can be comprehensively studied. A suitable route can be outlined, and extraneous steps can be eliminated.

Supervisory personnel are often involved in facilitating evaluation. Their assistance in selecting instruments and carrying out the data collection may be needed, and they frequently assume some responsibility for the reports and their dissemination.

EVALUATION OF CURRICULUM AND MATERIALS

Although teachers and students informally evaluate the curriculum and materials used in the classroom on a daily basis, a more structured approach is needed to improve the instructional program. The Model for Curriculum Development includes an area for evaluation. (See the Models for Curriculum Development section of Chapter 7.) This area incorporates program philosophy, goals, and general and specific objectives, as well as the materials, resources, strategies, and classroom lessons. A comprehensive evaluation of curriculum includes an examination of goals and the achievement of the goals. Content is evaluated on the basis of student needs, as well as on the viewpoints of experts in the discipline. In situations involving accreditation, as with the North Central Association of Colleges and Schools, general questions, as well as procedures, are suggested. Items related to student competencies which are considered important in a secondary school program need to be included. Students, teachers, parents, and community members might be asked to indicate how well they think a graduate from the school can:

1. Use the basic skills of reading for information, opinions, and recreation.
2. Express ideas in speaking and writing clearly and correctly.
3. Demonstrate mathematical thinking.
4. Show some artistic and literary taste and some enjoyment of the arts.
5. Exhibit an interest in, and understanding of, world events.
6. Indicate development of an understanding of the role of science in society today.

Supervisors often find the self-study materials of accrediting agencies useful in assessing the instructional program of a school.

When specific materials are being considered, they should be assessed as they relate to the proposed use. Since so many new packages, units, and texts are available, decisions regarding their purchase should be based on careful appraisal. The checklist below, prepared by Richard I. Miller (Klein, 1978, pp. 33-45), may be helpful. Although this instrument assumes the instructional units are being evaluated, it can be adapted to audiovisual materials, textbooks, and other instructional aids.

I. Initial probing
   A. Is this needed?
   B. What are anticipated accomplishments?
      1. More effective learning?
      2. Greater economy and more efficiency?
      3. Better teaching?
      4. Stronger support from the community?
      5. Greater receptivity to change?
      6. Better morale?
   C. Is this the best alternative to achieve objectives?
   D. What major problems and obstacles can be anticipated?
II. Developing an action plan
   A. What is the purpose of the investigation?
   B. Who should be involved—teachers, curriculum specialists, subject matter specialists, pedagogical specialists, school administrators, citizens, students, consultants?
   C. When should the study be made?
   D. How should the investigation be done?
III. Accomplishing the plan—materials should be analyzed from the following perspectives:
   A. Objectives
   B. Relevance and validity of content
   C. Compatibility with principles of human growth and development
   D. Organizational considerations: time and space
   E. Personnel factors

F. Community factors
G. Cost analysis
H. Instructional and curriculum factors
I. Evaluative procedures
J. Dissemination
K. Implementation
IV. Decision about purchase and/or use
V. Revision and recycling

The checklist recognizes a need for further appraisal of the materials after they are in use. If the materials are approved, secured, and used, there should be some provision for assessing whether or not the anticipated results have been attained. Sometimes, teachers find that the usefulness of specific aids changes as other factors in the learning environment are modified. The purchase of specific materials should not be a commitment to use them forever. If conditions change, the revision and recycling stage provides an opportunity to find other uses for these instructional aids.

Supervisory staff members are sometimes expected to direct committees in the evaluation of curriculum, pilot programs, and materials. A structured approach (such as the checklist) provides a pattern for committee action. Work can be begun without spending time and effort originating a procedure.

EVALUATION OF TEACHERS

Whenever evaluation is mentioned to teachers, they tend to become defensive, and show little enthusiasm. Few regard the process of assessment as an essential part of professional growth. Too often, teachers associate evaluation with getting rid of a teacher. Some teachers are discouraged because appraisal seems to focus on details unrelated to student learning. Evaluation should emphasize the ultimate goal of instructional improvement. However, there seems to be little constructive evaluation of experienced teachers (Commission on Public School Personnel Policies in Ohio, 1972). Teachers consider their classrooms as private domain. When an observer invades this territory, an antagonistic response from the teacher should be expected, and often, creating a helping relationship under such circumstances seems almost impossible.

In spite of the problems, some supervisors have established good rapport with teachers. By providing support, information, and materials, supervisors have developed a trust relationship with these teachers. In such cases, evaluation to promote teaching and learning may be realized. The purpose of teacher evaluation should be clarified for both appraiser and appraisee. Ideally, the supervisor should not evaluate for hiring, firing, or promotion, since a helping relationship is difficult to maintain with a person who makes decisions about termination. No teacher wants to seek help from an individual who may use the request as evidence of inability to cope. In reality, the supervisory staff may be evaluating teachers to provide the data for administrative decisions. Although final administrative decisions are not delegated to a supervisor, the supervisor is often expected to share information about teaching competency and teacher growth with administrators.

Evaluation of teaching requires collection of data in the classroom. Some educators claim that they "know" who the good teachers are simply by walking past classrooms. Such claims may be a rationalization for avoiding observation and conference procedures. Today, when litigation is so commonplace, documentation of observations is necessary for both the observer and observed. Hearsay evidence, generally not admissible in court, should not be tolerated by educators. If improvement of instruction is the goal, then information about the teaching behavior must be analyzed before alternative teaching strategies can be proposed. No problems in a teacher's classroom can be understood without hard evidence of what is happening. Solving problems depends on insightful analysis of this data. To accomplish this, observations are necessary.

Clinical supervision is one approach to teacher evaluation of professional development. (Procedures for collecting observational data and student feedback have been included in Chapters 4 and 6.) Rating scales and checklists can also be used for teacher assessment. An example of a rating scale is given in Figure 28, and a checklist is provided in Figure 29. Rating scales and checklists often deal with general behaviors which are not specific enough to be useful in the analysis and improvement of teaching. The items on these instruments may have little, if any, relation to instructional effectiveness. In addition, these instruments are difficult to interpret, because there is no standard for comparison. Situations are different; the noise level and participation in an open classroom will necessarily vary from those in a self-contained classroom taught by a traditional teacher. The observer response may reflect different expectations for the situations, and there is the possibility that the observer's biases will be reflected in the ratings. Furthermore, since rating scales and checklists include items which are not behaviorally defined, the appraisal they provide is less objective, for the rater's perception and memory may distort the results (Borich, 1977, p. 24).

One of the facets of teacher evaluation is student achievement—usually indicated by standardized test results. This information can be a part of the data collected in the evaluation of teaching, but it must be used with caution, since many factors affect student learning—family prob-

Figure 28. Supervisory Rating Scale.

SUPERVISOR: _____

DIRECTIONS: The purpose of the following questionnaire is to record your assessment of teachers. To record your assessment, first read the statement in capital letters. Place an X in one of the positions that best represents your view of the statement in capital letters.

A. YOUR VIEW OF THE TEACHER'S MAINTENANCE OF STUDENT INTEREST.

	1	2	3	4	5	6	7	
1. high	—	—	—	—	—	—	—	low
2. strong	—	—	—	—	—	—	—	weak
3. existing	—	—	—	—	—	—	—	nonexisting
4. superficial	—	—	—	—	—	—	—	deep
5. much	—	—	—	—	—	—	—	little

B. YOUR VIEW OF THE TEACHER'S WARMTH AND UNDERSTANDING OF PUPILS.

	1	2	3	4	5	6	7	
1. sensitive	—	—	—	—	—	—	—	insensitive
2. inferior	—	—	—	—	—	—	—	superior
3. humane	—	—	—	—	—	—	—	inhumane
4. cold	—	—	—	—	—	—	—	warm
5. unstable	—	—	—	—	—	—	—	stable

C. YOUR VIEW OF THE TEACHER'S CLARITY IN PRESENTATION OF CONCEPTS.

	1	2	3	4	5	6	7	
1. steady	—	—	—	—	—	—	—	changing
2. definite	—	—	—	—	—	—	—	indefinite
3. scarce	—	—	—	—	—	—	—	abundant
4. reliable	—	—	—	—	—	—	—	unreliable
5. weak	—	—	—	—	—	—	—	strong

D. YOUR VIEW OF THE TEACHER'S ENTHUSIASM.

	1	2	3	4	5	6	7	
1. narrow	—	—	—	—	—	—	—	wide
2. warm	—	—	—	—	—	—	—	cold
3. rare	—	—	—	—	—	—	—	abundant
4. easy	—	—	—	—	—	—	—	difficult
5. insensitive	—	—	—	—	—	—	—	sensitive

E. YOUR VIEW OF THE TEACHER'S METHODOLOGY.

	1	2	3	4	5	6	7	
1. learned	—	—	—	—	—	—	—	ignorant
2. uninfluential	—	—	—	—	—	—	—	influential
3. excellent	—	—	—	—	—	—	—	not excellent
4. insignificant	—	—	—	—	—	—	—	important
5. valuable	—	—	—	—	—	—	—	worthless

Figure 29. Teacher Evaluation.

Check statements that apply:
 1. Is interested in the student as a person.
 2. Encourages students.
 3. Has a good sense of humor.
 4. Doesn't talk about students to other students.
 5. Is friendly and understanding.
 6. Knows subject and sticks to subject in class.
 7. Has a good reason for giving punishment to students.
 8. Explains the subject and tries to help the students.
 9. Is patient with the student.
10. Has irritating personal habits.
11. Is clean and neat in appearance and is clean minded.
12. Is liberal—not picky at every little thing.
13. Gives proper kind of punishment and punishes all students the same for the same wrong.
14. Treats all students alike—has no pets.
15. Uses modern teaching methods and makes the subject interesting.
16. Treats students appropriately for their age.
17. Speaks clearly and writes clearly so all students can see what has been written.
18. Gives reasonable amount of homework.

lems, health, nutrition, economic and social status, death, and divorce. Although standardized tests may indicate general trends, specific implications about effective teaching are risky and inappropriate.

TEACHER SELF-APPRAISAL

One professional approach toward the improvement of teaching is self-evaluation. A mature individual who thoughtfully assesses his/her own teaching behavior can often locate areas for growth. Effective teachers are continuously evaluating their lesson plans, tests, and teaching strategies as part of the teaching process. Many self-evaluation forms are available. Figure 30 is a form that is suitable for secondary teachers. It includes several factors of teaching, such as knowledge of subject, enthusiasm, assignment, motivation, and tests. Dunn and Dunn's self-evaluation instrument (1977, pp. 77-87) is designed to reveal a teacher's teaching style. This "Teaching Style Inventory" results in a profile which provides information about the teacher's planning, teaching strategies, grouping of students, room design, environment, evaluation, philosophy, and teaching characteristics. The profile enables an individual to locate

Figure 30. Teacher Self-Evaluation.

Circle one of the numbers or the letter to the right of each statement.
Use this scale for rating:
5. Excellent   4. Above Average   3. Average
2. Below Average   1. Unsatisfactory   X. Unknown or Undecided

I would rate my:

1. Knowledge of the subject matter as	5 4 3 2 1 X
2. Ability to organize and present material effectively as	5 4 3 2 1 X
3. Willingness to answer questions as	5 4 3 2 1 X
4. Enthusiasm for teaching as	5 4 3 2 1 X
5. Enthusiasm for my teaching field as	5 4 3 2 1 X
6. Ability to motivate students to do their best work as	5 4 3 2 1 X
7. Tolerance for differing opinions as	5 4 3 2 1 X
8. Willingness to concede errors as	5 4 3 2 1 X
9. Willingness to entertain student suggestions about methods, materials or procedures as	5 4 3 2 1 X
10. Assignments as having value for students as	5 4 3 2 1 X
11. Assignments as being reasonable in amount and length as	5 4 3 2 1 X
12. Tests as being a realistic evaluation of the students' knowledge as	5 4 3 2 1 X
13. Fairness and impartiality of grading as	5 4 3 2 1 X
14. Promptness in grading and returning student assignments and tests as	5 4 3 2 1 X
15. Interest in students as	5 4 3 2 1 X
16. Availability to students as	5 4 3 2 1 X
17. Overall effectiveness as	5 4 3 2 1 X

him/herself on a continuum from individualized to traditional teaching. This can help teachers look more objectively at their behavior and analyze the consistency between practice and philosophy.

One sophisticated diagnostic instrument for self-evaluation is the Battelle Self-Appraisal Instrument. The valid standards for effective teaching it includes were developed through a search of literature and through the collection of critical incidents of teaching. The three fields of psychology, learning, and measurement and child development were the sources of principles which, if applied in the classroom, would produce the intended instructional results. More than 800 examples of effective and ineffective teaching were collected from effective teachers. These incidents were reviewed, and principles of effective teaching were abstracted. These principles of effective teaching were compiled and revised by a group of teachers and administrators, and four teaching roles were delineated.

Figure 31 shows the four roles—instructional leader, social leader, promoter of healthful emotional development, and communicator with parents and colleagues. Each role incorporates several principles. The general statement of each principle is then made more explicit. For example, ten principles are used to explain and apply the first guideline of the instructional leader. (See Figure 32.)

To use the Battelle Self-Appraisal Instrument (SAI) a teacher assesses him/herself on each principle with regard to relevance and the success of application. Since evaluation instruments are used for all situations—kindergarten through twelfth grade; required and elective classes; academic, vocational, and laboratory courses; special education classes—there are principles that are less applicable to certain groups. The form in Figure 33 allows a teacher to indicate which guidelines have little importance for his/her classes. The scoring provides a weighting of these ratings, and the final quantification is then graphed.

As a teacher completes each section of the instrument, a profile of the individual is produced. From this graph, the teacher's strengths and weaknesses are revealed. The teacher who tends to rate him/herself high will still show highs and lows on the profile, as will the teacher whose ratings tend to be lower. Through an examination of the specific principles in the low areas, a teacher can more knowingly set job targets. For example, from the sample profile given in Figure 34, the teacher would study the statements for A of Role II and C of Role III. This teacher's job targets should include establishing a democratic classroom atmosphere and strengthening student's weak skill areas to aid their adjustments.

Although the SAI is designed to be used in toto, a supervisor or principal may find such a commitment of time and effort is not feasible. If this is the case, only parts of the instrument can be used, when appropriate. For example, if a school is experiencing an increasing number of students with emotional problems, the section of the Battelle instrument which deals with the teacher as "promoter of healthful emotional development" could be employed.

If there is a committee that works on revision of the evaluation forms for a school system, this research-based instrument should surely be available. The four roles of the teacher and the procedure for weighing the relevance of specific items are unique features which should be considered in the committee's study.

One elementary principal who was impressed with the SAI used the principles as a basis for discussion in faculty meetings. Teachers were encouraged to give examples of how they applied or might apply the

Figure 31. Roles of Effective Teacher.*

I. Instructional Leader
    A. The teacher understands and applies psychological-readiness principles.
    B. The teacher provides a favorable success-failure ratio for each student.
    C. The teacher plans skillfully for an effective teaching-learning situation.
    D. The teacher individualizes instruction where appropriate.
    E. The teacher facilitates student motivation toward academic and social achievement.
    F. The teacher facilitates intellectual development.
    G. The teacher facilitates motor-skill development.
    H. The teacher uses effective reinforcement techniques.
    I. The teacher states and assesses behavioral objectives effectively and efficiently.
    J. The teacher accurately interprets obtained scores on tests and uses the information to improve the conditions of learning.
    K. The teacher understands and applies other principles of learning.

II. Social Leader
    A. The teacher establishes a democratic classroom atmosphere.
    B. The teacher guides peer interactions effectively.
    C. The teacher adjusts social interaction activities to group norms.
    D. The teacher adapts classroom activities to the pupil who is atypical in terms of social skills.
    E. The teacher facilitates development of moral character and moral behavior.

III. Promoter of Healthful Emotional Development
    A. The teacher recognizes symptoms of poor adjustment.
    B. The teacher reduces disabling levels of anxiety.
    C. The teacher strengthens weak skill areas as an aid to adjustment.
    D. The teacher uses effective case-study methods and employs necessary referral techniques.

IV. Communicator with Parents and Colleagues
    A. The teacher communciates information and suggestions to parents and colleagues about the intellectual, social and emotional development of students.

*Source: D.N. McFadden. *Increasing the Effectiveness of Educational Management*. (Columbus, OH: School Management Institute and Battelle Memorial Institute, 1970). Copyright © 1970 by Battelle Memorial Institute. Reprinted by permission.

Figure 32. Instructional Leader. A.*

> The Teacher Understands and Applies Psychological Readiness
> Principles
>
> A-1   The teacher ascertains each student's mastery of simpler tasks pre-
> requisite to the task at hand.
>
> A-2   The teacher recognizes that there are often wide variations in
> psychological-readiness levels within each pupil, and adjusts in-
> structional techniques accordingly or provides experiences designed
> to raise low levels of readiness.
>
> A-3   The teacher persists in efforts to raise skill level in cases of indi-
> viduals who have apparently reached plateaus, since some may be
> "late bloomers" capable of surpassing formerly superior students.
>
> A-4   The teacher attempts in the remediation of defective skills a different
> approach than original skill teaching, because there may be the need
> to extinguish ineffective habits and reduce emotional blocks built up
> through failure experiences.
>
> A-5   The teacher gives the child enough practice with several materials
> that incorporate the same concept, words, or skill before shifting to
> another concept, word, or skill that has inhibiting responses.
>
> A-6   The teacher allows the child opportunity to thoroughly learn the task
> in one situation before presenting the same task in a totally new or
> exciting situation.
>
> A-7   The teacher obtains knowledge of the child's past achievement,
> intellectual ability and the rate at which he/she might be expected to
> learn, and the teacher utilizes this knowledge in preparing for the
> classwork and assignments.
>
> A-8   The teacher gives the child time to assimilate new stimuli or new
> information before the presentation of further stimuli.
>
> A-9   The teacher uses objective evaluation as one technique of assessing a
> student's readiness to proceed to a new level.
>
> A-10 The teacher uses standardized readiness tests skillfully, when the
> maturational level of a child is important, to help make educational
> decisions relative to placement.

*Source: D.N. McFadden. *Increasing the Effectiveness of Educational Manage-
ment.* Columbus, OH: School Management Institute and Battelle Memorial Institute, 1970), p. A2. Copyright © 1970 by Battelle Memorial Institute. Reprinted
by permission.

Figure 33. Response Blank for the SAI.*

Role: I. Instructional Leader
Category: A. The teacher understands and applies psychological readiness
principles.

Principle	Personal Relevance	Success of Application	Appraisal = (P.R.) × (S.A.)
	1 = Little or none 2 = Moderate 3 = High	1 = Little or none 2 = Moderate 3 = High	
A-1	1 2 3	1 2 3	
A-2	1 2 3	1 2 3	
A-3	1 2 3	1 2 3	
A-4	1 2 3	1 2 3	
A-5	1 2 3	1 2 3	
A-6	1 2 3	1 2 3	
A-7	1 2 3	1 2 3	
A-8	1 2 3	1 2 3	
A-9	1 2 3	1 2 3	
A-10	1 2 3	1 2 3	
Totals	R = _____	//////////	A = _____

Profile Index = $\dfrac{A-R}{2R}$ = _____ (To be plotted on Profile Blank)

*Source: D.N. McFadden. *Increasing the Effectiveness of Educational Management.* (Columbus, OH: School Management Institute and Battelle Memorial Institute, 1970), p. 15. Copyright © 1970 by Battelle Memorial Institute. Reprinted by permission.

Figure 34. Profile Blank for SAI.*

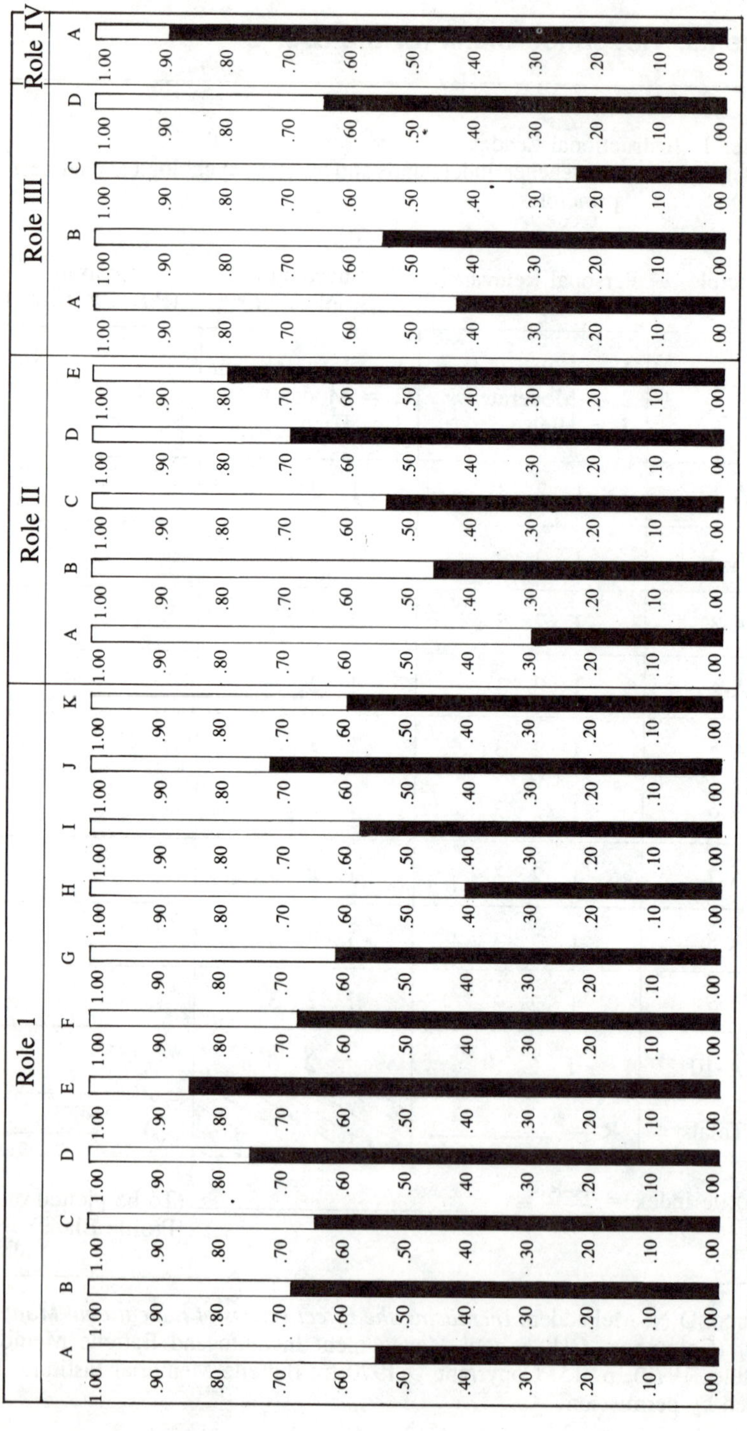

*Source: D.N. McFadden. *Increasing the Effectiveness of Educational Management.* (Columbus, OH: School Management Institute and Battelle Memorial Institute, 1970). Copyright © 1970 by Battelle Memorial Institute. Reprinted by permission.

statements in their teaching. The consideration of these principles of effective teaching was scheduled over a semester. At the conclusion of the project, the principal was convinced that instruction in the school had improved. Review of ideas about effective teaching and concern about applying these principles resulted in changed teacher behavior and a better instructional program.

SUPERVISOR AND SUPERVISORY PROGRAM APPRAISAL

Supervisors have a wonderful opportunity to provide a model for evaluation as they appraise their programs and procedures. Teachers can participate by providing feedback on inservice activities, as well as in the appraisal of the total supervisory program. Joy Clark, an English supervisor, videotaped a meeting of the curriculum committee which was working on revision of the English curriculum. She explained that she was using the tape to assess her own skills in conducting a meeting. This demonstration of willingness to analyze one's own behavior and concern for professional development can encourage the self-evaluation of teachers. Enthusiasm for continued learning can set the stage for better attitudes and efforts toward evaluation.

Evaluation of the total supervisory program should relate to the year's goals and objectives. Specific aspects of the program should also be appraised as individual projects. Each inservice meeting, for instance, must be assessed. (See the Evaluation section in Chapter 3.) Then, the contribution of the session to the overall objectives must be considered. Some questions which should be considered in the total evaluation include (Wiles and Lovell, 1975, pp. 282-46):

1. How many teachers are experimenting?
2. How many calls from teachers have requested assistance?
3. Has the nature of these problems changed?
4. Is there a demand for professional materials?
5. Is there sharing of material among faculty members?
6. Is there acceptance of differences among faculty members?
7. Are faculty becoming involved in planning and evaluating school program?

Evaluations of supervisors require teacher input. One form which could be used for this is presented in Figure 35. It can also be used by administrators and other supervisors who can provide information about the supervisor's work.

Self-evaluation is essential for supervisors. Not only analysis of time use, but examination of behavior in group leadership roles and in conference situations are valuable in indicating needed skills and demonstrated

Figure 35. Supervisory Checklist.

Please check those questions you consider to apply to your supervisor.

DOES S/HE

1. Conduct meetings and conferences effectively?   _____
2. Accept the rule of the majority while respecting the rights of   _____
   the minority?
3. Promote communication among staff members?   _____
4. Give teachers credit for creative activities?   _____
5. Provide opportunities for teachers to develop their leadership   _____
   potential?
6. Encourage teachers to try new methods and techniques?   _____
7. Allow teachers to choose the methods by which they will   _____
   work?
8. Make professional educational materials available to   _____
   teachers?
9. Willingly share the credit for achievements and successes?   _____
10. Always seem friendly and approachable?   _____
11. Maintain a sense of humor?   _____
12. Accept criticism gracefully?   _____
13. Encourage free discussion?   _____
14. Always try to be consistent in manner and performances?   _____
15. Allow professional disagreements without personal conflicts?   _____
16. Gather significant data for evaluating teacher performance?   _____
17. Evaluate the effectiveness of his/her supervision by follow-up _____
    activities?
18. Plan cooperatively with teachers who need help?   _____

Figure 36. Self-Evaluation Form for Supervisors.

The following listing of questions to be answered by the supervisor may prove helpful in evaluating the supervisory program.

1. Do I maintain cordial relationships with teachers?
2. Is communication with the staff on a personal basis?
3. Do I seek out the strong points in teachers and build upon these?
4. Do I seek and accept the contributions of all members of the staff, no matter how inconsequential the contribution may seem at the time?
5. Do I provide opportunities wherein teachers can make decisions in matters in which they are vitally concerned?

Figure 36. Self-Evaluation Form for Supervisors (cont'd).

6. Do I seek to uncover and encourage the development of leadership on the part of staff members? (It is the supervisor who knows that, the more people who feel a personal responsibility for the supervisory program, the more successful it probably will be.)

7. Do I pretend to be expert in all subjects and grade levels, or am I a specialist in working with teachers on the requirements of successful instruction?

8. Do I provide an ample supply of textbooks and supplementary materials and equipment, and then make sure that it is very easy for teachers to obtain these materials?

9. Do I keep teachers informed about free and inexpensive materials which are available?

10. Do I facilitate the participation by teachers and students in educational field trips?

11. Are my plans for supervision concrete and specific?

12. Are my plans for supervision consistent with the aspirations, goals and level of development of the teaching personnel and the citizens of the community?

13. Do I base planning, so far as possible, upon the realities of the situation that are discovered through the use of the techniques of research and careful experimentation?

14. Do I consult parents to find out what they think the school should be doing?

15. Do I contribute to and help coordinate and integrate the efforts of all agencies and institutions in the community that are interested in the improvement of education?

16. Do I actively cooperate with, and draw upon, the available local, state, national and international departments that are interested in the improvement of education?

17. Do I establish a schedule for my supervisory activities on a yearly, monthly, weekly, and daily basis?

18. Do I encourage teachers to assume more responsibility for self-supervision?

19. Have I been successful in elevating the quality and quantity of cooperative planning among staff members?

20. Have I been successful in stimulating more teachers to experiment and do research related to the instructional program and the curriculum?

21. Am I flexible, making changes easily when pertinent and when qualified data indicate changes are in order?

22. Do I realize that self-evaluation is the real key to the effective analysis of my contribution to the improvement of instruction?

strengths. Checklists and rating scales can assist the supervisor in such diagnosis. Figure 36 is an example of an instrument which might prove helpful.

SUMMARY

Evaluation has become a procedure that is accepted in all phases of life—business, industry, family, education. Supervisors are involved with evaluation of curriculum, materials, and teachers, as well as with their own programs and job performance. Evaluation may be formative, summative, or prescriptive.

A good evaluation is preplanned. First, the purpose of the assessment is determined. Then, the persons who will collect the data and perform other tasks, the instruments and procedures, the timing, and the interpretation and reporting of data should be decided. A variety of sources and methods of collecting information provide a more comprehensive picture of the situation.

Evaluation should be a continuous process. Teacher evaluation, a perennial problem for supervisory staff members, is a necessary part of promoting professional development. Rating scales and checklists may be useful in teacher appraisal, but the evaluator should recognize some of the disadvantages of these forms. Self-evaluation is another approach. Professional use of instruments, such as the Battelle Self-Appraisal Instrument, provides a sound basis for establishing job targets and encouraging staff development.

Supervisors should provide models for evaluation. Through a well-planned program of getting information from teachers and administrators, staff development activities can be modified to better meet teacher needs. The total supervisory program should also be assessed, so that appropriate goals are set. Self-evaluation for supervisors can lead to more effective management of time and talents.

REFERENCES

Bolton, D.L. *Selection and Evaluation of Teachers.* Berkeley, CA: McCutchan Publishing Co., 1973.

Borich, G.D. *The Appraisal of Teaching: Concepts and Process.* Reading, MA: Addison-Wesley Publishing Co., 1977.

Commission on Public School Personnel Policies in Ohio. *Teacher Evaluation to Improve Learning.* Cleveland, OH: Greater Cleveland Associated Foundations, 1972.

Dunn, R., and Dunn, K.J. *Administrator's Guide to New Programs for Faculty Management and Evaluation*. West Nyack, NY: Parker Publishing Co., Inc., 1977.

Harris, B.M. *Supervisory Behavior in Education*. 2d ed. Englewood Cliffs, NJ: Prentice-Hall Inc., 1975.

Klein, M.F. *About Learning Materials*. Washington, DC: The Association for Supervision and Curriculum Development, 1978.

McFadden, D.N. *Increasing the Effectiveness of Educational Management*. Columbus, OH: School Management Institute and Battelle Memorial Institute, 1970.

McGovern, E.G., and Loparo, C.A. *Teacher Evaluation: Trends in Ohio*. Medina, OH: Ohio Association for Supervision and Curriculum Development, 1980.

North Central Association for Colleges and Schools. *Policies and Standards for the Approval of Secondary Schools 1980-81*. Boulder, CO: Commission on Schools, 1980.

Owens, T.R., and Evans, W.D. *Program Evaluation Skills for Busy Administrators*. Portland, OR: North West Regional Educational Laboratory, 1977.

Wilhelms, F.T., ed. *Evaluation as Feedback and Guide*. 1967 Yearbook. Washington, DC: Association for Supervision and Curriculum Development, 1967.

Using Human Resources

Chapter 13
Communication

Communication is more than words. Communication involves a wide spectrum of human expression—printed words in a textbook, spoken words of a teacher, spoken and unspoken student responses, voices in the school hallways, the television show the kids watched the night before, even the publication of menus for the school lunch room. Communication is phone calls, school newsletters, the affective relationship between a teacher and the students in the classroom, memos from administrators, and the conferences between supervisor and teacher. Kelley (1952, p. 78) considered communication to be "the process by which one individual can to a degree know what another thinks, feels or believes. . . . It is . . . the key to human relatedness." The communication process is vitally important in supervision, since the supervisor deals with human relationships—working with an individual, a small group, or a large group to change behavior which will result in the improvement of instruction.

Good communication skills are essential in assessing the cognitive and affective development of the individual or individuals, in analyzing and planning for professional growth, and in carrying out the program so that student learning is positively affected. Whether the supervisor encourages one teacher to continue his/her efforts to challenge a gifted student, or presents information on new materials for interdisciplinary activities to a middle school staff, the supervisor hopes to motivate and inform through communication. In fact, the success of the supervisor depends on the effectiveness of communication. Oral and written, verbal and nonverbal, one-to-one, small group and large group, cognitive and affective—all of these are aspects of supervisory communication. Although cognitive and affective aspects of communication cannot in actuality be separated, they can be discussed more easily if they are defined arbitrarily.

AFFECTIVE COMMUNICATION

The affective domain refers to interests, attitudes, and values—those feelings which an individual brings to a situation. Sometimes, these emotive behaviors are unrecognized by the person exhibiting them. At other times, they are recognized but cannot be explained. A supervisor may have an immediate negative reaction to a new teacher and have no explanation for such a response. Perhaps the teacher looks like Aunt Emma, who was always sarcastic to the supervisor as a child, but this resemblance has not been consciously recalled.

Open communication is facilitated when such emotional blocks are recognized. Supervisors should be aware of their own feelings and try to put them in a reasonable perspective. In addition, sensitivity to the feelings and values of others is a skill which must be cultivated. Specific efforts to check on the reactions of others are helpful. In a conference, when a teacher is telling about an encounter with a student, a supervisor can practice interpreting his/her cues by questioning. S/he might ask, "It seems Joe's behavior made you angry; is that right?" The teacher's answer can give an indication of how well the situation is understood. Watching for nonverbal signals, as well as active listening, can build sensitivity. Nonverbal communication is the source of most misunderstandings and misinterpretation of emotive reactions, so frequent checking is worthwhile. A sincere concern for others and their professional development can be the base for empathy. Because self-analysis can become so absorbing, the supervisor is challenged to maintain a balance between his/her own feelings and the feelings of clients. The successful supervisor must keep a focus on other individuals.

A common fallacy in the affective area is the assumption that all teachers have similar values. The fact that educators are similar in socioeconomic status, work with students in a school environment, and live in the same geographic area does not assure that they have identical attitudes, interests, or values. Teachers disagree about grading policies, student behavior, and school regulations, because their values are often divergent. Effective supervisors recognize that differences exist, and they get to know the individual teachers, learn their interests and attitudes, and use this information to facilitate professional growth for each individual.

Modeling is one of the productive teaching strategies. Supervisors, as teachers of teachers, may help teachers develop positive approaches by modeling (demonstration). Some of the attitudes which are helpful and can be communicated are:

1. Enthusiasm—for learning, for the school, for students, and for activities. This zeal indicates a commitment to get involved and to find opportunities. It reveals that a supervisor honestly enjoys working with people in an educational setting.

2. Optimism—about better situations in the future, faith in the adaptability of individuals, confidence in the problem-solving skills of

students, and trust in education as a way to improve the quality of life. There are many pessimistic views of world tension, national crises, local political conflicts, social and economic dysfunction, school problems, and student misbehavior. Amid these gloomy prospects, a teacher needs to hear an encouraging word. The supervisor may be introducing an optimistic outlook when s/he builds on strengths, instead of dwelling on weaknesses. Presenting inservice programs as opportunities for professional progress, rather than "remedial" work to overcome teacher deficiencies, is an important strategy. A cheerful approach to daily activities sets an expectation of positive experiences.

3. Willingness to listen—not just to answers which are responsive to the supervisor's questions, but also to topics which the teacher chooses and to ideas which are in disagreement with the supervisor's point of view. The complete attention of an active listener says, "You are important and I am interested in hearing your ideas . . . ," a flattering and supportive message.

4. Open-mindedness—to consider dissenting opinions, to solicit ideas from all involved, to weigh all the evidence, and to evaluate alternatives. An administrator or supervisor loses credibility if a decision has been made before the teachers are involved. For example, a textbook committee of teachers has spent hours selecting an elementary math series. The members worked as individuals and as a group evaluating the different texts. Representatives of each of the three most favored publications met with the committee at different times to discuss the advantages of their textbooks and to answer questions. When the chairperson proudly took the report to the central office for the mathematics supervisor, the secretary looked at the report and remarked, "This isn't the series the superintendent had me order last month!" Obviously, those teachers who worked on the selection committee will not only resent the time they wasted, but they will also respond with little interest if asked to serve on other school committees.

5. Disposition to treat a problem as unique—to make each teacher feel special and to project sincere concern about finding a satisfactory solution. A supervisor may have as many as 200 teachers to work with, but s/he must show a sincere concern when one teacher describes a problem which reminds the supervisor of about 123 other teachers with the same problem. Although misery loves company, a flippant response from the supervisor ("I've heard that one before!") may preclude any future "helping relationship" between the two. A supervisor listening to a teacher

describe a familiar circumstance should recognize the individuality of the person. Together, they should analyze the situation and evolve an appropriate plan for alleviating or solving the problem.

6. Time-awareness—to save the supervisor's schedule and the teacher's self-respect. Since schools function on time schedules, teachers and administrators have time commitments which must be recognized. If a supervisor uses a teacher's preparation time to recount the details of his/her vacation trip, the teacher may label the supervisor an inconsiderate bore and avoid further conversation. This reaction may be completely different from the perception of the supervisor who felt s/he was building good rapport. If a supervisor in a conference is sensitive to the passing of time, the interchange can move along to the analysis of pertinent information and to an agreement on plans for professional growth. In contrast, a supervisor who is unaware of time may find that the teacher must return to the classroom, even though their conference has failed to solve some of the major problems.

COGNITIVE COMMUNICATION

The cognitive domain is concerned with thinking processes. Knowledge, comprehension, application, analysis, synthesis, and evaluation comprise one hierarchy, as described in Bloom's *Taxonomy* (1956). Other classifications include convergent and divergent thinking, understanding, generalization, and problem solving. Regardless of the descriptive terms used to designate the mental activities, supervisory messages are usually in the cognitive domain—they deal with content or professional information.

Sometimes, there is a conflict about whether a supervisor should be a subject specialist or a generalist. The services of both specialist and generalist can promote improved instruction, although the assistance provided to teachers by a specialist in content will be different from that of a generalist. The former can be a resource on materials and planning specific lessons, while the latter can be helpful in motivation, classroom management, and teaching strategies. In his/her supervisory role, the principal acts as a generalist; a department head with supervisory responsibilities acts as a specialist.

A supervisor sometimes finds it is necessary to work with a teacher who teaches a subject that is not a part of the supervisor's academic experience. In this instance, the main bond is not the basic knowledge of subject matter but, instead, the atmosphere of the class, the maintenance of student interest, and the development of a learning atmosphere. Instructional expertise involves more than lecture techniques; it means moving students into active participation, instead of letting them remain at a level of passive acceptance. A supervisor can help a teacher pace the instruction and vary the modes of presentation. Individualized instruction to provide success experiences for every student can also be facilitated.

American education reflects the democratic principles on which the nation was founded. All citizens have a voice—including students in our public schools. Our political and social climates mold the educational climate. Although the teacher retains the position of authority in the classroom—organizing materials for instruction, providing information, facilitating learning and evaluating—s/he must recognize that, in today's schools, student are citizens with inalienable rights. Since articulate citizens are needed in a democratic society, the teacher in the United States has a responsibility to teach communication skills. Simultaneously, the supervisor provides a model for these skills. Supervisors help teachers build communication skills for themselves, so they can proceed to teach students how to communicate effectively. Without responses from the students, a teacher cannot be sure what level of intellectual receptivity the individual class members are maintaining.

Students have after-school access to television, stereo, radio, and movies; "media-influenced" youngsters require more interesting learning activities than children in the 1800s. The twentieth century, therefore, puts many pressures on teachers which their predecessors never experienced. Communication in the classroom then should expand to include audio and video messages. Slides, films, photographs, and records are also useful communication tools that can introduce a variety of media in instruction.

Encouraging a teacher to stay current in his/her subject content areas is important in a rapidly changing world. An alert supervisor routes appropriate articles to teachers and occasionally circulates book reviews in a memo or newsletter. At other times, supervisors may induce teachers to attend professional meetings. The supervisor can provide verbal support for a teacher, and even substitute for the teacher in the classroom, so the teacher can participate in a workshop or conference. Such cooperative actions on the part of a supervisor signal his/her willingness to cooperate with teachers. Teachers who have not returned for refresher courses or recertification may believe that what they learned long ago in college will always be applicable. The supervisor may have to dispel this false belief and motivate a teacher to take a course or, in some cases, extensive programs of graduate work.

A teacher does not have a problem until s/he recognizes it. For instance, a supervisor and principal may decide that a teacher, Mr. Jessop, is having discipline problems in his classroom. But, the problem is theirs only, until Mr. Jessop decides that students sitting on window ledges, writing notes, and crawling under tables are distractors in a learning environment. If either the supervisor or principal told Mr. Jessop that he had a discipline problem, he would probably deny it, explain the student behavior, defend his actions, or try to satisfy his superordinates by doing whatever they suggested. However, after he sees his own problem, he will become concerned with finding ways of eliminating student misbehavior.

On the other hand, a teacher may recognize a problem which seems insignificant to the supervisor. Mary Jackson, the shy new English teacher in the junior high school, is embarrassed when Mr. Cranshaw, an experienced social studies teacher, talks to her in the hall. "He has his hands all over me," she explains. "I hate his pawing me, but I don't know how to fight him off without making a scene." A supervisor may have what s/he considers more serious concerns but, in order to help Ms. Jackson, s/he must deal with what Ms. Jackson describes as her problem. Perception of problems is a personal interpretation, and the supervisor must investigate the teacher's perceptions. Otherwise, communication is blocked.

A final caution in cognitive communication relates to meaning of words, phrases, and messages. Semantic differences can lead to unsatisfactory communication, and such problems may result in misunderstandings and confusion. An illustration of such usage was discovered in a study of males and females in an organization. The women were described as poor team members. A closer study of the situation revealed that the male team concept was based on a football team scheme, where each member had a specific job to do—the success of the team depended on each one doing the assigned task. The women, on the other hand, considered teamwork as a cooperative enterprise; they looked at group progress and tried to help in those tasks which seemed to be less effectively done. The females appeared to be intruding on male turf when they offered to help with jobs that were assigned to men. Only when group members understand what teamwork is, and they develop their roles in accordance with accepted definitions, can communication be meaningful. In the interest of open communication, defining and clarifying meanings is always appropriate. To achieve desired goals, the cognitive aspects of communication require careful supervisory attention.

ORAL COMMUNICATION

Verbal communication uses words to carry a message, in either spoken or written form. In oral communication, the supervisor should adapt the tone and volume of his/her voice to the situation. A firm yet gentle approach may be generally appropriate. Volume of speaking must be clearly audible to a group, i.e., loud enough to command attention, but not so loud as to be overpowering. In a confidential exchange with a teacher, a soft voice can assure the teacher that no one else can hear the conversation, as well as create a feeling of mutual cooperation.

Rate of speaking influences the retention of the comments which a supervisor exchanges with a teacher. Variation in speaking rate can provide a change of pace which makes the voice easier to listen to. If a supervisor wants to affirm an idea which has been described by the teacher, the supervisor should speak lightly and quickly. But, if the supervisor is responding to a request for an opinion on a serious matter, the rate of speech should be slower. A decelerated rate of speaking gives the listener a chance to assimilate content and indicates the speaker's willingness to consider a situation carefully before making a reply.

Vocabulary also has an impact on the receiver, for the choice of words transmits a message about how the sender regards the receiver. Careless speech tends to indicate lack of respect. Teachers who deal with young people on a daily basis can quickly recognize the use of slang, contemporary phrases, or "in" words. Teachers can accept this vocabulary from their students, but they will not respond affirmatively to a supervisor who uses this style of language. Surprisingly, some supervisors have a tendency to use excessively casual words, while others seem deliberately to use esoteric words. The ideas may be excellent, but the vocabulary used may dilute the ultimate effect. Supervisors should make a point of expanding their vocabularies, trying to speak in a literate manner, and avoiding overuse of colloquial speech or jargon.

Pitch of voice can be controlled to some extent. People in our culture are conditioned to expect a deep sound from an authority figure and a high pitch from an adolescent or effeminate character. From the standpoint of auditory irritation, a low pitch can be tolerated longer than a high one. Whether male or female, a supervisor should strive to lower the pitch of his/her voice when speaking, since this effort may be conducive to better acceptance of supervisory ideas.

Inflection of voice refers to the use of rising and falling tones in the sentences which are being articulated. A well-inflected voice can carry a listener, giving him/her an expectation of hearing something interesting. A badly-inflected voice can be stultifying and is best described as monotone. Inflection emphasizes the meaning, indicates punctuation, and shows emotion, when appropriate.

NONVERBAL COMMUNICATION

Nonverbal communication, or body language, does not require words. In the last 20 years, scientists and the public have become fascinated with nonverbal communication and its complexities. Body language conveys an important part of the message that a person sends to others. Gestures, posture, and the speed of movement give impressions about the feelings, relationships, and status of a person. Dress and hair style can also be indicators of economic status, interests, activities, and characteristics. An analysis of the elements of nonverbal communication can contribute to understanding of interpersonal responses. Broad categories of nonverbal influence include haptic, optic, proxemic, labic, pedic, and chromatic.

Haptic communication is a transfer of meaning by hand motion or touching. One of the most frequently used and universally accepted haptics is the handshake. A supervisor can make a personal decision about when and where to use a handshake, but it is possible to use it at all greetings. If a supervisor sees the teacher daily, a handshake may be excessive; but, considering the frequency of most supervisional observations, a handshake is probably appropriate. If the handshake is chosen as a form of greeting, the supervisor should reach out, grasp the teacher's hand firmly, and actually shake it in a warm greeting.

Other haptics which are feasible in a supervisor-teacher relationship are patting on the shoulder at the time of a compliment or reaching out to touch a hand when support is needed. The warmth of body contact can lighten the force of a disappointment or negative feeling.

Not only should a supervisor decide when haptic communication should be used, but s/he should also observe the teacher's haptic responses. For example, if a supervisor extends a hand for a warm handshake and the teacher reluctantly puts out a hand and delivers a limp handshake, a negative message is being communicated to the supervisor.

As with most communications that express sympathy or warmth, a supervisor must use good judgment. If the supervisor is male and the teacher is female, a friendly hand on on the shoulder or a pat on the arm may be acceptable but, if protracted or repeated, such behavior may be inappropriate.

Optic communication involves the use of eyes in the communication of a message from the sender to the receiver. Through its use, the sender imparts a feeling which words cannot transmit. One of the traditional optics is the wink, which indicates a flirtatious mood or, as is more likely in a job circumstance, implies a form of in-joke understanding between two people or a sharing of special information.

A more serious use of optics is in the maintenance of eye contact between two people during a conversation. In the conference situation, if a supervisor tries for eye contact and notices that the teacher's eyes keep roaming to the window, the bond of communication will be weakened. Also, if a supervisor cannot get a gaze from the teacher which meets the supervisor's eyes squarely, an inevitable lack of rapport is the result. In the North American culture, eye contact indicates a trusting relationship; therefore, it should not be ignored by educators who must live with the personal impressions they create.

Proxemic communication deals with personal space. Proxemics are probably the least well-known of the body language elements. They relate not to a specific use of parts of the body, but instead to the physical placement of the two or more human beings who are communicating.

Etymologically, the word *proxemics* is connected with the more familiar word *proximity*. Nearness is part of proxemics—consider how much more personal a conversation is when the sender and the receiver are within a few feet of each other. Compare this proxemic situation with another when the sender speaks to a receiver from about 10 yards away. The distance between the two communicators affects the confidentiality of the interchanged messages. Short distances give a view of smiles and other facial expressions and also make auditory perceptions sharper so the receiver detects nuances of speech. In short, all of the other aspects of both verbal and nonverbal communication are affected adversely or beneficially by the amount of space between the sender and the receiver.

A supervisor should also consider that a proxemic element is the placement of furniture in a conference setting. Open communication lines are easier to maintain when there is no desk or table between the conferees. If the two participants speak to one another, sitting side by side, they can easily share comments. This room arrangement creates a friendlier atmosphere than one in which participants confront each other across a furniture barrier. A supervisor who stays behind a desk automatically sets up the proxemic situation of superordinate and subordinate. The person on the other side of the desk may feel that s/he has been called in for a reprimand, and this response sometimes obviates a helpful discourse between supervisor and teacher.

Labic communication relates to messages sent by the mouth—entirely separate from the words spoken. Study of labics is an area of nonverbal research which results, in part, from closeup camera shots of television performers. Enlarged views of lips on TV screen have made viewers mouth conscious. Although studies of the effects of smiles were begun over 40 years ago, interest in other aspects of labic communication has developed recently. Educators should recognize and assess this type of human sender-to-receiver interaction.

Labic communications include pursing of lips (displeasure, disapproval); rounding of mouth (surprise, anticipation); or frequent licking of lips (nervousness, low confidence level). Sometimes, loosely held lips indicate health problems (sinusitis, adenoids, nasal congestion, or slackness related to fatigue); biting of lips may be construed as a symptom of security level (lack of confidence, stagefright, fear); and visible tongue pressures on roof of mouth can indicate readiness to respond to a question (enthusiasm, energy). Supervisors need to be aware of labic activity—their own and others'—so that a complete picture is drawn of the communication flow in the classroom or conference environment.

Pedics communication was identified by communication analysts who recognized that almost all parts of the body in motion impart additional information about senders and receivers. The study of pedics, as the word implies, relates to nonverbal messages sent out by the feet—foot-tapping, foot-swinging, and foot-nudging. Nonfunctional action by one foot or both feet often indicates repressed nervous energy or the presence of inner agitation and/or impatience. Foot-tapping is a cue which supervisors can notice in teachers sitting near them in a conference setting. Teachers have long been aware of student foot activity in confined classroom environment, and since many supervisors have had classroom teaching experience, they can easily make a transfer of symptoms and arrive at another stage of understanding communication between supervisors and clients.

Many times, the supervisor will receive nonverbal cues about the reactions of the conferee. The basic cause of the body language may be some comment or criticism by the supervisor. In other words, the pedic nonverbal action may be a response, rather than an initiating message. Does it mean that the supervisor is asking a question and not waiting for an answer? Does it mean that the supervisor has offered a suggestion which the teacher would like to reject? Often, the answer to these questions is affirmative. Just because the response is inaudible, the supervisor cannot assume that no reply has been given.

Chromatic communication is a pervasive category in the educational scene. These communications are related to color, which can be part of clothing, cosmetics, skin, nails, automobiles, hair, wallpaper, bulletin board decorations, or floor coverings. In short, chromatics are part of every message, and they involve color on any person, place, or thing. Many colorations are not within the range of control, but many others are definite exhibitions of taste and selection.

Since colors influence the impact an individual has on others, such questions as the following might be considered by a supervisor: Would a bright red dress be the costume to wear for a job interview? Would a bright yellow jacket be appropriate for the first teacher's meeting? What makeup is suitable to wear when visiting in schools? Is a deep suntan an advantage or disadvantage? What is the best color to paint the walls of a classroom? Do brightly colored papers add or detract from the effectiveness of a bulletin board? Would a purple letterhead be satisfactory for memo paper on which the supervisor sends comments to a teacher following a conference? Since there is no correct answer to such questions, each person must respond based on the desire to express individualism, personal choice, and the possible interpretation of others.

Supervisors must acknowledge that color is an element in human communication. Color provides a message of boldness or caution, assuredness or uncertainty, good taste or insensitivity, and attractiveness or drabness. Individuals achieve selected goals by being highly visible or by coming into a situation on a low key. Chromatic communications are part of life-style, a realization fundamental to the right choice of chromatic transmission—almost as important as right choice of words and phrases.

A supervisor must be aware of his/her own nonverbal communication, which can be periodically analyzed by observing videotaped records of conferences or meetings. Sensitivity to nonverbal messages of others can also benefit the supervisor, as s/he strives for open communication lines. The fact that cultural and individual differences exist makes nonverbal communication interesting, but its accurate interpretation is difficult.

WRITTEN COMMUNICATION

There is no more respected and useful mode of message transmission than putting words on paper. Since ancient Egypt, significant events have been recorded and retained on flat surfaces. Whether on papyrus or on a word processing printout, the written/printed word provides several advantages over oral and nonverbal communication. Some of these major considerations follow:

1. Words on paper can become permanent records. Often, an informative written communication is valuable at several points in time—initially, it transmits a timely message and, later, if properly filed and retained, it can become a reference for subsequent study. The materials which supervisors retain in notes, minutes, and reports are often the only accurate historical records of faculty activities, such as workshops and inservice programs.

2. Words on paper, reflecting formal actions of teachers, supervisors, and administrators, are the data on which legal and political judgments are based. These words become a basis for decisions in matters of contract continuance, tenure, salary raises, delegation of authority, assignment of faculty responsibilities, and other areas which vitally affect the job environment and career success of many educators.

No one doubts the force of the spoken word. But, it is important to consider how much more lasting the same message can be when put in written form.

3. Written words which are affirmative, descriptive, and informative can often be a bonding force in a school system. Well-timed, well-distributed printed pieces can be influential in creating positive attitudes. Both internal and external publications combine as powerful elements in building and maintaining good morale in a school system. Conversely, publications put together quickly and thoughtlessly can cause morale of both teachers and students to decrease.

Continuing improvement within a school does not just evolve; it must be painstakingly developed by supportive attitudes. Supervisors must often take the initiative in building school morale by writing messages in such a way that the self-confidence levels of others are raised. Notes congratulating teachers on completing a curriculum project or receiving a community award create good feelings. Evidence that individuals are important contributors to school progress is always appreciated. Such written notes take little time, but they produce positive feelings.

4. Written communications are often seriously considered by those who read them. Without conscious consideration, receivers of messages are aware that writing takes time. In fact, writing requires premeditation, and the results are apt to be more carefully noticed. Some people tend to be less skeptical and more accepting of ideas in printed form. Not only are written messages heeded at the time of their receipt, but they also become a source of information to which the receiver can return. There may be a tendency for senders of spoken messages to offer information without explanatory matter. In contrast, the same person presenting the message in writing would probably explain why s/he had taken the time to write and send a memo to the faculty.

A presupervisor is repeatedly told that s/he will be expected to use words creatively as a successful practitioner. Yet, most educational institutions do not require special writing courses in their programs for those who specialize in supervision. Responsibility for developing word skills usually falls directly on the individual. Some supervisors take credit or noncredit college courses to improve their language skills. Others work alone at becoming more skillful in sentence structure, oral delivery, written format, and concise explanations. A good source of information—a traditional requirement for journalism majors—is Flesch's book, *Art of Plain Talk* (1946). In it, he decries the use of gobbledygook and enumerates ways to communicate understandably. Some of his suggestions are applicable to supervisors:

1. Speak and write consistently. Do not write up or down to your audience.
2. Do not use sarcasm or irony in your writing.
3. Avoid cute word rhymes and rhythms which divert instead of inform.
4. Use concrete instead of abstract words. For instance do not say, "He will observe the utilization of the kitchen facility." Instead, say, "He is going to the kitchen to see how the dishwasher is used."
5. Watch use of colloquial speech, especially in writing. Often, it is slang or "trend talk" which may go out of style before the printed material itself becomes obsolete.
6. Avoid use of subtle hints in writing. Usually, people want to be told in forthright fashion what is to be done or what is not to be done. For example, do *not* write in a student orientation book: "It is less tiring to all considered if low decibel levels can be maintained when in transit from one institutional site to another." State a school rule so it is clearly understood, for example, "Please keep your voices down when passing classes!" or "No shouting in the hallways!"

In order to respond to communication responsibilities, a supervisor should accept the fact that much of his/her writing will be anonymous. By-lines are seldom included on publicity releases sent to the local paper; authors of brochures and booklets are rarely credited; and a supervisor who writes out a few words for a colleague to speak to the PTA meeting can expect to be an educational ghost writer.

This anonymity extends to helping supervisees prepare materials which will be part of proposals to foundations and federal agencies for monetary grants. Sometimes a supervisor, aiding a supervisee, will collect documentation for a proposal, interview teachers about specific needs, work with the budget officers in arriving at reasonable financial requests, and correspond with a federal office to keep the proposal within strict guidelines. If the proposal is accepted, usually the school administrators will be credited with gaining the additional funding, and the supervisor must gain a feeling of satisfaction from knowing that the writing job was well done. Such unrecognized effort is a facet of human nature that is part of the supervisory environment.

A productive supervisor, wanting to use communication skills to improve learning circumstances for the students, should be determined to develop good writing habits, an understanding of grammar, and a flexible style. Writing a newsletter for teachers requires a different approach from one that is suitable for an article which a teacher wants to produce and submit to a professional journal.

In addition to being able to write about events and situations, supervisors also should be able to identify situations which merit attention. Writing well requires looking, seeing, and deducing before writing. Also, it requires facts and figures. For instance, if a supervisor observes that Ms. Jones had a good class, the supervisor does not provide a good report by merely indicating such generalities. A good report includes the supervisor's precise description: "Ms. Jones involved 20 children in a discussion of colonial life in Massachusetts." The activities of the colonists which the students included should be specifically listed, as should the comparisons to aspects of life today (e.g., the newspaper is the modern pillory in some communities). The supervisor who writes knowingly about a teacher's skill is a boon to the teacher, because an accurate recording of data enriches the permanent file.

SUMMARY

Communication plays a vital role in supervision. As the supervisor works with individuals and groups to improve instruction, many facets of communication are involved. Both affective and cognitive messages must be considered by supervisors who need to develop skills in sending and receiving communications. Effective use of verbal and nonverbal communication (haptic, optic, proxemic, labic, pedic, and chromatic) is essential in supervisory activities.

Furthermore, supervisors are involved in a variety of written messages which include grant proposals, articles, news articles, personal notes, newsletters, and professional reports. Those who produce written communications successfully will be the ones who help others work productively in the schools.

REFERENCES

Aranguren, J. *Human Communication*. New York: McGraw-Hill Book Company, 1967.

Birdwhistell, Ray L. *Kinesics in Context*. Philadelphia: University of Pennsylvania Press, 1970.

Bloom, B. S., ed. *Taxonomy of Educational Objectives. Handbook I: Cognitive Domain*. New York: David McKay Company, Inc., 1956.

Cogan, M. "Supervision at the Harvard-Newton Summer School." Boston: Harvard Graduate School of Education, 1961.

Flesch, R. *Art of Plain Talk*. New York: Harper and Brothers Publishers, 1946.

Forsdale, Louis. *Nonverbal Communication*. New York: Harcourt Brace Jovanovich, Inc., 1974.

Galloway, C. M. *Silent Language in the Classroom*. Bloomington, IN: Phi Delta Kappa Education Foundation, 1976.

Hall, Edward T. *Beyond Culture*. Garden City, NY: Anchor Press/Doubleday, 1976.

——. *The Hidden Dimension*. New York: Doubleday & Co., 1966.

——. *The Silent Language*. New York: Fawcett Books Groups, 1959.

Kelley, E. C., and Rasey, M. I. *Education and the Nature of Man*. New York: Harper and Brothers, 1952.

Morris, Desmond. *Manwatching*. New York: Harry N. Abrams, Inc., Publishers, 1977.

Mosher, R., and Purpel, D. *Supervision: The Reluctant Profession*. Boston: Houghton-Mifflin Company, 1972.

Nierenberg, G., and Calero, H. *Metatalk*. New York: Trident Press, 1975.

Nine-Curt, C. *Non-Verbal Communication*. Bronx, NY: Northeast Center for Curriculum Development, 1976.

"Nonverbal Communication." *Theory into Practice* 10 (4) (October 1971).

Ornstein, Robert E. *The Psychology of Consciousness*. San Francisco, CA: Freeman, 1972.

Rossi, P., and Biddle, B. *The New Media and Education: Their Impact on Society*. New York: Doubleday & Company, Inc., 1967.

Weitz, Shirley. *Nonverbal Communication*. New York: Oxford University Press, 1979.

Chapter 14
Change

An effective supervisor makes a significant contribution to a school system when s/he causes visible, desirable change in a supervisee. Such change can be achieved in many ways, both formal and informal. Change can affect the curriculum, the learning environment, and/or the teacher's behavior. A supervisor develops human contacts through the visitation and conference route, a structured clinical method, or frequent communications. By whatever combination of means, the alteration of circumstances and actions often is the result of a chain of activities. The actions in the role of a change agent are important in the lives of supervisors, no matter whether their supervisees are beginners, mid-career teachers, or senior teachers in their most productive years.

The need for change may come from the failure to achieve educational goals. Sometimes, this result can be attributed to ineffective teaching; other times, the disappointing outcomes may be related to curriculum and learning environment. Change may be proposed as a means of improving the educational scene—a growth opportunity, rather than a remedial action. However, developing technologies, shifting social scenes, and varying economic conditions often create a need for modifications in the schools. Sometimes, teaching strategies, curriculum offerings, organizational patterns, and learning sites must all be adapted. The decade of the 80s is expected to present many "future shock" occurrences. Toffler (1970, pp. 2-3) states that "earnest intellectuals talk bravely about 'education for change' or 'preparing people for the future.' But we know nothing about how to do it. In the most rapidly changing environment to which man has ever been exposed, we remain pitifully ignorant of how the human animal copes."

Educators must begin to learn coping skills. Studying what the futurists have to say may be a good way to begin. Another way to learn how to deal with change is to analyze change as a social phenomenon.

EXTRINSIC AND INTRINSIC CHANGE

One should be aware that there are two broad categories of change—extrinsic and intrinsic. Assessing which of these is responsible for a faulty school circumstance may well be one of the first responsibilities of the supervisor who is acting as change agent, since supervisory action will be different depending upon the type of change.

Extrinsic change occurs in an environment and proceeds from outer sources toward the affected individuals. Although it may be of human origin, extrinsic change springs essentially from sociological or environmental forces. For example, an extrinsic change among this nation's teenagers in the early part of the twentieth century was a change of mobility, as automobiles became part of the American scene. Teachers of the period, therefore, had to deal with this extrinsic change element which was beyond their sphere of influence.

Intrinsic change occurs within an individual. This kind of change is caused—in fact, in some instances is necessitated—by varying extrinsic forces. Essentially, an intrinsic change is a personal altering of an attitude or an action. In other words, as teachers of the early twentieth century faced the situation of increased mobility of students, they also felt the need to modify their outlooks. A major adaptation of teachers in this period was the recognition that children who had attended rural, one-room schools were brought to schools in towns and cities by bus. The simplest change in the teacher may have been the adjustment to more students in the schoolroom, but the situation also demanded that village teachers learn to understand the children of farmers, as well as the children of townspeople.

As those early teachers grappled with the changes, they learned to cope with new situations by trial and error. There were few knowledgeable change agents, such as supervisors, on hand to help them make logical alterations. Today, however, supervisors have much of the responsibility of anticipating problems and preparing teachers to handle them. These procedures are directly beneficial to teachers but, indirectly, just as advantageous to students whose learning is less hampered as a teacher struggles with unanticipated crises. Instead of relying on improvised survival tactics, teachers have a supervisory support system to help them avoid a traumatic experience which unexpected change can cause. Teacher effort then can be turned to improvement of instruction.

Intrinsic change deals with individual perceptions. Because of the uniqueness of perception, the supervisor may find that influencing intrinsic change is a difficult task. The creativity of supervisors must be used to broaden the teacher's experience and enable him/her to find ways to teach effectively, since a teacher's perceptions are influenced by beliefs, values, needs, opportunities, and self-concept.

A modern supervisor must develop a multitude of skills in order to help today's teachers cope with changing events. Among these skills is an awareness of sociological/economic events which have universal impact on school systems and all citizens involved. Also, a supervisor must develop continuing patience in activating the chain of events which can bring about successful implementation of change and thoughtful conceptualization of the detailed processes of change. Only as supervisors become cognizant of social and economic trends can they predict their potential effects on the school. This recognition allows for the planning and developing of strategies for dealing with the new situations. Some communities have been able to adjust facilities and personnel to decreasing enrollment without public confrontation; other communities have experienced demonstrations and emotional upheaval. When planned change transpires, the process is slow. Involvement of persons affected by a proposed change takes time and effort. Laying the proper groundwork for a transition and instructing those who implement change are essential steps for the supervisor who believes that significant changes can be produced only through group action. The supervisor must have a theory of change for planning and proceeding in a systematic way. Without such concepts, the complex process of change becomes unpredictable and erratic.

MODELS OF CHANGE

Change can be produced by evolution or revolution, or it can be planned. Educators usually select the planned approach, eliminating the conflict of revolution and the slow development of evolution. Models of planned changes have been suggested by numerous writers. Havelock (1973) stressed a six-step series of actions that would lead to ideal education in the future. These steps included building a relationship between the change agent and the client, diagnosing the problem, acquiring relevant resources, choosing the solution, gaining acceptance and stabilizing the innovation, and generating self-renewal. Harris (1975) recommended that a chain of activities should first emphasize a simulation of reality and a soliciting of reaction to this simulation. By recording, analyzing, and feeding back to a client, Harris indicated that data can be interpreted so that applied change can be achieved. Rogers (1962) wrote that changes consist of antecedents, process, and results. The antecedents represent the psychological factors of the persons involved, i.e., their perceptions of the situation and readiness for change; the process includes the stages of awareness, interest, evaluation, trial, and adoption; and the results are the outcomes which must be compared to specific goals for the project and to the school philosophy. Each of these models can be applied by a supervisor.

Another model which emphasizes the decision process as an essential element is presented in Figure 37. The six steps here show the process an individual teacher or a group of educators experiences in meeting the challenge of a situation which might be improved by an alteration of structure and/or activity. Each step (or "coping link") is a part of the process of adapting to change. The sequence of events is rapport development, teacher adaptiveness, reality sharing, decision box activity, pro/con-change choices, and crystallization. Each period is explained below in relation to a group which is considering a new program, for example, teachers who are considering replacement of reading in each class by a nongraded reading program in grades one through three.

1. Coping Link I—Rapport Development
   In this period, the group of teachers who will be affected by the projected change meets together. The supervisor hopes to develop empathy among the individuals. Even though the teachers may work in the same building, they may not know how others feel about teaching students. There is encouragement to speak openly and to employ active listening. Establishing a trust relationship requires an investment of time and patience. In the sharing process, the supervisor works to develop an understanding and acceptance of different attitudes by the group. The individuals who feel a need for change express their views as a background for considering possibilities. Often, the supervisor simply convenes the group and sets the stage for the teachers who are proponents of an innovation.

2. Coping Link II—Teacher Adaptiveness
   Group members indicate a willingness to consider a change, either by adapting to an extrinsic change or initiating an intrinsic change, since such change seems essential to alleviate problems or to improve instruction. Receptivity to the idea of change may evolve if the group has developed rapport and if the supervisor has created an environment which supports and rewards new ideas. As teachers view alternatives, they speculate about potential outcomes. They think about their own behavior and the modifications required if a new program is adopted. They interpret the proposed changes in terms of the required personal adjustments.

3. Coping Link III—Reality Sharing
   This is a period of facing the situation as it is. Teachers look at available facilities and resources. They consider the possible re-

Figure 37. The Decision Process.

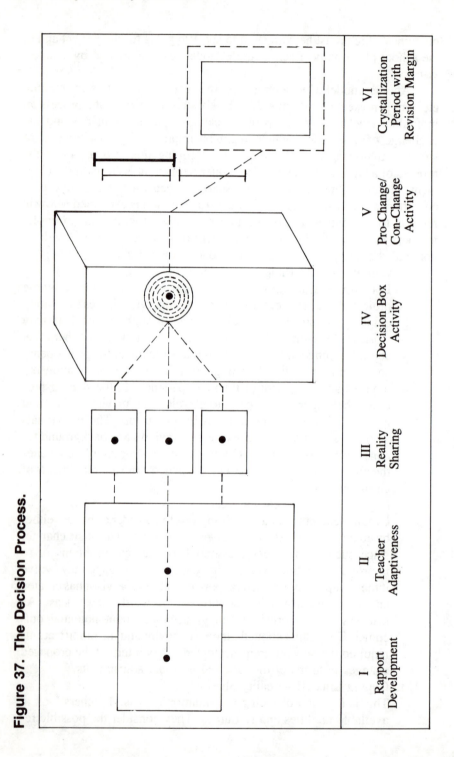

sults of continuing the status quo, of instigating the new program, and of developing alternatives. What teacher effort is required to begin a new program must also be carefully defined. After what may have been a period in which many philosophical ideas have been exchanged, reality sharing involves narrowing professional action to specifics. Activities should be indicated and simplified so that appropriate resources can be selected. If individuals are identified as resources, the altered work pattern becomes a human relations project, as well as a cognitive one.

4. Coping Link IV—Decision Box Activity
   At this stage of the process, general ideas of future professional activity are organized as specifications. Here, the group may invite its participants to join in the consideration of a reasonable course of action. Parent and community reactions may be sought at this time. Although administrators have been informed of the group work, they may now share their concerns with the group. Teachers who will be working with the students before and after the new program (kindergarten and fourth-grade teachers for non-graded reading) may be involved. Also, content specialists in the school system should be invited. Interaction skills are essential. Participants should be assertive in presenting their ideas but receptive in considering choices proposed by others. The interchange of opinions should produce new insights as different aspects of the situation are viewed by new persons who react to the proposed actions. All positive and negative elements should be classified.

5. Coping Link V—Pro-Change/Con-Change Choices
   After thoughtful consideration of the choices, a consensus of the group should be sought. Should there be a change? If so, what change should be implemented? These questions must be answered. If there is a decision to make no change, then the proposal is discarded or perhaps deferred until a later date. If a pro-change choice is made, then a specific proposal must be approved and implementation commenced.

6. Coping Link VI—Crystallization Period with Revision Margin
   At this stage, the supervisor and those members of the group who will put the new program into operation should finalize their plans. The resources are mustered and innovation is underway. The general approval and cooperation of peers and others involved in the decision box and the pro-change/con-change activities provide a supportive environment for the venture. The supervisor can work in a helping relationship to allocate time, facilities, and resources to the teachers involved. A revision margin, which allows for

modification of plans, is a necessity for every new understanding. Based on data from evaluation, appropriate revisions can be made. Unanticipated problems will arise and solutions must be found. The supervisor will need to continue support of these activities, provide inservice meetings to coordinate efforts, work out difficulties, and consolidate revisions, as well as orient new teachers to the program. Using the talents of the teachers involved is an important opportunity to reward these teachers, to publicize the innovation, and to stimulate creativity within the system.

RESISTANCE TO CHANGE

When a new idea is introduced, resistance to change is a common reaction. An individual who is familiar with procedures and expectations in a situation is comfortable and secure in knowing what to do and how to do the job. Almost any innovation introduces new activities and different possibilities. The unknown and unfamiliar can be frightening and uncomfortable, although some people consider the unknown a challenging, exciting adventure. Teachers in this latter group are the ones who should be involved in pilot programs and experimental projects, since they can provide the background and enthusiasm to move their peers toward innovation.

Whenever change is considered, there are always pressures to make the change and pressures to resist it. In each situation, the forces urging change will vary. Often, special groups, such as parents of gifted children, want new programs, so they collect local data and push the proposals. They publicize their viewpoints and seek to gain advocates. Resistance to this type of change frequently comes from teachers who feel that they lack the necessary skills, knowledge, time, and materials to make the change successfully. Some teachers may feel a commitment to the present practice, because they were instrumental in originating the plan. Others who consider the classroom as private territory may feel that change is a threat to their autonomy. Since peer support and administrative support have been part of the status quo, teachers may doubt that their administrators and peers will shift loyalty to the new program.

When these factors are recognized, they can be diminished or eliminated. Successful implementation of change requires that resistance forces be minimized. Inservice activities can help teachers develop needed skills; supervisors can provide information and materials for carrying out the new program; and time management can be studied by the teachers involved in the change. Perhaps volunteers, student aides, or paraprofessionals can be obtained to help work on the plan. Indications of administrative support for change should be evident, and peers should be informed about the proposal. Whenever possible, their reactions should be used in revising the program.

CHANGE FOR AN INDIVIDUAL TEACHER

Before initiating a significant change process with a teacher, a supervisor should organize resources so that s/he can suggest several courses of action for the teacher. Teachers should be reminded that they are in charge of their own lives and that a supervisor only provides suggestions, encouragement, and guidance—the teachers make the choices.

Frequently, a conscious selection of a change pattern is not necessary. If a supervisor senses dissatisfaction in a teacher, pointing out available alternatives may be sufficient help. If a teacher feels inadequate in handling students who have been recently transferred into the classroom, arrangements to visit other schools may help. Seeing that other teachers have similar problems often relieves a teacher's self-doubt and distress. At other times, a supervisor can point out relevant reading material in professional journals and publications.

Attending appropriate conferences, classes, or clinics may give teachers a chance to join a group which shares problems and discusses possible solutions. After such experiences, a teacher may decide that there is indeed a problem in his/her management of a classroom situation and that a change is necessary. When the teacher reaches this awareness, the supervisor can initiate Coping Link I to establish the rapport necessary to probe into the specific problem. On the other hand, the teacher may feel that the attending of meetings or the reading of material has resolved the problem. The supervisor can be a sounding board for the teacher, and s/he can provide feedback when a teacher shares reactions to the activities or materials which have been experienced. A supervisor may decide that a teacher's problem is a personal one and that no outsider—including the supervisor—should provide assistance. This teacher reaction is difficult to handle. Often, a supervisor will initiate Coping Link I, even though the teacher feels that s/he needs no further help. By friendly action, a supervisor can sometimes build an open relationship and eventually effect change.

Goodlad (1965) made recommendations for educational change, suggesting that a teacher is the workable human unit with whom a supervisor most successfully functions. But, he also pointed out that the culture of a school must be taken into consideration and that the pupil responses should be accurately assessed. In a paradigm reflecting the dynamics of change, Goodlad put teacher behavior in a central location.

A teacher's behavior screens the culture of the school so that its influence is controlled before it affects students. When a teacher either cannot or does not accurately project the beliefs and culture patterns of the school community, classroom groups can become restless, because they do not have an accurate environmental image.

For example, a group of vocational students learning how to build frame structures might lack sufficient motivation to work in class unless the teacher has assessed future job prospects for the students and made specific recommendations about builders, real estate, and development opportunities. Students in a remedial reading class might observe their own academic inadequacies and develop a low self-image. They may be ashamed that they are not in classes with peers who are able to read and write satisfactorily. In the second case, a teacher might invite successful businesspeople to speak with the remedial reading group about some shortcoming which they experienced in school years and which they overcame by remedial measures. Often, members of advanced courses feel that they are separated from their peer group. Teachers directly associated with them must handle the ambivalent task of maintaining humility in these students, providing assurance that they are normal young people, and encouraging intellectual satisfaction in their achievements.

In any of the cases above, a teacher must develop sensitivity to student needs. When a teacher is unsuccessful, a supervisor can sometimes identify solutions and guide the teacher to suitable behavior patterns. The change may be a general design for an altered teaching operation, or it may be a unique teacher action which can resolve a transient situation.

In working as a change agent, the supervisor may find that a teacher's collection of data is important. For example, a teacher who is dissatisfied with student behavior in the classroom should begin by compiling lists of exact occurrences. A supervisor should not settle for a statement that "some of the students are unruly during math class." The teacher should make a log of specific acts, keeping track of students who are unruly, and describing the unsatisfactory behavior. A record sheet could be as simple as a listing of items like this:

John . . . . began to talk out of turn when he finished his problems early.

Susan. . . . . left the room without asking permission when the teacher was helping another student hunt a new work packet.

Tommy . . . . hit Billy on the arm when the two of them were in line at the supply shelves.

Donna & Betty . . . . got the giggles near the end of the class period when they were waiting to put their protractors and rulers back on the shelves after completing their math assignment.

At first consideration, it might appear that the teacher had five problems that affected five students. Close examination of the data would, however, indicate that one problem seemed evident: Children waiting to receive or return math working materials are apt to be disruptive—talking, leaving the room, hitting fellow students, or giggling. A quick solution would be to arrange materials so that each item is easily found and returned. This arrangement, combined with a separation of items so that all students would not need to form only one line to get to the supply shelves, might do away with the behavior problems in math class.

Solving this logistic problem is not dealing with a complex behavioral issue. Nonetheless, an important part of a supervisor's job is to look at a situation and come up with a simple solution. Whenever an adjustment of inanimate things can be an element in ameliorating a discipline problem, a supervisor is lucky. Merely moving the rulers, protractors, and calculators to other shelves is an easy matter, far less involved than setting up the process of change which may be necessary for more serious problems.

Creative teachers can contribute to change efforts, and their ideas often stimulate proposals for change. Their enthusiasm may be an important factor in gaining peer support for innovative programs. Supervisors should identify creativity in the classroom and nurture it.

In solving problems, supervisors in an educational milieu should move decisively forward to institute change. Educational supervisors can look into supervisional activities in other fields and adapt successful patterns of operation. Small (1980), when writing about time management, stated that "the speed with which corporations can act and make change, when they want to, has surprised (many) consultants. 'Whole staffs have been shuffled or a product canceled,' one consultant reports. 'Some of us who come from academia are used to things limping along.' " Supervisors functioning in academia must dispel the notion that improvements must move slowly. By observing and by putting corrective measures into action, the benefits of change can be enjoyed by the teachers involved, by their students, and, of course, by the supervisors who help to bring it all about.

SUMMARY

A significant part of a supervisor's activities is devoted to change. Extrinsic change occurs in the environment and intrinsic change occurs within the human being. Both types of change can alter teacher and student attitudes and affect the instructional program.

The Coping Link model for describing change has six steps: rapport development, teacher adaptiveness, reality sharing, decision box activity, pro-change/con-change choices, and crystallization period with revision margin. Resistance to change must be overcome before change can be successfully implemented. A supervisor frequently helps individual teachers modify their behavior to produce better learning situations. Creative teachers should be identified and involved in change efforts.

REFERENCES

Goodlad, J. *Dynamics of Educational Change*. New York: McGraw-Hill, 1965.

Harris, B. *Supervisory Behavior in Education*. Englewood Cliffs, NJ: Prentice-Hall, Inc., 1975.

Havelock, R. *The Change Agent's Guide to Innovation in Education*. Englewood Cliffs, NJ: Educational Technology Publications, 1973.

Lippitt, R; Watson, J.; and Westley, B. *The Dynamics of Planned Change*. New York: Harcourt, Brace, and World, Inc., 1958.

Postman, N., and Weingartner, C. *The Soft Revolution: A Student Handbook for Turning Schools Around*. New York: Dell Publishing, 1971.

Rogers, E. M. *Diffusion of Innovations*. New York: Free Press, 1962.

Sarason, S. *The Culture of the School and the Problem of Change*. Boston: Allyn and Bacon, 1971.

Small, L. "Goodmeasure: Selling Corporations on Change." Ms (July 1980: 53–54.

Toffler, A. *Future Shock*. New York: Bantam, 1970.

Chapter 15
Public Relations

Students of supervision might find it difficult to historically trace the rise of public relations activity by supervisors in American schools. Many of the public relations acts of a supervisor are not identified or defined; in fact, a supervisor's anomalous role misleads the general public in two different directions: At one end of the spectrum, supervisors are thought to be unnecessary, vaguely assigned educators who do not do very much to help improve the learning of young people and, at the other end, supervisors are assessed to be Wonder People who can work with and do anything which is school related. As a matter of fact, most supervisors could probably be located on the continuum between doing nothing and achieving everything. One of the responsibilities which adds to the perplexity of a supervisor's job analysis is that of public relations.

Frequently, a supervisor is considered a person behind the scenes or a ghost writer. Neither of these titles lessens thē importance of the public relations activities, however. Open communication lines must be built and maintained. When the supervisor observes that lines are not open, and that nobody appears to be carrying out an effective communication project, a responsible supervisor offers assistance or, in some cases, just pitches in and takes care of the public relations job that needs attention.

At times, a supervisor's diplomatically offered suggestion to another educator can do the trick. The educator, often an administrator or a longtime teacher with established credibility, reacts like an automobile in which someone has turned the ignition key. The person, once started, shifts gears and moves forward to write a news release, arrange a program or special event, call the newspaper, appoint a committee, reach for the phone, or stand up in a meeting and inform the gathered parents and teachers. Such basic public relations effort is spontaneous and, sometimes, it is most effective because it is timely and natural. Whatever is postponed and agonized over may be delivered self-consciously and too late. It is the supervisor's job to make the suggestion and hope for quick action. But, if the communication is not taken care of, the supervisor may take the circumstance on his/her own shoulders as a professional "do-it-yourself" project.

Administrators should be encouraged to plan writing and speaking with public relations in mind. In these situations, a supervisor enacts the role of facilitator. Once in a while, the best facilitation requires direct action, i.e., staying with a project past the "sparking" stage. Even when this driving effort is necessary—whether the activity is brief or sustained—the supervisor usually works at developing a plan for somebody else. Seldom is the supervisor identified as the originator of a successful innovation which improves a school system, since even when a supervisor has designed a public event, written new releases about it, lined up committees, checked dates, sketched out signs and posters, and made innumerable phone calls, the citizens eventually give credit or discredit to the person at the administrative helm.

REQUISITE SKILLS

Because of the difficult working conditions in the realm of informing the public and building good relations between a school and the surrounding communities, a supervisor needs several special qualities to be effective and happy in this work. Some suggestions follow:

1. A supervisor handling public relations should be aware of how and when to offer help. A supervisor needs to learn to sense when supervisory assistance would be resented or ignored. Sometimes, rescheduling meetings is necessary, since at another time, suggestions might be offered indirectly so that the persons involved feel no resentment.

2. A supervisor should have a well-developed ability with words, both written and spoken. Relating to the public requires literacy in many areas—the writing, editing, and printing of newsletters; the arrangement of outlines for speeches; and the preparation of informative news releases which are sent to newspapers, radio stations, television studios, or to the principal's office for reading over the public address system.

3. A supervisor should be self-assured and good humored when somebody else takes an idea and claims it. Sometimes the loss of a supervisor's identification with a school-related action is the first step in someone's taking the idea and putting it into action. Occasionally, a teacher or administrator becomes convinced that a public relations idea was his/her own and that the supervisor just happened to be on hand when the great idea switched on. In these cases, a supervisor must take the long view and gain satisfaction from knowing that improved education will be achieved. The

quality which is essential to a supervisor in these cases is ego-restraint or humility. In most cases, the supervisor who gives words and ideas freely will turn into an effective, successful professional. A supervisor's career recognition comes when an astute administrator in the central office observes how a supervisor has improved an educational climate.

As the "sparking" element in a public relations activity for other people, the supervisor needs to develop the three qualities described above, but the value of these traits does not end when a supervisor motivates others to move forward. Good timing, an ability to express ideas in written and spoken format, and a sense of humor about getting credit for supplying ideas to other people are all valuable traits for a supervisor to have in all human contacts.

A supervisor's public includes the supervisees with whom s/he works; therefore, relating to one supervisee after another is often a major public relations activity for the supervisor. Behind this relationship is the strong bond which should be developed between the supervisor and the administrators in charge of the supervisory areas. In actual chronological order, a supervisor usually has to establish an affirmative connection with the principal of a school before s/he can work effectively with an individual who teaches in that building.

A supervisor working with an individual teacher in a specific building must learn about the procedures, relationships, and climate of that school so the entire environment is taken into consideration as the teacher's responsibilities are analyzed. For example, a supervisor should be fully cognizant of a new bussing situation—its causes, its results, its success—before going into an affected school. If a teacher in that school is having difficulty with discipline, not because of management techniques but because the atmosphere of the entire building is restless and disruptive, the supervisor might spend time with the principal to try to determine how several teachers could work together to gain control of student groups.

To understand the environment of a school or a system, a supervisor must develop observation skills. Very simple activities can supply the materials a supervisor needs. For example, short drives through the school district can be enlightening; careful reading of media coverage of school matters can provide vital information; and attending occasional meetings and conferences at which the supervisor is not an active participant can be a real learning experience. Putting together the observed facts and circumstances requires the ability to observe, screen the information, and generalize. When a supervisor feels well-informed about the environment, visitations to classrooms can be scheduled. New supervisors are usually aware that such orientation is necessary; experienced supervisors who are assigned to different schools, or who work in neighborhoods that are changing, should also recognize this need.

When both the supervisor and supervisee are well-informed about the school and its community, public relations activities can be devised to encourage positive attitudes, to promote educational progress, and to alleviate difficulty in the school, as well as in the individual classrooms.

There are two broad categories of public relations activities which supervisors deal with directly (on their own) and indirectly (through the teachers they are assigned to help). These categories are (1) internal public relations, which are confined to the in-house activities of one school or one school system, and (2) external public relations, which pertain to the communications that go out to the public at large.

Both internal and external activities require similar skills—human sensitivity, patience, and the ability to speak or write.

INTERNAL PUBLIC RELATIONS

Often, a pattern of internal public relations is established so a supervisor can help in the development of school morale. Open lines of communication are sometimes simple to establish and easy to maintain. Their results may be dramatic—hostilities can be cooled, enmities dissolved, and working conflicts can be eased into cooperative relationships. Open communication means frequent and accessible interaction and two-way interchange. Not only is this two-way communication important among peers in horizontal patterns, but it is also important in vertical patterns with administrators, supervisors and teachers. Too often, messages come from an office—the central office or the building principal's office—to teachers who are given no opportunity to respond. Neglect of the upward channel may produce frustration and discontent among staff members, which a simple procedure for reply could relieve. The reply procedure has other advantages: Good ideas will be received and misunderstandings will be discovered.

Kindred (1965) suggested that careful orientation of new teachers may be the single most important event in developing good internal public relations. As new staff members are acquired, they need to know where to go, what to do, whom to contact, when to arrive, and how to proceed. In many ways, the five Ws of basic journalism can be transferred to in-school communication. A supervisor can help prepare an orientation meeting and distribute handouts with simple who, what, why, when, and where questions and succinct answers. A half-hour meeting and a two-page handout can make the difference between shaky relations and positive good will. If the supervisor's presentation reflects well-organized thinking, and if the printed handout is prepared in literate, readable form, new staff members can begin their jobs with knowledge and confidence.

Follow-up inservice meetings—further opportunities to foster favorable public relations—should be regularly scheduled throughout the school year. Usually, a building principal will take initiative for these meetings and call on supervisors as resource people, since the supervisor can offer practical hints and information about current developments. Since the supervisor is a teacher of teachers in these meetings, s/he should recognize that the media and teaching methods s/he uses are models for the teachers who are attending. Thus, the supervisor should plan carefully so that the content and the methodology are worthwhile. A supervisor faces a somewhat more complex challenge than a classroom teacher because his/her cognitive range is wider and often more abstract. For example, a supervisor might spend 30 minutes on the subject of teacher stress and ways to control it, and a teacher might spend 30 minutes exploring causes of the American Revolution in history class. The supervisor is dealing with an emotional and physical human problem; in contrast, the teacher is drawing on factual material. Teaching and supervising require many similar competencies, and the activities of the two areas are understandably interwoven in today's educational milieu.

In assisting with inservice meetings for faculty during the school year, a supervisor often supplies information and cooperates with committees which arrange for workshops, clinics, and a variety of other inservice sessions. Although the nomenclature for these meetings may be interpreted flexibly, a workshop usually extends over a longer period of time to allow the participants to become involved in experience-centered study. In other words, it is a continuing study group in which members pool their experiences and share their knowledge. It may last several days, extend over several weeks, or continue through a semester with regularly scheduled meetings. Workshops usually involve consultants who are specialists. Activities during a workshop might include role playing, small group activities, large group interaction, lectures, field trips, audiovisuals, and games. Individuals are often given the opportunity to work on specific tasks or problems that they choose. Group dynamics are very important, as the workshop attendees eat, work, and relax together.

A clinic is usually limited in time to several hours. Often, it deals with a specific problem or problem area. A supervisor working with administrators or faculty organizations will sometimes recommend a clinic as a means of bringing conflicting or confused opinions out in the open. A clinic differs from most of the other sessions in that a conclusion is usually sought. A businesslike opening and closing of the meeting is common and, at the end of the clinic, a committee or chairperson sums up the ideas presented and offers a course of action which can be accepted and followed.

Inservice sessions for academic credit may be arranged singly or successively. When credit is earned, the presenters are usually brought into the school from an institution of higher education. Varying arrangements are made about time involvment and payment for these sessions. Scheduling is frequently done by an administrator from the school, and the school facilities are sometimes used for meetings. When an individual teacher gets academic credit for inservice programs, there is usually direct payment by the teacher to the institution granting the credit.

Other types of inservice sessions may be planned. Although most are professional and serious in nature, some are developed for entertainment. The best meetings provide a core of professional content and have some humor and diversion as well. The experience of laughing and enjoying common experiences can help build morale within a school. A supervisor can help to maintain a balance between the entertaining and the informing portions of inservice programs. A file of teacher and student talent is a good resource for a supervisor to have when arranging such programs.

All inservice meetings are internal public relations opportunities. Carefully planned sessions which meet the needs of teachers are positive; those which teachers see as boring and unproductive are negative.

School or systemwide newsletters can be an effective public relations instrument. In addition to using them to recognize teacher ideas and activities, information about current developments and research results can be included, if the presentation is concise and meaningful. Here, too, cartoons and humor can be shared. A regular news bulletin, which is readable and interesting, can contribute to the morale of the group receiving it.

While assisting teachers and opening communication lines, supervisors should foster internal public relations by building a work atmosphere of relaxation and good will. Otherwise, the best laid and executed plans may be valueless. William H. Whyte, former editor of *Fortune* magazine and student of human relations, wrote that "only with trust can there be any real communication" (1952). Although programs to prepare educational administrators and supervisors may neglect writing and speaking courses, they often stress the value of trust-building between human beings. One helpful recommendation for supervisors is that they learn how to be "active listeners." Listening is done regularly by supervisors— sometimes in direct communication with a supervisee in the conference setting. Just as frequently, however, a supervisor must listen, indicate interest, and be supportive in large and small group meetings, as well as in informal conversations with another person.

At the University of Tennessee, the College of Communications established a "listening clinic." During sessions at the clinic, students are scheduled for short periods when they go to an advisor's office to express their opinions and ideas. Little feedback is offered. The principal value to the student is that s/he actually puts opinions and feelings into words as someone listens attentively. Now and then, there is an "active listening" expression from the faculty member who receives the student's expressed ideas. Paraphrasing and summarizing are often used to indicate attentiveness. Although to the uninitiated, the listening clinic appears to be merely a gesture of attention to students, in actuality it is not. When a student talks and tells about concerns, tension is relieved. The student puts ideas into words and watches the listener's response upon receiving the message. Sometimes, an astonishing clarity is the result—not just for the speaker, but for the listener as well. The listening clinic is a formal activity in some college settings. Supervisors perform a similar service when they listen to supervisees who need a verbal outlet.

Any indication of sincere concern is good public relations. A birthday card, a thank-you note for doing a particular task, or a note or phone call in case of family illness or hospitalization are thoughtful communications that show that the supervisor cares. Such actions take only a few minutes. Although the tendency is to postpone doing anything or to decide the effort is insignificant, most people appreciate receiving such messages, and they respond well to such personal attention.

EXTERNAL PUBLIC RELATIONS

Participation in external public relations is one of the activities of a supervisor. Although writing publicity releases and planning school events which should be publicized are usually not on a supervisor's job description, these tasks may fall upon the supervisor if the principal of the school is not skilled in these areas. A supervisor is wise to build friendly relations with the newspaper office and the radio station.

Abraham Lincoln said in an open debate with Stephen Douglas, that "with public sentiment nothing can fail; without it nothing can succeed." The name of the game in the 1860s was public sentiment; it is still the same today. In this century, television cameras, microphones, and press photographers expand the range of obtaining public sentiment considerably, but the events and the actions are similar.

A supervisor needs to understand the difference between public relations and publicity. O'Brien (1977) defined publicity as "a means of spreading ideas." Doing so at a local level is the tactical process of sending out releases. Public relations, a common term in a media-oriented society, constitutes an umbrella, or overall, campaign. Public relations, therefore, is strategic and pertains to any organization's plan for sending to and receiving messages from the public at large.

A public relations expert works closely with an administrator to devise a course of action. Then, s/he delegates portions of the follow-up plan to various publicists. These publicists cover events and write releases describing them. They anticipate or preview events and send releases, which make the events sound exciting and worth public attention, to the media.

Most educational public relations plans are established in the superintendent's office. A supervisor hears what the plan is all about and learns to write or speak in accordance with the plan. All materials prepared by supervisors should be approved by the administrators or by the designated public relations person. Professionals associated with a school can function more efficiently and more happily if they work in harmony with a general plan of action—whether the plan pertains to school rules, school sports, school vacations, school expansions, or school programs.

Supervisors offer public relations/publicity skills to make a plan of action successful. News releases are written, newsletters are composed, school announcements are written, skits for the PTA program are prepared, and, in some cases, school songs are composed—often by the supervisor. When there is a program, tournament, fair, carnival, awards dinner, disco night, or bingo game in the gym, the word gets around—often sent out by the supervisor.

The tone of school announcements should be affirmative and confident. If there is no game or program to write about, a supervisor who helps with school publicity should look around the school building to find a successful, winning experience. The best publicity releases are based on good news. Some examples of worthwhile releases are a bus driver who finishes his fifth year of safe driving, a cook in the school cafeteria who invents a new recipe, a maintenance man who helps a young boy get back in the building to hunt a lost book, a teacher who takes a letter signed by an entire class to a sick class member in the hospital, or an athlete who goes to visit a young disabled student whose leg is in traction. Human interest items which show human concern, kindness, or valor run the best chance of acceptance by the local paper.

Sometimes, acknowledging a less than perfect situation is unavoidable. If there are controversies at board meetings, criticism of the school budget, or disagreement about the hiring or firing of some special teacher or coach, news releases must be informative and fairly stated. A wise supervisor analyzes and writes and then routes the copy through school channels so that releases are in accordance with school policy. A supervisor should feel that administrative approval of releases is essential to maintaining consistent and credible communication. Once a release is routed to the central office, and after it receives the principal's approval, it may influence someone on the central policy publicity staff to get behind the story and give it some additional clout.

Much could be written about the public relations skills that are beneficial to supervisors. Basically, the willingness to use words and the ability to express ideas in an articulate, interesting fashion are fundamental to public relations. Less frequently mentioned, but almost as important, is the ability to use important communications tools, e.g., the typewriter and the telephone. Most supervisors must type their own material, and most of them must make the initial phone contacts and follow-up expressions of gratitude to the media.

It is helpful for supervisors to have some knowledge of photography, since the best stories deserve illustration, and a newspaper will frequently accept a glossy print submitted by a school representative. Less conspicuous, but equally valuable, tools are notebooks and pencils. A good supervisor keeps notes about teachers, students, plans, ideas, promotable events, winning activities, and heartwarming story material contributed from anybody in any part of the school.

Supervisors can contribute to a better informed community by inviting citizens into the schools. Bringing reporters and news media personnel to a school for on-site interviews and filming may arouse their interest in the school. Inviting community members to participate in special projects with individual students or small groups of students is an appropriate way of encouraging involvement. Although they are often neglected, retired citizens are an excellent resource for tutoring and for historical and career information. As the number of community members who have children in the schools decreases, educators must find ways of getting older citizens to participate in school activities and to support the schools.

In short, spreading the good word can grow into one of the most rewarding of a supervisor's activities. With a basic interest in informing the community and recognizing educational accomplishments, a willing supervisor can bring about dramatic improvements in the teaching/learning climate.

SUMMARY

Although public relations is usually not considered a part of supervisory responsibility, a supervisor is often involved in activities which influence staff relations and community understanding. Recognition of these opportunities should encourage a supervisor to develop the appropriate skills. Qualities which facilitate building public relations, both internal and external, include good timing, ability with words, and a willingness to work without acclaim. The situations in which a supervisor can promote positive morale within the school (internal public relations) include inservice and personal contacts. Communication with the community (external public relations) emphasizes publicizing interesting school events and situations. A supervisor is in a position to know about these activities, and s/he can help publicize them, mentioning the ultimate goal of improvement in the school climate.

REFERENCES

Blumenthal, R. *Practice of Public Relations*. New York: McGraw-Hill, 1972.

Fine, B. *Educational Publicity*. New York: Harper and Brothers Publishers, 1943.

Haney, W. V. *Communication and Organizational Behavior, Text and Cases*. Homewood, IL: Richard D. Irwin, Inc., 1973.

Johnson, M. *Current Thoughts on Public Relations*. New York: Harper and Row, 1977.

Kindred, L. *School Public Relations*. Englewood Cliffs, NJ: Prentice-Hall, Inc., 1957.

O'Brien, R. *Publicity: How to Get It*. New York: Harper and Row, 1977.

Whyte, W. *Is Anybody Listening?* New York: Simon and Schuster, Inc., 1952.

Appendix A
Microteaching Manual

Microteaching is à scaled-down teaching encounter. Its focus is on one specific task or skill of teaching. The number of students is limited—usually two to eight are involved. Since the time is generally limited to from 5 to 15 minutes, the selection being taught is only a small segment of the total content. Usually, the teacher selects a concept which can be dealt with in this short time span. Although this setup is different from the typical one in a classroom, the teacher is still teaching selected content to learners—a vital part of education!

The sequence of microteaching (approximately an hour and a half is required) provides feedback to the teacher and gives him/her an opportunity to revise and improve the lesson. If the lesson is 10 minutes in length, the following time schedule will be approximated:

8:00	Teach
8:15	View videotape and confer with supervisor
8:30	Revise lesson
9:00	Reteach a different group of students
9:15	View portions of videotape and evaluate changes with supervisor

The feedback from the videotape, the supervisor, and students who complete a rating scale should provide ideas for improving the lesson. These changes should be incorporated in the follow-up teaching session—the reteach. If the feedback indicates an excellent lesson with no need for improvement, try a different approach to the concept or set up a specific group situation (slow students, advanced students, nongraded group) so that the reteach is a challenge.

THE PLAN

A basic lesson plan indicates what the student will be able to do as a result of the lesson, what activities should produce these results, and how the teacher and student know whether goals have been achieved. The plan includes objectives, teacher and student activities, and evaluation. The objectives are the basis for selection of activities. Feedback from the students (evaluation) is specifically related to the objectives. This last section provides the data from which the teacher decides whether to proceed to new concepts or to try a different approach to the same material. Lesson plan forms may include some further delineation of these basic parts, such as materials needed and time estimates.

If the objectives of a lesson are that (1) the student will be able to demonstrate a chest pass, and (2) the student will be able to describe a situation in which the chest pass is appropriate, then the activities may include a movie or videotape demonstration, live demonstration, oral or written description, pictures, slides, discussion, or any combination of these. The evidence regarding the success of the experience, however, must come from the student. Can the student demonstrate the pass? Can s/he tell when to use it? Without such feedback, a teacher cannot determine whether to proceed or backtrack. Since, in microteaching, the plan must be carried out in under 15 minutes, the teacher must carefully select goals that are reasonable for the limitations and provide an opportunity to get information about whether or not goals have been accomplished.

Here are some brief examples of these relationships:

Objective	Possible Activities	Evaluation
The student can make a chart of a mixture problem.	Problems are given and the students supply the information to build the chart on a transparency on the overhead projector.	Student is given a problem and sets up the chart on his/her own paper.
The student can state five procedures helpful in memorizing Latin vocabulary.	The teacher presents the Latin numerals 1 to 10. As each is presented, the students hear, pronounce, write, give English derivatives, and use the word in simple addition and subtraction problems.	The students are asked to list on the board the steps in learning a new word.
The student can describe three rock types according to their formation.	The teacher explains the terms applied to rock types and illustrates each with pictures as s/he points out the differences.	The students summarize the material orally, including rock types and their formation.

In the plan itself, the teacher states objectives in terms of specific student behavior which can be observed. Two to three objectives are sufficient for each microteaching session. Then, the activities are indicated in detail. If the teacher presents material, an outline of the points with examples should be given. For a discussion, key questions should be listed along with the main concepts to be covered. Specific examples, illustrations, pictures, and sketches should also be included. Evaluation provides both teacher and students with information about whether the teaching was effective; i.e., whether objectives were accomplished. Each student may not be required to demonstrate each objective; a sampling will be suitable for the microteaching situation.

TEACHING TASKS

The four teaching tasks which have been selected for microteaching sessions are clarity of instructional objectives, presentation and making an assignment, getting and keeping student attention, and questioning. Rating scales for these tasks are included at the end of this Appendix.

In the clarity of instructional objectives task, it should be noted that students perform better when they know what they are expected to do. Communication of the goals often hastens attainment, particularly when a student is involved in the learning experience and sees the relevance for him/herself. The rating scale gives some clues about the lesson, why the goal is important, and how the activities can lead to the goal. The student should be able to show that the goal was accomplished. Since learning is active, student involvement is expected.

If the students realize that, at the end of the lesson, they will be expected to list five specific ways in which they can improve the ecology of the environment, then the learning has more direction. This learning will be facilitated when the students feel that ecology is important to them personally. The activity of the lesson, perhaps a discussion of some local projects or a viewing of slides taken in the community, should include very definite contributions a citizen can make to improve his/her environment. Some lessons for this task that have been successful include teaching a few computational short cuts ($\times 25 = \times 100 \div 4$), effects of geography on weather (ocean currents on temperature, mountains on rainfall), introduction of a select French or Spanish vocabulary, or an analysis of ballads to establish the characteristics of ballads.

The second task is presentation and making an assignment. The teacher in secondary schools often does a poor job giving assignments. Asking students to read the next 10 pages provides neither motivation nor guidance for effective study. The teacher should set the stage by arousing student interest, developing relevance and meaning for the topic, and providing specific procedures for accomplishing the assigned job. Sometimes, the actual process is performed by the group to demonstrate how to begin and what steps to follow. The rating scale emphasizes that the student should be able to tell why the lesson is relevant. It is the teacher who provides motivation for this lesson. Then, the student can tell not only how to start but also the steps to complete the assignment. Item three on the scale indicates that the teacher should use an audiovisual aid that relates to the lesson, trying something other than the chalkboard, such as the overhead, some pictures, slides, or a model. The fourth item encourages student involvement; relating the lesson to the student and his/her active involvement should be planned. Some responses are difficult to express as observable behavior, and item five includes some of these. The questions relate to student interest, teacher voice, teacher enthusiasm, and eye contact; the responses should give the teacher information to utilize in the presentation.

When the assignment for an office practice lesson is to solve problems in situations which may face a secretary, one of the situations may be worked out by the group in sequential steps. Each student should be given a description of the situation. Then, the group should define the problem, analyze the given data, suggest possible solutions with probable outcomes, and select the most appropriate procedure. After doing this together, the class should summarize the steps so the process can be followed in the assigned problems. The planning of a speech, preparing a dinner menu with a limited budget, solving some kind of mathematical problems, and testing solutions to determine their properties have all been used for this task.

The third task, getting and keeping student attention, requires some technique for arousing student interest. The teacher must provide enough variety and student participation to maintain student attention through the use of role playing, games, use of all the senses, and other strategies. The rating form provides checklists for the first two items. In the first, evidence that the student is paying attention is sought; the reason for this attention is requested in item two. Item four is concerned with how the teacher responds to student participation. Item five deals with whether the teacher distracts students with his/her voice, gestures, or manner. Finally, if student attention has been held, the student should be able to state the main idea of the lesson. Three ways that the teacher can help the students retain the main points are: practice, relationships, and tips for remembering.

Student attention can be attained by selection of topics, activities, and examples. Students might be interested in student rights, if some pertinent examples or a role-playing situation is used. The teacher might involve the group in a communication with other students—using the bulletin board, a news article, or some publicity gimmick. The teacher is encouraged to surprise the student with content, procedures, or both. For this task, one teacher had each student replace damaged plugs on electric cords. Keep in mind that students can learn using touch and smell as well as sight and sound. Teachers can also create games. Although "Twenty Questions" and "I've Got a Secret" can be used, original games are more interesting.

Questioning, the fourth task, is a skill that can be developed in various ways. Emphasis can be on student thinking and the use of processes more complex than recall. The student can be guided to discover relationships for him/herself, and the group can become involved in interaction through questions. The first item in the rating scale deals with this concept. Items two and three indicate that the teacher probes to get expanded answers and rephrases to clarify questions. Sometimes no answer is given because the question is too difficult, and the teacher must move to a simpler question. The teacher may simplify several times before an answer is supplied. When a student can give a specific example, s/he indicates an understanding of the concept. The ideal discussion involves more student talk than teacher talk; however, the microteaching situation makes such involvement virtually impossible. The sixth item deals with wording of questions, use of student ideas, participation, and logical development of the lesson.

Experienced teachers are continually trying to improve their questions. Often, they write down questions that seem clear and stimulating. The purpose of a question determines the way it can be stated. A review session may start with simple short-answer questions, e.g., *What is a short story?* However, when the teacher wants to encourage sudents to analyze and show relationships between concepts, the question should be formulated in different terms, e.g., *How are Poe's poems and stories similar?* When students find the question confusing or too broad to answer, the teacher must simplify and limit the question. The previous question might be revised as follows: *What are similarities between "The Raven" and "The Tell-Tale Heart?"*

Sometimes, teachers rush on before students have had time to organize responses. If a question is clear to the students, someone will respond if the teacher waits expectantly. Silence is hard to endure, and the teacher usually fills in with an answer. Cultivate waiting for an answer, since this procedure gives students an opportunity to organize and express their ideas. Questioning to encourage higher-level thinking contributes to the development of the learner's mental processes. A student cannot be expected to solve problems, analyze, synthesize, and evaluate, unless s/he has experienced these processes. Questioning should provide opportunities for students to practice these processes. Questioning in microteaching can present a problem if the students have no information; consequently, choose a topic that everyone knows something about or provide background information with a handout or common experience. Experiences such as listening to music, reading a poem, observing an incident, and tasting or smelling selected materials might be used.

I. Clarity of Instructional Objectives

Teacher's Name _____ _____ Teach

Your Name _____ _____ Reteach

Please rate the lesson on these items and write comments to help the teacher improve the teaching.

1. The student can explain what s/he is supposed to learn in the lesson.
   _____a. Definitely
   _____b. Partly
   _____c. Not really

2. The student can give reasons why the lesson is important for him/her.
   _____a. Yes
   _____b. Somewhat
   _____c. No

3. The student can explain how each activity of the lesson leads toward the goal.
   _____a. Not at all
   _____b. Partly
   _____c. Completely

4. The student can demonstrate that s/he accomplished what s/he was supposed to in the lesson.
   _____a. No
   _____b. Somewhat
   _____c. Yes

5. The student was active in the lesson by answering questions, volunteering ideas, asking questions, writing on the board and helping in other ways.
   _____a. Not at all
   _____b. Somewhat
   _____c. Greatly

6. Comments about the lesson.

II. Presentation and Making an Assignment

Teacher's Name ————————————————————— ——————— Teach

Your Name ————————————————————— ——————— Reteach

Please rate the lesson on these items and write comments to help the teacher improve the teaching:

1. The student can state why the lesson is relevant for him/her.
   _____a. Yes
   _____b. In part
   _____c. No

2. The student can tell how to begin the work and what steps are necessary to complete the assignment.
   _____a. Yes
   _____b. Partly
   _____c. No

3. The student can relate audiovisual aids to the lesson by telling what ideas were emphasized.
   _____a. Well
   _____b. In part
   _____c. Not at all

4. The student participated in the lesson by answering and asking questions, volunteering ideas, and contributing in other ways.
   _____a. Never
   _____b. Sometimes
   _____c. Frequently

5. Please answer *yes* or *no* and make any comment you wish:
   a. Were you interested in the lesson?
   b. Was teacher's voice pleasant and varied?
   c. Did teacher seem enthusiastic?
   d. Did teacher look at you during the lesson?
   e. Comments:

III. Getting and Keeping Student Attention

Teacher's Name _____   _____ Teach

Your Name _____   _____ Reteach

Please check correct responses and write any comments which would help the teacher do a better job:

1. The student shows that s/he is paying attention because s/he
   _____a. follows directions.
   _____b. answers questions.
   _____c. makes appropriate comments.

2. The student pays attention because
   _____a. the teacher is enthusiastic.
   _____b. the introduction of the lesson is unique.
   _____c. the material is relevant.

3. The student is encouraged to participate because
   _____a. an unusual activity is used.
   _____b. there is a variety of ways for students to become involved.
   _____c. students can express their own ideas and feelings.

4. After the student participates, the teacher
   _____a. frowns and looks unpleasant.
   _____b. smiles and looks happy.
   _____c. goes right on.

5. The student is distracted by the teacher's voice, gestures, or presentation.
   _____a. Not at all
   _____b. Sometimes
   _____c. Frequently

6. The student can state the main ideas in the lesson.
   _____Yes
   _____Partly
   _____No
If yes, the reason is
   _____a. the relationships are clearly indicated.
   _____b. helps for remembering are provided.
   _____c. practice in using the material is provided.

7. Comments about the lesson:

IV. Questioning

Teacher's Name _____ _____ Teach

Your Name _____ _____ Reteach

1. The student gave answers which showed thinking, not just remembering.
   ____a. Usually
   ____b. Occasionally
   ____c. Never

2. The student explained and developed his/her own answer and other student answers in response to teacher questions.
   ____a. Frequently
   ____b. Sometimes
   ____c. Not at all

3. The student answered because the teacher rephrased the question or moved to another question.
   ____a. Often
   ____b. Occasionally
   ____c. Never

4. The student can give examples or illustrations related to the lesson.
   ____a. Usually
   ____b. Sometimes
   ____c. Never

5. The students talked
   ____a. more than the teacher.
   ____b. as much as the teacher.
   ____c. less than the teacher.

6. Answer the following questions briefly:
   a. Did the teacher phrase questions clearly?
   b. How did the teacher use ideas from students?
   c. Which students were participating?
   d. Was the lesson developed in logical steps?
   e. How could the lesson be improved?

Appendix B
Helpful Hints for Using Equipment in Microteaching

The television instruments used in the microteaching process are similar to those used in commercial telecasting. The rerun of a videotaped microteaching sequence is just another filmed replay, the kind most Americans have learned to accept in watching sports events. "Shoot, rewind, replay" is the standard pattern in giving commercial TV viewers an understanding of activities, such as end runs in football, smash serves in tennis, and birdie-putting in golf. The shoot, rewind, and replay of microteaching is quite similar and requires many of the skills which network camera operators use.

For these and other reasons, teachers and supervisors often approach the microteaching laboratory with an ambivalent feeling of ease and insecurity. Television may be as familiar as the telephone to most educators, yet they have a feeling that something new is about to occur. It is wise for a novice in the microlab to remember that a television camera is just a camera. Even though the videotape deck or recorder which houses the cassette may be a new electronic device, it functions on the same principle as the familiar tape recorder which most educators have used. Thus, a student of supervision or a supervisor at work can move forward, ready to enjoy the opportunity of experimenting with TV and, at the same time, discover the potential of one of the best educational uses of electronic media in the school world today.

Specific technical instructions for various brands of TV cameras and recorders will not be included here. These should be available either in the microlab orientation by an experienced operator or in handouts describing the equipment. Some suggestions which can make a microteaching videotape more useful and eliminate some of the blunders which may occur follow:

1. Keep in mind that an audiovisual record is going to be made of a professional experience. The videotape is not a work of art. Therefore, concentrate on subject matter first and artistic balance second. Get as much of the teacher as possible in the picture, especially the head and upper torso.

2. Set up the filming area before the teacher comes into the room to meet with the students. A maximum inclusion of students should be arranged in the camera viewer. Student reactions are important indications of the teacher's effectiveness. If there is one camera, arrange the chairs in profile with the teacher so that, with a minimum of camera movement, as many faces are visible as possible. If there are two cameras, focus one on the teacher and the other on the students; in this case, each camera is filming only half of what can be seen on the camera's viewer. Check the TV monitor to see how much and which half of the screen each camera is filming.

3. Make sure the record button is lighted during recording. Failure to depress this button properly is the most frequent error in the first use of the lab.

4. Whenever possible, have windows behind the camera so that the lens does not include light blurs in the taping. Avoid shooting into a camera field where bright lights are visible. Don't aim the camera at an overhead projector light.

5. Check all camera and recorder switches before the teacher and students are in place. Delayed filming of a class activity is distracting to all concerned. In all ways possible, the eye of the television camera should be unobtrusive.

6. As the class begins, use the camera eye to introduce each of the participants in the videotaped sequence. Focus briefly on the teacher. Then, maintain a long shot for about 30 seconds and pan slowly across the room. This will provide information to subsequent viewers of the tape; they can see the number of students, age, responsiveness, and the classroom arrangement. This introduction brings about relaxed viewing; otherwise, a viewer spends valuable time wondering who is sitting where.

7. Avoid fast cuts from one person to another as the videotaping progresses. A camera lens is not as quick as the human eye. Panning (or "providing a panoramic view") must be done in a slow, steady way. Otherwise, the film shows jerky, hard-to-view pictures, and some of the value of the sequence is lost.

8. Avoid using the zoom lens, unless a tight closeup view is valuable. Zooming is a quick moving-in for concentrated attention on a very

small area. Generally, this is an aspect of commercial TV which does not translate well into the educational environment.

9. Before leaving the camera, retighten the screws which allow the vertical and horizontal camera movement. If the camera is loose, there is danger that it may topple over.

10. Feeling unsure about a first videotaping can be remedied by viewing tapes which others have made. Seeing both well-done and poorly-done sequences can be beneficial. Remember also that facility with the equipment comes from working with it when there is no pressure to get things done on a tight schedule.

A final suggestion to anyone who is being newly introduced to televising a classroom experience is "Try your own ideas!" The whole field of supervising with audiovisual media is a relatively new professional area, and all practitioners can come up with ideas that improve and expand its potential uses.

Index